CONTENTS
and
EXPLANATORY NOTES

TABLE DES MATIÈRES
et
NOTES EXPLICATIVES

UNITED NATIONS CONFERENCE ON TRADE AND DEVELOPMENT,
Geneva

The least developed countries 1985 Report

Addendum: Basic data

Prepared by the UNCTAD secretariat

UNITED NATIONS

New York, 1986

NOTE

Symbols of United Nations documents are composed of capital letters combined with figures. Mention of such a symbol indicates a reference to a United Nations document.

*

*   *

The designations employed and the presentation of the material in this publication do not imply the expression of any opinion whatsoever on the part of the Secretariat of the United Nations concerning the legal status of any country, territory, city or area, or of its authorities, or concerning the delimitation of its frontiers or boundaries.

*

*   *

Material in this publication may be freely quoted or reprinted, but acknowledgement is requested, together with a reference to the document number. A copy of the publication containing the quotation or reprint should be sent to the UNCTAD secretariat.

TD/B/1059/Add.1
TD/B/AC.17/25/Add.1/Rev.1

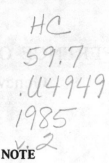

UNITED NATIONS PUBLICATION

Sales No. E.86.II.D.2

ISBN 92-1-112217-1
(complete set of two volumes)
ISBN 92-1-112220-1 (Vol. II)
ISSN 0257-7550

04500P, Vols. I and II
Not to be sold separately

CONTENTS

TABLE DES MATIÈRES

EXPLANATORY NOTES

A. Definition of country groupings

LEAST DEVELOPED COUNTRIES (LDC)

The 36 countries at present identified by the United Nations as least developed are: Afghanistan, Bangladesh, Benin, Bhutan, Botswana, Burkina Faso, Burundi, Cape Verde, Central African Republic, Chad, Comoros, Democratic Yemen, Djibouti, Equatorial Guinea, Ethiopia, Gambia, Guinea, Guinea-Bissau, Haiti, Lao People's Democratic Republic, Lesotho, Malawi, Maldives, Mali, Nepal, Niger, Rwanda, Samoa, Sao Tome and Principe, Sierra Leone, Somalia, Sudan, Togo, Uganda, United Republic of Tanzania and Yemen. Except where otherwise indicated, the totals and the tables for least developed countries as a group, in this document, refer to these 36 countries.

MAJOR ECONOMIC AREAS

The classification of countries and territories according to main economic areas used in this document has been adopted for purposes of statistical convenience only and follows that in the UNCTAD *Handbook of International Trade and Development Statistics, Supplement 1985*.[1] Countries and territories are classified according to main economic areas as follows.

Developed market-economy countries: United States, Canada, EEC (Belgium, Denmark, France, Germany, Federal Republic of, Greece, Ireland, Italy, Luxembourg, Netherlands, United Kingdom), EFTA (Austria, Finland, Iceland, Norway, Portugal, Sweden, Switzerland), Faeroe Islands, Spain, Yugoslavia, Israel, Japan, Australia, New Zealand, South Africa.

Socialist countries of Eastern Europe: Albania, Bulgaria, Czechoslovakia, German Democratic Republic, Hungary, Poland, Romania, USSR.

Socialist countries of Asia: China, Democratic People's Republic of Korea, Mongolia, Viet Nam.

Developing countries and territories: all other countries, territories and areas in Africa, Asia, America, Europe and Oceania not specified above.

In some tables the group of *all developing countries* excludes, as indicated, *major petroleum exporters*. *Major petroleum exporters* are defined as those countries for which petroleum and petroleum products accounted for more than 50 per cent of their total exports in 1978, namely, Algeria, Angola, Bahrain, Brunei, Congo, Ecuador, Gabon, Indonesia, Iran (Islamic Republic of), Iraq, Kuwait, Libyan Arab Jamahiriya, Mexico,

---

[1] United Nations publication, Sales No. E/F.85.II.D.12.

NOTES EXPLICATIVES

A. — Définition des groupements de pays

PAYS EN DÉVELOPPEMENT LES MOINS AVANCÉS (PMA)

Les 36 pays ainsi identifiés par l'Organisation des Nations Unies sont à présent les suivants : Afghanistan, Bangladesh, Bénin, Bhoutan, Botswana, Burkina Faso, Burundi, Cap-Vert, Comores, Djibouti, Ethiopie, Gambie, Guinée, Guinée-Bissau, Guinée équatoriale, Haïti, Lesotho, Malawi, Maldives, Mali, Népal, Niger, Ouganda, République centrafricaine, République démocratique populaire lao, République-Unie de Tanzanie, Rwanda, Samoa, Sao Tomé-et-Principe, Sierra Leone, Somalie, Soudan, Tchad, Togo, Yémen, et Yémen démocratique. Les totaux et les tableaux concernant l'ensemble des pays les moins avancés, qui figurent dans ce document, se rapportent à ces 36 pays.

GRANDES ZONES ÉCONOMIQUES

Le classement des pays et territoires par grandes zones économiques, utilisé dans ce document, n'a été adopté qu'aux fins de présentation des statistiques et il suit celui qui est utilisé dans le *Manuel de statistiques du commerce international et du développement, Supplément 1985*[1]. Les pays et territoires sont classés en grandes zones économiques, constituées comme suit :

Les *pays développés à économie de marché :* Etats-Unis, Canada, Communauté économique européenne (Allemagne, République fédérale d', Belgique, Danemark, France, Grèce, Irlande, Italie, Luxembourg, Pays-Bas, Royaume-Uni), AELE (Autriche, Finlande, Islande, Norvège, Portugal, Suède, Suisse), Espagne, îles Féroé, Yougoslavie, Israël, Japon, Australie, Nouvelle-Zélande, Afrique du Sud.

Les *pays socialistes d'Europe orientale :* Albanie, Bulgarie, Hongrie, Pologne, République démocratique allemande, Roumanie, Tchécoslovaquie, URSS.

Les *pays socialistes d'Asie :* Chine, Mongolie, République populaire démocratique de Corée, Viet Nam.

Les *pays et territoires en développement :* tous les autres pays, territoires et zones d'Afrique, d'Asie, d'Amérique, d'Europe et d'Océanie non mentionnés ci-dessus.

Dans certains tableaux, il est indiqué que l'*ensemble des pays en développement* ne comprend pas les *principaux pays exportateurs de pétrole*. Par *principaux pays exportateurs de pétrole,* on entend les pays pour lesquels les exportations de pétrole et de produits pétroliers ont représenté plus de 50 % de leurs exportations totales en 1978, c'est-à-dire : Algérie, Angola, Arabie saoudite, Bahreïn, Brunéi, Congo, Emirats arabes unis, Equa-

---

[1] Publication des Nations Unies, numéro de vente : E/F.85.II.D.12.

Nigeria, Oman, Qatar, Saudi Arabia, Syrian Arab Republic, Trinidad and Tobago, United Arab Emirates and Venezuela.

teur, Gabon, Indonésie, Iran, Iraq, République islamique d', Jamahiriya arabe libyenne, Koweït, Mexique, Nigéria, Oman, Qatar, République arabe syrienne, Trinité-et-Tobago et Venezuela.

OTHER COUNTRY GROUPINGS

DAC member countries. The countries members of the OECD Development Assistance Committee are Australia, Austria, Belgium, Canada, Denmark, Finland, France, Germany, Federal Republic of, Italy, Japan, Netherlands, New Zealand, Norway, Sweden, Switzerland, United Kingdom and United States.

OPEC member countries. The countries members of the Organization of the Petroleum Exporting Countries are Algeria, Ecuador, Gabon, Indonesia, Iran (Islamic Republic of), Iraq, Kuwait, Libyan Arab Jamahiriya, Nigeria, Qatar, Saudi Arabia, United Arab Emirates and Venezuela.

B. Terms, definitions and sources used

The estimates of *population* are for mid-year and are primarily based on data from the Population Division of the Department of International Economic and Social Affairs of the United Nations Secretariat.

National accounts data are mainly based on information from the United Nations Statistical Office, the United Nations Economic Commission for Africa, the World Bank and national sources.

The estimates relating to *agricultural production, food* and *nutrition,* are derived mainly from information provided by FAO.

Trade data are estimates by the UNCTAD secretariat mainly derived from the UNCTAD *Handbook of International Trade and Development Statistics, Supplement 1985.* Exports are valued f.o.b. and imports c.i.f.

The figures concerning *aid flows* are mainly based on information provided by the OECD secretariat. Following the DAC definitions[2] *concessional assistance* refers to flows which qualify as official development assistance (ODA), i.e., grants or loans undertaken by the official sector, with promotion of economic development and welfare as main objectives, and at concessional financial terms (if a loan, at least 25 per cent grant element.

Non-concessional flows include grants from private agencies (private aid) and transactions at commercial terms: export credits, bilateral portfolio investment (including bank lending) by residents or institutions in donor countries; direct investment (including reinvested earnings); and purchases of securities of international organizations active in development. Figures for *commitments* reflect a firm obligation to furnish assistance specified as to volume, purpose, financial terms and

AUTRES GROUPEMENTS DE PAYS

Les *pays membres du Comité d'aide au développement* (CAD) sont les suivants : Allemagne, République fédérale d', Australie, Autriche, Belgique, Canada, Danemark, Etats-Unis, Finlande, France, Italie, Japon, Norvège, Nouvelle-Zélande, Pays-Bas, Royaume-Uni, Suède et Suisse.

Les *pays membres de l'Organisation des pays exportateurs de pétrole* (OPEP) sont les suivants : Algérie, Arabie saoudite, Emirats arabes unis, Equateur, Gabon, Indonésie, Iraq, Iran, République islamique d', Koweït, Jamahiriya arabe libyenne, Nigéria, Qatar et Venezuela.

B. — Définitions, terminologie et sources utilisées

Les estimations de la *population* sont des estimations de milieu d'année fondées essentiellement sur des données fournies par la Division de la population du Département des affaires économiques et sociales internationales de l'ONU.

Les données se rapportant aux *comptes nationaux* ont été établies principalement d'après des informations provenant du Bureau de statistique des Nations Unies, de la Commission économique pour l'Afrique et de la Banque mondiale, ainsi que de sources nationales.

Les estimations concernant la *production agricole,* l'*alimentation* et la *nutrition*, sont surtout tirées d'informations communiquées par la FAO.

Les données se rapportant au *commerce* sont des estimations du secrétariat de la CNUCED tirées en grande partie du *Manuel de statistiques du commerce international et du développement, Supplément 1985*. Les exportations sont données en valeur f.o.b. et les importations en valeur c.a.f.

Les chiffres se rapportant aux *apports d'aide* sont principalement fondés sur des informations communiquées par le secrétariat de l'OCDE. Suivant les définitions du CAD[2], l'*aide concessionnelle* désigne les apports qui sont considérés comme une « aide publique au développement » (APD), c'est-à-dire les dons ou les prêts accordés par le secteur public, dans le but essentiel d'améliorer le développement économique et le niveau de vie, et assortis de conditions financières libérales (dans le cas des prêts, 25 % au moins d'élément de don).

Les apports *non concessionnels* comprennent les dons des organismes privés (aide privée) et les transactions assorties de conditions commerciales : crédits à l'exportation, investissements bilatéraux de portefeuille (prêts bancaires compris) effectués par les résidents ou des institutions des pays donneurs; investissements directs (bénéfices réinvestis compris) et achats de titres d'organisations internationales s'occupant du développement. Les données concernant les *engagements* se rapportent

---

[2] See OECD, *Development Co-operation, 1983 Review* (Paris, 1983), p. 176.

[2] Voir OCDE, *Coopération pour le développement, examen 1983* (Paris, 1983), p. 200.

conditions, while figures for *disbursements* represent the actual provision of funds. Unless otherwise specified, disbursement figures are shown net, i.e., less capital repayments on earlier loans. Grants, loans and credits for military purposes and loans and credits with a maturity of less than one year, are excluded from aid flows.

The data for the years 1977-1983 concerning aid flows from OPEC member countries and multilateral agencies mainly financed by them have been supplied directly by the donors to the UNCTAD secretariat. In a few cases the figures represent estimates by the UNCTAD secretariat based on secondary sources.

Tables 35 and 48 present data for individual DAC and OPEC member countries respectively, on the estimated amount of official development assistance provided to LDCs expressed as a percentage of the GNP of each donor. So as to give a clear picture of the total flow, an attempt has been made to estimate the share of multilateral flows to LDCs which is provided by each donor. In order to do so, two different methods have been used. Under method A, the percentage share of contributions to each multilateral agency from each donor was applied to the total net disbursements from each multilateral agency to LDCs in each year; the resulting amounts for each donor country were then added to its bilateral ODA and shown as a percentage of its GNP. Under method B, the share of each agency's disbursement to LDCs, expressed as a percentage of its total disbursements to developing countries, was applied to the donor's contributions to the agency in question; the sum for all agencies thus calculated was then added to the donor's bilateral ODA and expressed as a percentage of its GNP.

Balance-of-payments data are estimates by the UNCTAD secretariat based on the IMF balance-of-payments tapes and other information mainly provided by the IMF.

Debt data cover total external long-term and medium-term debt (including private debt) and are based on information provided by the OECD secretariat.

With regard to other economic and social indicators, data on *area* are from the United Nations, *Demographic Yearbook 1983*[3] and the FAO *Production Yearbook 1982*.

The estimates relating to *urban population* are not strictly comparable from country to country because of differences in definitions and coverage. They have been

au moment où le donneur prend l'engagement ferme de fournir une aide déterminée quant à son volume, sa destination, ses conditions financières et ses modalités, tandis que les données concernant les *versements* correspondent à la fourniture effective des fonds. Sauf indication contraire, les chiffres des versements sont indiqués « nets », c'est-à-dire déduction faite des remboursements effectués au titre de prêts antérieurs. Les dons, les prêts et les crédits de caractère militaire, ainsi que les prêts et les crédits dont la durée de remboursement est inférieure à un an, sont exclus.

Les données pour les années 1977-1983, concernant l'aide en provenance des pays membres de l'OPEP et des institutions multilatérales essentiellement financées par ceux-ci, ont été généralement fournies directement par les donneurs eux-mêmes. Dans quelques cas, les chiffres sont des estimations du secrétariat de la CNUCED à partir de sources secondaires.

Les tableaux 35 et 48 présentent des estimations, pour les divers pays membres du CAD et de l'OPEP, sur le montant de l'aide publique au développement qui a été fourni aux PMA, exprimé en pourcentage du PNB de chaque donneur. Afin de donner un aperçu précis des apports totaux, on a essayé d'estimer la part des apports multilatéraux qui a été fournie par chaque donneur aux PMA. A cette fin, on a utilisé deux méthodes différentes. Selon la méthode A, on a alloué les versements annuels nets totaux aux PMA en provenance de chaque institution multilatérale d'après la part en pourcentage des contributions annuelles des divers donneurs à chaque institution multilatérale en question. Les montants totaux ainsi obtenus pour chaque pays donneur sont ajoutés à l'aide bilatérale et montrés en pourcentage de son PNB. Selon la méthode B, on a appliqué, aux contributions du pays donneur à chacune des institutions multilatérales, la part respective des versements nets de chacune de ces institutions aux PMA exprimée en pourcentage des versements nets correspondant à l'ensemble des pays en développement. La somme ainsi obtenue pour l'ensemble des institutions est ajoutée à l'aide bilatérale du pays donneur et exprimée en pourcentage de son PNB.

Les données concernant la *balance des paiements* sont des estimations du secrétariat de la CNUCED d'après les bandes magnétiques de la balance des paiements du FMI et d'autres renseignements fournis surtout par le FMI.

Les données concernant la *dette* recouvrent la dette extérieure totale à long et moyen terme (y compris la dette privée) et sont fondées sur des renseignements communiqués par le secrétariat de l'OCDE.

En ce qui concerne les autres indicateurs économiques et sociaux, les données relatives aux *superficies* sont tirées de l'*Annuaire démographique, 1983* des Nations Unies[3] et de l'*Annuaire de la production, 1982* de la FAO.

Les estimations concernant la *population urbaine* ne sont pas toujours comparables d'un pays à l'autre en raison des différences qui existent dans les définitions et la couverture. Elles sont principalement tirées du *Rap-*

---

[3] United Nations publication, Sales No. E/F.84.XIII.1.

[3] Publication des Nations Unies, numéro de vente : E/F.83.XIII.1.

mainly derived from the World Bank *World Development Report 1985*.

The *labour force participation rate* refers to economically active population as a percentage of total population of sex(es) specified of all ages, as shown in the World Bank, *Social Indicators Data Sheets* (Jan. 1984).

Crude birth rates and *crude death rates* indicate respectively the number of births and deaths per thousand of population. Together with *life expectancy at birth* and *infant mortality rates, crude birth* and *death rates* have been derived mainly from the United Nations, *Demographic Yearbook 1981*[4] and *1983*; United Nations, *Demographic indicators of countries: estimates and projections as assessed in 1980*[5] and United Nations, *World population prospects: estimates and projections as assessed in 1982.*[6]

Life expectancy at birth indicates the average number of years the newly born children would live, if subject to the same mortality conditions in the year(s) to which the life expectancy refers, while the *infant mortaliy rate* is the number of infants who die before reaching one year of age per thousand live births in the reference year.

Under the heading *health at birth, low birth weight* directly reflects the nutritional status of mothers and indirectly, mediated through the status of women, that of the population in general. The figures are drawn from WHO, *World Health Statistics Quarterly*, 33 (3) (1980) and *Weekly Epidemiological Record*, No. 27, 6 July 1984.

The *percentage of women attended during childbirth by trained personnel* is a good indicator of the availability of medical services. It reflects the geographical distribution of the facilities and hence their accessibility, and indeed whether the hospitals had the equipment and supplies to dispense effective medical care. The percentage of women attended during childbirth by trained personnel also to a degree reflects the status of women. Data are drawn from WHO, *World Health Statistics Quarterly*, 38 (3) (1985).

The estimates of *average daily calorie intake per capita* was calculated by dividing the calorie equivalent of the food supplies in an economy by the population. Food supplies comprise domestic production, imports less exports, and changes in stocks; they exclude animal feed, seeds for use in agriculture, and food lost in processing and distribution. The daily calorie requirements used as a basis for calculating average daily calorie intake as a *percentage of requirements* refers to the calories needed to sustain a person at normal levels of activity and health taking into account age and sex distributions, average body weights, and environmental temperatures. The data in this table are weighted by

port sur le développement dans le monde, 1985, de la Banque mondiale.

Le *taux d'activité* est le rapport (en pourcentage) entre la population active et la population du ou des sexes indiqués, tous âges confondus. Les chiffres sont tirés des *Social Indicators Data Sheets* (janvier 1984) de la Banque mondiale.

Les *taux bruts de natalité et de mortalité* indiquent respectivement le nombre de naissances vivantes et de décès pour mille habitants. Ces taux, ainsi que l'*espérance de vie à la naissance* et les *taux de mortalité infantile*, sont principalement tirés de l'*Annuaire démographique, 1981*[4] *et 1983; de Demographic indicators of countries: estimates and projections as assessed in 1980,*[5] et de *World population prospects: estimates and projections as assessed in 1982*[6] des Nations Unies.

L'*espérance de vie à la naissance* indique le nombre moyen d'années que vivrait un nouveau-né pour autant que les conditions de mortalité ne changent pas, alors que le *taux de mortalité infantile* exprime le nombre de décès d'enfants de moins d'un an pour mille naissances vivantes survenus pendant l'année de référence.

Sous la rubrique *santé à la naissance,* le *poids insuffisant à la naissance* reflète directement le statut nutritionnel des mères et indirectement, compte tenu du statut de la femme, celui de la population en général. Les chiffres sont tirés du *Rapport trimestriel de statistiques sanitaires mondiales,* 33 (3) [1980], et du *Relevé épidémiologique hebdomadaire n° 27,* du 6 juillet 1984 de l'OMS.

Le *pourcentage de femmes ayant reçu des soins prodigués par du personnel qualifié pendant l'accouchement* constitue un indicateur de la disponibilité des services médicaux. Il reflète la distribution géographique de l'équipement, et par conséquent leur accessibilité, et dans quelle mesure les hôpitaux disposent du matériel et des fournitures qu'il faut pour offrir des soins médicaux efficaces. Le pourcentage de femmes ayant reçu des soins prodigués par du personel qualifié pendant l'accouchement reflète aussi dans une certaine mesure le statut de la femme. Les données sont tirées du *Rapport trimestriel de statistiques sanitaires mondiales,* 38 (3) [1985] de l'OMS.

On a calculé les *disponibilités alimentaires* en divisant l'équivalent en calorie de l'offre de denrées alimentaires disponible dans un pays par sa population totale. Cette offre comprend la production intérieure, les importations diminuées des exportations et les variations de stocks; elle ne recouvre ni l'alimentation du bétail, ni les semences utilisées dans l'agriculture, ni les pertes en cours de traitement et de distribution. Les besoins caloriques par habitant et par jour ayant servi à calculer les *disponibilités alimentaires en pourcentage des besoins* expriment le nombre de calories nécessaires pour maintenir une population dans un état d'activité et de santé normal, compte tenu de sa structure par âge et par sexe,

[4] United Nations publication, Sales No. E/F.82.XIII.1.
[5] United Nations publication, Sales No. E.82.XIII.5 and corrigendum.
[6] United Nations publication, Sales No. E.83.XIII.5.

[4] Publication des Nations Unies, numéro de vente : E/F.82.XIII.1.
[5] Publication des Nations Unies, numéro de vente : E.82.XIII.5 et corrigendum.
[6] Publication des Nations Unies, numéro de vente : E.83.XIII.5.

population and are taken from World Bank, *World Development Report 1985*.

The *percentage of population with access to safe water or adequate sanitation* are estimates by WHO. The percentage with access to safe water refers to the share of people with "reasonable" access to treated surface waters or untreated but uncontaminated water, such as that from protected boreholes, springs and sanitary wells, as a percentage of their respective populations. In an urban area a public fountain or standpost located not more than 200 metres from a house is considered as being within "reasonable" access to that house; in rural areas, "reasonable" access would imply that the housewife or members of the household do not spend a disproportionate part of the day in fetching the family's water needs.

The percentage of population with access to adequate sanitation includes the share of urban population served by connections to public sewers or by systems (pit privies, pour-flush latrines, septic tanks, communal toilets, etc.) and the share of rural population with adequate disposal such as pit privies, pour-flush latrines, etc.

With respect to both water and sanitation, the figures for 1980 are derived from *The International Drinking Water Supply and Sanitation Decade: Review of National Baseline Data* (as at 31 December 1980), WHO offset publication No. 85, Geneva, 1984, The corresponding data for 1983 were provided by WHO.

Data relating to *education and literacy* are mainly derived from UNESCO, *Statistical Yearbook* 1984 and *Statistical Digest 1982* and other information provided by UNESCO. The *adult literacy rate* is the percentage of people aged 15 and over who can read and write. The data on *school enrolment ratios* refer to estimates of total, male, and female, enrolment of students of all ages in primary/secondary school, expressed as percentages of the total, male, and female, population of primary/secondary school age.

Newsprint consumption is estimated from imports, except in Bangladesh, which also produces newsprint for domestic consumption. The estimates are based on UNESCO, *Statistical Yearbook*, 1984.

Data on *mail traffic* cover letters, postcards, printed matter, merchandise samples, small packets and photopost packets. The figures are from the Universal Postal Union, *Statistiques des services postaux*, 1980 and 1983.

Data on *telephones per 1000 inhabitants* are based on ITU, *Yearbook of Common Carrier Telecommunica-*

du poids moyen des habitants, et des températures ambiantes. Les chiffres présentés sur ce tableau sont pondérés par la population. Les données sont tirées du *Rapport sur le développement dans le monde, 1985* de la Banque mondiale.

Les *pourcentages de la population disposant d'eau saine ou de mesures suffisantes d'hygiène du milieu* sont des estimations de l'OMS. Le *pourcentage de la population disposant d'eau saine* indique la part (en pourcentage) de personnes jouissant d'un accès « raisonnable » aux eaux superficielles traitées ou à une eau non traitée mais non contaminée, provenant par exemple de forages, de sources et de puits protégés, par rapport à la population en question. Dans une zone urbaine, une fontaine publique ou une borne-fontaine située dans un rayon de 200 mètres est considérée comme étant d'accès « raisonnable ». Dans les zones rurales, pour que l'accès soit « raisonnable », il faut que la ménagère ou toute autre personne faisant partie du ménage ne passe pas une trop grande partie de la journée à se procurer l'eau nécessaire à la famille.

Le *pourcentage de la population disposant de mesures suffisantes d'hygiène du milieu* comprend la part de la population urbaine jouissant de raccordements aux égouts publics ou de systèmes ménagers (cabinets à fosse, latrines à entraînement par eau, fosses septiques, toilettes communales, etc.) et la part de la population rurale jouissant de moyens suffisants d'évacuation (cabinets à fosses, latrinements à entraînement par eau, etc.).

Tant pour l'eau que pour l'hygiène du milieu, les données pour 1980 se basent sur *The International Drinking Water Supply and Sanitation Decade: Review of National Baseline Data* (au 31 décembre 1980), publication de l'OMS, nº 85, Genève 1984. Les données correspondantes pour 1983 ont été fournies par l'OMS.

Les données concernant l'*enseignement et l'alphabétisme* sont principalement tirées de l'*Annuaire statistique, 1984,* et du *Résumé statistique, 1982* de l'UNESCO, et d'autres renseignements fournis par l'UNESCO. Le *taux d'alphabétisation des adultes* est le pourcentage de la population âgée de 15 ans ou plus, sachant lire et écrire. Les données concernant les *taux d'inscription scolaire* sont des estimations du nombre total de garçons et de filles inscrits à l'école primaire et secondaire, de tous âges, exprimées en pourcentage de la population totale, masculine et féminine, en âge de fréquenter l'école primaire ou secondaire.

La *consommation de papier journal* est estimée à partir d'importations, sauf pour le Bangladesh qui, outre qu'il en importe, produit aussi du papier journal pour sa consommation intérieure. Les estimations sont basées sur l'*Annuaire statistique, 1984* de l'UNESCO.

Les données relatives au *trafic postal* couvrent les lettres, les cartes postales, les imprimés, les échantillons, les petits colis et les colis renfermant des travaux photographiques. Les données sont tirées des *Statistiques des services postaux, 1980* et *1983* de l'Union postale universelle.

Les *données sur les téléphones pour mille habitants* se basent sur l'*Annuaire statistique des télécommunica-*

tion Statistics (12th edition) and ITU, *Telecommunications for all*, November 1983.

Data on radio receivers per 1000 inhabitants is derived from UNESCO, *Statistical Yearbook*, 1984. The ratio uses the number of receivers in use and/or licences issued, depending on the method of estimation used in each country reporting.

Data on *energy consumption per capita* refer, on the one hand, to forms of primary energy, including hard coal, lignite, peat and oil shale, crude petroleum and natural gas liquids, natural gas, and primary electricity (nuclear, geomethermal, and hydroelectric power)—often called "commercial energy"—and on the other hand, to the use of fuelwood, charcoal and bagasse. All data are converted into coal equivalent and are based on information from United Nations, *Energy Statistics Yearbook,* 1982[7] and on the World Bank, *Social Indicators Data Sheets* (various issues).

The data on *installed electricity capacity* are also derived from United Nations, *Energy Statistics Yearbook,* 1982.

C. Other notes

References to dollars ($) are to United States dollars, unless otherwise stated.

Annual rates of growth and change refer to compound rates.

Details and percentages in tables do not necessarily add to totals, because of rounding.

The following symbols have been used:

A dash (—) or a zero (0) indicates that the amount is nil or negligible.

Two dots (..) indicate that the data are not available or are not separately reported.

Use of a hyphen (-) between dates, representing years, e.g. 1970-1982, signifies the full period involved, including the initial and final years.

D. Abbreviations used

AfDB	African Development Bank
AfDF	African Development Fund
AFESD	Arab Fund for Economic and Social Development
AsDB	Asian Development Bank
BADEA	Arab Bank for Economic Development in Africa
CMEA	Council for Mutual Economic Assistance
CRS	Creditor Reporting System (OECD)
DAC	Development Assistance Committee (of OECD)
DRS	Debtor Reporting System (World Bank)
EDF	European Development Fund
EEC	European Economic Community
EIB	European Investment Bank
FAO	Food and Agriculture Organization of the United Nations

---

[7] United Nations publication, Sales No. E/F.84.XVII.4.

tions du secteur public (12e édition) et *Telecommunications for all* (novembre 1983) de l'UIT.

Les *données sur les postes récepteurs de radio pour 1 000 habitants* sont tirées de l'*Annuaire statistique, 1984* de l'UNESCO. Le rapport est calculé à partir du nombre de postes récepteurs en service et/ou de licences délivrées selon la méthode d'estimation employée dans chaque pays qui fournit des données.

Les données concernant la *consommation d'énergie par habitant* se rapportent, d'une part, aux formes d'énergie primaire (houille, lignite, tourbe et schiste bitumineux, pétrole brut et liquides extraits du gaz naturel, et électricité primaire [nucléaire, géothermique et hydraulique]) — souvent appelée « énergie commerciale » — et, d'autre part, à l'utilisation de bois de chauffage, de charbon de bois et de bagasse. Toutes les données sont converties en équivalent-charbon et ont été établies d'après l'*Annuaire des statistiques de l'énergie, 1982,* des Nations Unies[7] et les *Social Indicators Data Sheets* de la Banque mondiale (divers numéros).

Les données sur la *puissance électrique installée* sont également tirées de l'*Annuaire des statistiques de l'énergie, 1982* des Nations Unies.

C. — Autres notes

Sauf indication contraire, le terme « dollar » s'entend du dollar des Etats-Unis d'Amérique.

Les taux annuels de croissance et de variation sont des taux composés.

Les chiffres étant arrondis, les totaux indiqués ne correspondent pas toujours à la somme des composantes et des pourcentages portés dans les tableaux.

Les symboles suivants ont été utilisés :

Un tiret (—) ou un zéro (0) signifient que le montant est nul ou négligeable.

Deux points (..) signifient que les données ne sont pas disponibles ou ne sont pas montrées séparément.

Le trait d'union (-) entre deux millésimes, par exemple (1970-1982), indique qu'il s'agit de la période tout entière (y compris la première et la dernière année mentionnée).

D. — Abréviations utilisées

AID	Association internationale de développement
APD	aide publique au développement
ATNU	assistance technique des Nations Unies
BADEA	Banque arabe pour le développement économique de l'Afrique
BAfD	Banque africaine de développement
BAsD	Banque asiatique de développement
BEI	Banque européenne d'investissement
BID	Banque interaméricaine de développement
BIRD	Banque internationale pour la reconstruction et le développement (Banque mondiale)
CAD	Comité d'aide au développement (de l'OCDE)
CAEM	Conseil d'assistance économique mutuelle
CEE	Communauté économique européenne
CTCI	Classification type pour le commerce international (révision 1)

---

[7] Publication des Nations Unies, numéro de vente : E/F.84.XVII.4.

IBRD	International Bank for Reconstruction and Development (World Bank)	FADES	Fonds arabe de développement économique et social
IDA	International Development Association	FAfD	Fonds africain de développement
IDB	Inter-American Development Bank	FAO	Organisation des Nations Unies pour l'alimentation et l'agriculture
IFAD	International Fund for Agricultural Development	FSAAA	Fonds spécial d'aide arabe à l'Afrique
IFC	International Finance Corporation	FED	Fonds européen de développement
IMF	International Monetary Fund	FIDA	Fonds international pour le développement agricole
LDCs	least developed countries	FMI	Fonds monétaire international
mill.	millions	mill.	millions
OAPEC	Organization of Arab Petroleum Exporting Countries	NPSA	Nouveau programme d'action pour les années 80 en faveur des pays les moins avancés
ODA	official development assistance	OCDE	Organisation de coopération et de développement économiques
OECD	Organisation for Economic Co-operation and Development	ONU	Organisation des Nations Unies
OPEC	Organization of the Petroleum Exporting Countries	OPAEP	Organisation des pays arabes exportateurs de pétrole
SAAFA	Special Arab Aid Fund for Africa	OPEP	Organisation des pays exportateurs de pétrole
SITC	Standard International Trade Classification, Revision 1	PAM	Programme alimentaire mondial
		PMA	pays les moins avancés
SNPA	Substantial New Programme of Action for the 1980s for the Least Developed Countries	PNUD	Programme des Nations Unies pour le développement
UN	United Nations	SFI	Société financière internationale
UNDP	United Nations Development Programme	SNPC	« Système de notification des pays créanciers » de l'OCDE
UNICEF	United Nations Children's Fund	SNPD	« Système de notification des pays débiteurs » de la Banque mondiale
UNHCR	Office of the United Nations High Commissioner for Refugees	UNHCR	Haut Commissariat des Nations Unies pour les réfugiés
UNTA	United Nations Technical Assistance	UNICEF	Fonds des Nations Unies pour l'enfance
WFP	World Food Programme		

TABLES

TABLEAUX

Table 2

Real GDP, total and per capita: annual average growth rates 1970-1983

Percentages

Tableau 2

Produit intérieur brut réel, total et par habitant: taux annuels moyens d'accroissement 1970-1983

En pourcentage

Country	Total real product Produit réel total							Per capita real product Produit réel par habitant					Pays
	1970-1980a/	1980-1983	1978-1979	1979-1980	1980-1981	1981-1982	1982-1983	1978-1979	1979-1980	1980-1981	1981-1982	1982-1983	
Afghanistan b/	3.6	3.2	-2.5	-3.4	1.8	2.0	5.9	-5.0	-5.9	-0.8	-0.6	3.2	Afghanistan b/
Bangladesh c/	3.9	3.3	4.4	3.7	5.9	1.1	2.9	2.2	1.3	3.9	-1.2	0.7	Bangladesh c/
Benin	2.2	5.6	2.3	10.2	6.3	7.3	3.3	-0.4	6.9	3.0	4.0	0.1	Bénin
Bhutan d/	..	..	7.1	7.1	8.9	1.4	..	4.9	5.0	6.7	-0.6	..	Bhoutan d/
Botswana c/	9.1	11.6	11.9	15.2	11.2	4.1	20.1	7.8	11.1	7.4	0.5	16.0	Botswana c/
Burkina Faso	1.9	6.1	9.0	2.5	8.6	6.9	2.8	6.7	0.3	6.3	4.5	0.5	Burkina Faso
Burundi	3.8	1.9	1.3	3.7	2.0	-1.5	5.3	-0.5	1.3	-0.8	-4.1	2.5	Burundi
Cape Verde	0.3	3.1	4.3	3.3	12.3	5.2	-7.3	2.8	1.9	10.9	3.5	-8.5	Cap-Vert
Central African Rep.	2.1	-2.2	-3.0	-3.8	-2.1	-1.6	-2.9	-5.1	-5.9	-4.2	-3.8	-5.1	Rép. centrafricaine
Chad	1.8	-6.6	-4.8	-7.4	-9.0	-7.3	-3.4	-6.9	-9.4	-11.0	-9.4	-5.6	Tchad
Comoros	-0.9	4.4	9.7	7.3	3.6	6.0	3.7	5.6	3.4	0.3	2.7	0.6	Comores
Dem. Yemen	..	..	4.0	-7.3	3.1	-4.5	..	0.9	-10.1	-0.0	-7.4	..	Yémen dém.
Djibouti	3.0	2.5	3.9	3.4	2.9	1.6	2.9	-3.2	-2.3	1.5	-1.7	-0.1	Djibouti
Equatorial Guinea	-12.9	1.0	-8.8	-9.1	2.2	3.9	-2.9	-10.7	-10.9	0.2	1.7	-4.9	Guinée équatoriale
Ethiopia e/	2.6	2.8	6.0	4.4	2.5	1.4	4.7	3.5	2.2	-0.5	-1.6	1.7	Ethiopie e/
Gambia c/	3.6	3.3	5.8	-8.8	-3.2	9.9	3.6	1.7	-12.3	-5.4	7.5	1.4	Gambie c/
Guinea	3.0	3.1	0.0	5.6	2.1	5.7	1.4	-2.2	3.3	-0.2	3.3	-0.9	Guinée
Guinea-Bissau	1.4	1.8	2.3	-4.2	3.0	0.5	2.0	-2.6	-7.9	0.2	-1.5	0.4	Guinée-Bissau
Haiti f/	3.7	-0.4	7.3	6.4	-0.9	-1.3	1.0	5.4	4.5	-2.8	-3.2	-0.9	Haïti f/
Lao People's Dem. Rep.	-0.1	..	6.0	10.1	5.0	-1.1	..	3.3	7.3	2.3	-3.5	..	Rép. dém. pop. lao
Lesotho d/	9.6	-1.8	4.0	8.4	-0.2	-3.6	-1.3	1.5	5.7	-2.7	-6.0	-3.8	Lesotho d/
Malawi	7.6	2.1	5.7	2.0	-0.8	2.6	4.4	3.0	-0.6	-3.3	-0.0	1.8	Malawi
Maldives	..	7.8	10.7	18.6	7.9	9.6	5.9	7.0	15.5	4.5	7.0	2.8	Maldives
Mali	3.8	0.4	2.9	4.0	-1.8	-1.7	5.0	0.4	1.5	-4.2	-4.2	2.3	Mali
Nepal g/	2.7	3.5	2.4	-2.3	8.3	3.8	-1.4	-0.1	-4.6	5.8	1.4	-3.6	Népal g/
Niger	5.0	1.1	10.1	4.9	1.1	-0.5	2.7	7.2	2.1	-1.6	-3.2	-0.1	Niger
Rwanda	8.0	3.1	4.9	7.9	2.8	1.2	5.3	1.5	4.4	-0.6	-2.2	1.7	Rwanda
Samoa	..	-1.5	..	-5.5	-5.7	-1.6	3.0	..	-6.1	-6.3	-2.8	2.4	Samoa
Sao Tome & Principe	1.1	..	7.6	7.3	-10.6	2.9	..	6.3	6.0	-12.6	0.6	..	Sao Tomé-et-Prin.
Sierra Leone c/	2.1	1.3	7.4	3.0	6.2	-0.2	-2.0	5.7	1.3	4.4	-1.9	-3.7	Sierra Leone c/
Somalia	2.7	3.9	-15.7	-2.5	1.3	6.0	4.6	-22.2	-8.8	-4.1	1.5	0.9	Somalie
Sudan c/	6.7	1.5	-10.2	1.4	3.2	4.2	-2.7	-12.9	-1.6	0.2	1.3	-5.4	Soudan c/
Togo	2.4	-5.7	6.1	1.9	-5.0	-5.5	-6.5	3.5	-0.6	-8.1	-8.6	-9.6	Togo
Uganda	-2.4	7.1	-14.5	-4.9	5.7	8.3	7.3	-17.3	-8.1	2.2	4.6	3.6	Ouganda
United Rep. of Tanzania	4.5	-1.3	3.6	3.3	-3.9	-2.9	3.1	..	-0.2	-7.1	-6.2	-0.5	R.-Unie de Tanzanie
Yemen c/	9.2	4.8	6.6	5.5	5.8	5.3	3.4	3.5	2.4	2.7	2.3	0.4	Yémen c/
All LDCs	3.8	2.4	0.2	2.3	2.8	1.9	2.4	-2.3	-0.4	0.2	-0.8	-0.3	Ensemble des PMA
All developing countries	5.8	1.0	4.8	3.1	1.9	1.2	0.1	2.1	0.5	-0.7	-1.4	-2.5	Ensemble des pays en développement
Developed market economy countries	3.3	1.3	3.4	1.4	1.7	-0.2	2.3	2.8	0.8	1.0	-0.9	1.7	Pays développés à économie de marché
Socialist countries of Eastern Europe	5.3	3.2	2.4	3.1	2.4	3.3	3.9	1.5	2.2	1.5	2.4	3.0	Pays socialistes d'Europe orientale

Source: UNCTAD secretariat calculations based on data from the United Nations Statistical Office, the Economic Commission for Africa, the World Bank and other international and national sources.

Source: Chiffres calculés par le secretariat de la CNUCED d'après des données du Bureau de statistique des Nations Unies, de la Commission économique pour l'Afrique, de la Banque mondiale et d'autres sources internationales et nationales.

a/ Exponential trend function.
b/ Years beginning 21 March.
c/ Years ending 30 June.
d/ Years beginning 1 April.
e/ Years ending 7 July.
f/ Years ending 30 September.
g/ Years ending 15 July.

a/ Fonction exponentielle et tendance.
b/ Années commençant le 21 mars.
c/ Années finissant le 30 juin.
d/ Années commençat le ler avril.
e/ Années finissant le 7 juillet.
f/ Années finissant le 30 septembre.
g/ Années finissant le 15 juillet.

Table 3   Tableau 3

The agricultural sector   Le secteur agricole

Country / Pays	Per capita GDP in agriculture (dollars) / PIB par hab. dans le secteur agricole 1983	Labour force (% in agriculture) / Main d'oeuvre (% dans l'agriculture) 1983	% share of agriculture in total GDP / Part en % de l'agriculture dans le PIB total 1983	Agricultural production / Production agricole 1970-1980a/	1980-1981	1981-1982	1982-1983	1983-1984	Food production / Production vivrière 1970-1980a/	1980-1981	1981-1982	1982-1983	1983-1984
Afghanistan	(106)	77	(51)b/	0.0	-0.4	-3.1	-0.2	-3.3	-0.2	-0.0	-2.5	-1.0	-3.4
Bangladesh	53	83	47	-0.2	-2.2	1.3	0.3	-2.9	0.0	-2.1	1.2	0.1	-2.2
Benin	111	45	42	-0.5	-3.2	-2.5	-1.5	10.3	-0.3	-3.6	-3.2	-2.0	10.1
Bhutan	55c/	93	54c/	0.4	-0.3	0.7	0.9	0.2	0.4	-0.3	0.8	1.0	0.3
Botswana	67	78	7	-6.1	19.8	-1.8	-11.6	-1.4	-6.2	20.2	-1.8	-11.7	-1.4
Burkina Faso	57	79	33	0.0	4.3	-2.5	-1.8	-7.7	-0.2	5.4	-2.3	-2.8	-8.1
Burundi	160	82	53	0.3	8.6	-10.0	4.6	-10.2	0.4	2.2	-4.8	1.1	-10.3
Cape Verde	51	54	21	2.8f/	-28.8	-5.8	-9.2	14.6	2.8f/	-29.4	-5.8	-9.3	14.9
Central African Rep.	73	86	30	-0.2	-2.0	2.4	-6.8	1.4	-0.2	-1.2	-2.8	-3.6	-0.1
Chad	67	81	50	-0.4	-2.6	-0.8	2.4	-13.2	0.0	-1.7	-2.8	0.5	-12.3
Comoros	87	63	39	-1.7f/	-7.9	0.7	1.7	-3.2	-1.5f/	-8.0	0.6	1.7	-3.3
Dem. Yemen	(51)	57	10d/	-1.9	0.4	-2.9	1.9	-2.2	-1.5	0.4	-3.0	-1.7	-2.1
Djibouti	41	..	6	..	..	..	..	..	..	..	..	..	..
Equatorial Guinea	(77)d/	73	41d/	-0.8	-3.4	6.1	-3.5	-12.5	-0.8	-4.2	7.3	-4.0	-14.8
Ethiopia	58	77	41	-6.1	29.3	17.5	-30.4	4.1	-6.1	29.2	17.6	-30.4	4.0
Gambia	89	77	28	-1.8	9.9	-0.0	-5.3	0.3	-1.8	10.3	-0.0	-5.4	0.4
Guinea	157	79	38	-1.8	9.9	-0.0	-5.3	0.3	-1.8	10.3	-0.0	-5.4	0.4
Guinea-Bissau	85	80	45	-3.3	23.4	11.4	-17.0	15.2	-3.2	23.5	11.4	-17.0	15.2
Haiti	(105)	64	(32)	-0.4	-0.7	0.3	-2.0	0.4	-0.4	-1.6	-1.6	-0.1	0.0
Lao P.D.R.	(72)d/	72	(52)d/	-0.4	6.3	-2.0	-1.8	13.9	-0.4	6.4	-2.2	-1.6	14.0
Lesotho	39	81	15	-0.2	1.6	-6.2	-2.5	-1.4	-0.2	-4.6	-6.5	-2.5	-1.3
Malawi	78	82	38	-0.2	1.8	4.8	-3.3	-1.7	-0.2	1.5	1.8	2.2	-1.8
Maldives	(134)	54b/	34b/	-1.9f/	5.2	1.8	2.2	-2.1	-1.9f/	2.8	1.4	1.8	-2.1
Mali	41	85	26	1.1	1.0	1.0	-6.4	-5.5	0.7	1.4	1.4	-8.0	-6.1
Nepal	(86)	92	56d/	-1.6	0.7	-10.9	16.8	-2.5	-1.5	1.0	-10.7	17.1	-2.3
Niger	155	86	49	1.3	-3.5	-3.3	-1.0	-14.5	1.2	-3.5	-3.3	-1.0	-14.6
Rwanda	106	88	39	1.0f/	4.8	1.9	0.5	-10.3	1.0f/	4.0	2.8	0.1	-10.9
Samoa	(57)d/	75b/e/	(13)d/	5.2f/	2.2	-4.2	-1.8	-1.7	5.3f/	2.3	-4.3	-1.8	-1.7
Sao Tome & Principe	117	..	38	-0.3	3.5	-8.0	-3.9	14.2	-0.4	-1.0	-8.5	-3.9	14.3
Sierra Leone	129	63	29	-4.5	-1.3	7.2	-0.5	-15.8	-4.4	7.7	1.3	0.4	-16.4
Somalia	129	78	45	-1.5	9.7	1.4	-8.5	-4.2	-1.5	12.5	1.5	-8.5	-4.1
Sudan	(125)	75	33d/	-1.2	-12.5	-12.5	1.5	-4.0	-1.2	-17.2	-4.4	-1.7	-5.6
Togo	68	66	26	-1.2	2.7	-4.3	-5.8	-2.1	-1.2	2.2	1.4	-6.0	-2.2
Uganda	(176)	79	83d/	-2.2	1.6	2.7	1.4	-1.6	-1.3	1.4	-7.5	1.3	-2.1
U.R. of Tanzania	112	79	47	-0.1	-8.5	-8.5	-3.3	-2.5	1.5	-1.6	-1.7	-2.4	-2.1
Yemen	112d/	74	26d/	0.0	1.6	-1.6	-19.4	14.9	-0.4	1.6	-1.7	-19.7	15.3
All LDCs / Ensemble des PMA	85	80	42	-0.7	0.7	-1.5	-0.9	-3.1	-0.5	1.0	-1.9	-1.4	-3.2
All developing countries / Ensemble des pays en développement	152d/	56	17d/	0.3	2.3	-1.5	-0.2	0.0	0.5	2.2	-0.9	-0.4	0.0

Annual average growth rates per capita (%) / Taux annuels moyens d'accroissement par habitant (%)

Source: UNCTAD secretariat calculations based on data from FAO, the Economic Commission for Africa, the World Bank and other international and national sources.

a/ Exponential trend function.   b/ 1980.   c/ 1981.   d/ 1982.
e/ In subsistence agriculture.   f/ 1973-1980.

Source: Chiffres calculés par le secrétariat de la CNUCED d'après des données de la FAO, de la Commission économique pour l'Afrique, de la Banque mondiale, et d'autres sources internationales et nationales.

a/ Fonction exponentielle de tendance.   b/ 1980.   c/ 1981.   d/ 1982.
e/ Dans l'agriculture de subsistence.   f/ 1973-1980.

Table 4

Total agricultural production and food production: annual average growth rates 1970-1984

Tableau 4

Production agricole totale et production vivrière totale: taux annuels moyens d'accroissement 1970-1984

Percentages / En pourcentage

Country	Total agricultural production / Production agricole totale							Total food production / Production vivrière totale							Pays
	1970–1980a	1980–1984	1979–1980	1980–1981	1981–1982	1982–1983	1983–1984	1970–1980a	1980–1984	1979–1980	1980–1981	1981–1982	1982–1983	1983–1984	
Afghanistan	2.4	0.8	1.0	2.2	-0.6	2.4	-0.8	2.3	0.8	3.5	2.6	0.0	1.5	-0.9	Afghanistan
Bangladesh	2.5	1.3	5.3	-0.3	3.7	2.6	-0.8	2.7	1.4	7.5	-0.1	3.6	2.4	-0.0	Bangladesh
Benin	2.2	3.9	-6.9	-0.1	0.7	1.7	13.8	2.4	3.4	-6.5	-0.6	-0.1	1.2	13.6	Bénin
Bhutan	2.5	2.4	2.8	1.8	2.7	3.0	2.3	2.4	3.4	2.8	1.8	2.8	3.0	2.1	Bhoutan
Botswana	-2.5	4.2	-22.9	24.0	1.6	-8.5	2.0	-2.6	4.2	-23.2	24.4	1.7	-8.6	2.1	Botswana
Burkina Faso	1.9	0.3	-3.2	6.6	-0.3	0.5	-5.4	1.8	0.2	-4.6	7.7	-0.1	-0.5	-5.8	Burkina Faso
Burundi	0.6	0.6	-6.1	11.6	-7.5	7.5	-7.7	2.6	-0.4	-4.2	5.1	-2.2	3.9	-7.8	Burundi
Cape Verde	4.5b	-7.3	39.6	-27.9	-4.2	-8.0	16.1	4.4b	-7.5	41.4	-28.5	-4.3	-8.1	16.3	Cap-Vert
Central African Rep.	1.8	0.9	1.5	0.1	4.7	-4.7	3.8	2.0	1.1	2.4	1.0	2.7	-1.4	2.2	Rép. centrafricaine
Chad	1.7	-1.5	-0.7	-0.4	1.4	4.7	-11.1	2.0	-2.0	-0.3	0.5	-0.6	2.8	-10.2	Tchad
Comoros	2.2b	0.8	4.9	-4.8	4.0	4.8	-0.5	2.4b	0.7	5.5	-5.0	3.8	4.9	-0.6	Comores
Democratic Yemen	1.3	2.3	-5.1	3.5	0.1	5.0	0.8	1.7	1.5	-2.9	3.5	0.1	1.4	0.9	Yémen démocratique
Djibouti	..	..	..	..	..	..	..	..	..	..	..	..	..	..	Djibouti
Eq. Guinea	..	..	..	..	..	..	..	..	..	..	..	..	..	..	Guinée équatoriale
Ethiopia	1.6	-0.7	-3.9	-0.5	9.3	-0.6	-9.8	1.6	-1.4	-4.5	-1.3	10.5	-1.2	-12.2	Ethiopie
Gambia	-2.7	4.7	4.2	32.3	20.1	-28.9	6.5	-2.7	4.3	4.3	32.2	20.2	-28.9	6.4	Gambie
Guinea	0.3	3.5	-0.7	12.4	2.3	-3.0	2.7	0.2	3.6	-0.7	12.8	2.3	-3.1	2.8	Guinée
Guinea-Bissau	1.0	9.2	-12.0	26.9	13.6	-15.6	16.8	1.2	9.2	-12.1	27.0	13.7	-15.6	16.8	Guinée-Bissau
Haiti	1.3	1.6	-4.1	1.2	2.2	0.8	2.4	1.5	1.3	-2.8	1.4	0.2	0.8	2.0	Haïti
Lao P.D.R.	2.1	6.5	15.1	9.1	0.5	0.7	16.6	2.1	6.5	15.3	9.1	0.2	0.9	16.7	Rép. dém. pop. lao
Lesotho	0.5	-1.0	-2.3	-1.1	-3.8	-0.0	1.1	1.1	-1.1	-3.1	-2.2	-4.1	-0.0	1.3	Lesotho
Malawi	3.3	2.9	3.8	4.3	7.5	-0.8	0.9	2.4	2.6	6.8	4.1	5.5	0.1	0.7	Malawi
Maldives	1.1b	2.8	8.6	0.9	4.3	5.3	0.8	1.1b	2.8	8.6	4.3	5.3	0.8?	0.8	Maldives
Mali	3.1	1.0	3.7	7.9	3.5	-4.0	-3.0	2.7	1.1	8.6	10.7	4.0	-5.6	-3.7	Mali
Nepal	0.9	2.9	10.1	3.1	-8.8	19.6	-0.2	0.9	3.2	10.3	3.4	-8.5	19.8	0.0	Népal
Niger	3.8	-3.1	3.6	-0.8	-0.5	1.8	-12.0	3.8	-3.0	3.7	-0.8	-0.6	1.8	-12.1	Niger
Rwanda	4.6	2.5	0.0	8.4	5.5	4.0	-7.1	4.4	2.3	0.6	7.6	6.4	3.7	-7.7	Rwanda
Samoa	2.0b	-0.5	2.5	2.8	-3.0	-1.2	-0.5	2.1b	-0.5	3.0	3.0	-3.1	-1.2	-0.5	Samoa
Sao Tome & Pr.	-4.1b	3.7	-16.1	5.9	-5.9	-0.7	16.7	-4.1b	3.7	-16.2	6.0	-5.9	-0.7	16.8	Sao Tomé-et-Principe
Sierra Leone	1.3	-1.2	2.1	0.4	9.1	1.2	-14.2	1.1	-1.0	3.3	0.7	9.6	2.2	-14.8	Sierra Leone
Somalia	0.7	-0.1	5.4	0.5	6.0	-5.2	-1.4	0.7	-0.1	0.6	5.8	5.8	-5.2	-1.3	Somalie
Sudan	1.5	1.2	-3.8	13.0	-9.9	4.4	-1.3	3.1	-0.8	-2.4	15.9	-14.8	1.1	-2.9	Soudan
Togo	1.2	-0.3	4.3	1.2	-1.1	-2.7	1.2	1.3	-0.5	3.1	1.1	-1.2	-2.8	1.2	Togo
Uganda	0.7	4.6	1.0	5.2	6.3	5.0	1.9	1.6	4.3	5.8	5.8	5.0	4.9	1.4	Ouganda
U.Rep. of Tanzania	3.3	-0.8	5.4	1.1	-5.2	0.1	1.0	4.9	0.0	4.6	1.9	-4.2	1.1	1.4	Rép.-Unie de Tanzanie
Yemen	3.0	1.0	3.8	4.6	1.3	-17.0	18.3	2.6	1.0	4.0	4.7	1.3	-17.3	18.8	Yémen
All LDCs	1.9	1.4	2.0	3.3	1.2	1.7	-0.6	2.2	1.2	2.9	3.7	0.7	1.3	-0.7	Ensemble des PMA
All developing countries	3.0	2.8	2.5	5.0	1.1	2.4	2.6	3.1	2.8	3.0	4.9	1.7	2.2	2.6	Ensemble des pays en développement

Source: UNCTAD secretariat calculations based on data from FAO.

a/ Exponential trend function.
b/ 1973-1980.

Source: Chiffres calculés par le secrétariat de la CNUCED d'après des données de la FAO.

a/ Fonction exponentielle de tendance.
b/ 1973-1980.

Table 5 / Tableau 5

The manufacturing sector / Le secteur manufacturier

Annual average growth rates of real GDP arising in manufacturing (%) / Taux annuels moyens d'accroissement du PIB réel dans le secteur manufacturier (%)

Country / Pays	Per cap. GDP in manuf. (dollars) / PIB par hab. dans le secteur manuf. (dollars) 1983	% share of manuf. in total GDP / Part en % du secteur manuf. dans le PIB total 1983	Total 1970-1980a/	Total 1980-1983	Total 1978-1979	Total 1979-1980	Total 1980-1981	Total 1981-1982	Total 1982-1983	Per capita / Par habitant 1970-1980a/	Per capita 1980-1983	Per capita 1978-1979	Per capita 1979-1980	Per capita 1980-1981	Per capita 1981-1982	Per capita 1982-1983
Afghanistan	(20)	(10)	2.8	5.7	-3.5	-4.6	-1.7	3.2	16.3	0.3	3.0	-6.0	-7.0	-4.2	0.6	13.4
Bangladesh	8	7	11.8	1.8	4.5	0.2	5.4	1.6	-1.6	8.9	-0.4	2.3	-2.1	3.3	-0.7	-3.7
Benin	14	5	-2.5	4.5	-16.2	7.4	3.4	6.7	3.4	-5.0	1.2	-18.4	4.3	0.2	3.4	0.1
Bhutan	5e/	5e/	..	..	5.9	6.9	40.3	..	..	..	..	3.8	4.9	37.4	..	..
Botswana	74	8	13.1	12.8	34.6	-33.0	26.7	23.8	-8.5	8.9	9.0	29.7	-35.4	22.4	19.6	-11.6
Burkina Faso	18	11	2.1	2.8	4.4	0.9	4.4	2.9	1.4	0.1	0.5	2.3	-1.3	1.7	0.6	-0.9
Burundi	26	9	4.0	5.8	6.6	7.6	13.8	-2.4	6.8	1.8	3.0	4.6	5.2	10.7	-5.1	3.9
Cape Verde	13	6	1.6	0.0	2.4	7.1	6.7	2.1	-8.2	-0.1	-1.4	1.1	5.7	5.3	0.4	-9.3
Central African R.	16	7	-4.1	0.5	-4.8	-16.8	2.1	1.6	-2.1	-6.0	-1.7	-6.8	-18.6	-0.2	-0.7	-4.3
Chad	9	7	0.5	-14.0	-7.7	-12.0	-20.8	-13.0	-7.6	-1.5	-15.9	-9.7	-13.9	-22.5	-15.0	-9.7
Comoros	11	5	-4.9	5.1	2.5	5.8	6.5	4.9	4.0	-8.4	1.8	-1.3	2.0	3.1	1.6	0.8
Dem. Yemen c/	(47)	9f/	6.3	-1.5	1.3	-18.8	22.6	-11.2	..	-0.6	-5.0	-1.7	-21.2	18.9	-13.8	..
Djibouti	41	6	-12.2	0.0	5.5	3.0	-1.1	-4.7	1.4	-13.9	-2.1	-1.7	-2.7	-5.4	-7.8	-1.6
Equat. Guinea	10f/	5f/	2.3	4.0	-13.3	-9.2	1.7	5.0	-6.3	0.0	1.0	-15.1	-11.0	-0.3	2.7	-8.3
Ethiopia	14	10	8.8	31.0	15.0	6.7	4.1	3.4	4.6	5.1	28.1	12.3	4.5	1.1	0.4	1.6
Gambia	16	5	2.1	4.6	26.5	-46.9	92.3	15.1	3.0	0.0	2.3	21.7	-49.0	88.0	12.6	-0.7
Guinea	12	3	2.2	-1.2	-1.6	2.7	3.0	8.0	0.5	-0.2	-3.3	-3.7	0.4	0.7	5.6	-1.1
Guinea-Bissau	3	2	8.6	-2.6	3.3	-5.1	2.0	-5.7	1.0	6.8	-4.4	1.5	-6.9	0.2	-7.6	-0.9
Haiti	(57)	(17)f/	-3.2	-2.6	10.2	14.0	-9.5	1.1	1.0	-5.7	-4.4	8.3	12.0	-11.2	-0.7	-0.9
Lao PDR	(11)f/	(8)f/	..	..	0.0	10.1	13.2	4.4	..	..	..	-2.6	7.3	10.4	1.8	..
Lesotho	15	6	17.1	6.2	32.8	16.0	12.7	1.8	4.4	14.5	3.6	29.7	13.1	9.9	-0.7	1.8
Malawi	25	12	5.2	3.4	6.5	3.7	1.8	-6.1	15.4	2.6	0.7	3.8	1.0	-0.7	-8.5	12.5
Maldives d/	(17)	5b/	..	17.8	1.7	..	26.2	21.9	6.3	..	14.4	..	..	22.2	18.9	3.1
Mali	10	7	3.9	-1.7	6.0	1.5	-3.6	-4.3	3.1	1.9	-4.1	3.4	-1.0	-6.1	-6.6	0.5
Nepal	(6)	4f/	1.8	-1.1	13.9	4.7	-4.4	-0.8	2.1	-0.7	-3.8	10.9	1.9	-7.0	-3.5	-0.7
Niger	15	5	4.3	6.8	7.5	12.4	1.8	3.6	4.0	1.9	3.2	4.0	8.6	-1.6	2.3	0.5
Rwanda	36	14	26.7	9.4	1.7	12.4	7.2	15.1	17.7	22.7	8.4	4.0	8.6	6.5	11.2	17.0
Samoa	(28)f/	(7)f/	2.3	2.3	3.5	33.4	-27.9	3.1	0.8	0.9	0.6	1.8	32.5	-29.5	0.8	-0.6
Sao Tome & Pr.	(14)	5f/	4.3	2.3	4.7	126.1	7.2	3.1	17.7	1.9	0.1	3.0	123.5	6.5	2.3	17.0
Sierra Leone	19	4	2.4	5.1	2.4	4.7	-0.9	1.9	1.2	0.1	2.6	0.1	3.0	-2.9	-0.1	-1.0
Somalia	17	6	5.7	3.1	8.9	11.2	4.0	2.8	7.8	2.7	0.5	5.6	-4.2	1.0	0.1	4.0
Sudan	(26)	7f/	-3.9	-4.6	-16.4	27.1	4.4	4.2	2.6	-6.2	-7.7	-18.4	24.0	1.0	0.8	-0.2
Togo	18	7	-9.1	3.5	-33.9	6.1	-5.4	12.6	4.2	-11.7	1.0	-16.4	2.6	-8.6	8.7	0.6
Uganda	(8)	4f/	6.0	-27.4	12.7	-15.7	-27.4	-25.4	-29.5	2.5	-29.9	8.8	-18.6	-29.8	-28.0	-22.9
U. R. of Tanzania	15	6	12.2	16.8	16.8	15.2	24.0	13.0	13.7	9.0	13.4	13.4	11.9	20.4	9.7	10.4
Yemen	29f/	7f/	12.2	16.8	16.8	15.2	13.0	13.7	10.4	9.0	13.4	11.9	20.4	-29.8	-28.0	-31.9
All LDCs	14	7	4.5	0.5	5.0	1.1	-0.2	0.7	1.3	1.8	-2.1	2.3	-1.5	-2.8	-2.0	-1.4
All developing countries	151f/	17f/	6.9	-0.4 c/ e/	5.7	3.9	0.0 c/	-0.8 c/	..	4.2	-2.9 c/	3.0	-1.3	-2.6 c/	-3.3 c/	..

Pays (French country names): Afghanistan, Bangladesh, Bénin, Bhoutan, Botswana, Burkina Faso, Burundi, Cap-Vert, Rép. centrafricaine, Tchad, Comores, Yémen démocratique c/, Djibouti, Guinée équatoriale, Ethiopie, Gambie, Guinée, Guinée-Bissau, Haïti, Rép. dém. pop. lao, Lesotho, Malawi, Maldives d/, Mali, Népal, Niger, Rwanda, Samoa, Sao Tomé-et-Princ., Sierra Leone, Somalie, Soudan, Togo, Ouganda, R.-U. de Tanzanie, Yémen, Ensemble des PMA, Ensemble des pays en développement.

Source: UNCTAD secretariat calculations based on data from the United Nations Statistical Office, the Economic Commission for Africa, the World Bank and other international and national sources.

Source: Chiffres calculés par le secrétariat de la CNUCED d'après des données du Bureau de Statistique des Nations Unies, de la Commission économique pour l'Afrique, de la Banque mondiale et d'autres sources internationales et nationales.

a/ Exponential trend function. b/ 1980. c/ Total industry.
d/ Including electricity e/ 1981. f/ 1982. g/ 1980-1982.

a/ Fonction exponentielle de tendance. b/ 1980. c/ Ensemble des activités industrielles. d/ Y compris l'électricité. e/ 1981. f/ 1982. g/ 1980-1982.

Table 6 / Tableau 6

Investment[a] / Investissement[a]

Annual average growth rates of real investment (%)
Taux annuels moyens d'accroissement des investissements réels (%)

Country	Per cap. investment (dollars) 1983	% share of inv. in total GDP (Part en % des investissements dans le PIB total) 1983	Total 1970-1980b/	Total 1980-1983	Total 1978-1979	Total 1979-1980	Total 1980-1981	Total 1981-1982	Total 1982-1983	Per capita (Par habitant) 1970-1980b/	Per capita 1980-1983	Per capita 1978-1979	Per capita 1979-1980	Per capita 1980-1981	Per capita 1981-1982	Per capita 1982-1983	Pays
Afghanistan	..	..	..	..	..	..	..	..	..	..	..	..	..	..	..	..	Afghanistan
Bangladesh	19	17	1.9	-2.5	-1.3	37.7	7.6	-24.7	14.3	-0.7	-4.6	-3.4	34.5	5.5	-26.4	11.8	Bangladesh
Benin	53	20	-0.5	9.6	-1.2	6.4	16.8	9.9	2.5	-3.7	6.2	-3.7	3.3	13.2	6.5	-0.7	Bénin
Bhutan	..	..	..	..	..	..	..	..	..	..	..	..	..	..	..	..	Bhoutan
Botswana	282	31	4.7	-12.0	22.3	32.1	1.5	15.0	-41.6	0.8	-15.0	17.8	27.4	-2.0	11.1	-43.6	Botswana
Burkina Faso	32	19	3.9	3.9	-9.0	3.4	16.1	-12.5	10.4	1.9	1.6	-10.9	1.2	13.6	-14.5	7.9	Burkina Faso
Burundi	50	17	17.3	21.9	4.0	-4.4	37.6	25.0	75.2	14.8	18.6	2.1	-6.5	33.9	-27.0	70.5	Burundi
Cape Verde	55	22	-0.3	-3.7	15.7	20.3	7.5	6.4	-21.9	-2.0	-5.0	14.1	18.7	6.1	4.7	-22.9	Cap-Vert
Central African R.	35	14	2.3	-5.5	-9.7	-7.2	-6.3	-4.8	-5.5	0.2	-7.6	-11.7	-9.3	-8.1	-7.0	-7.6	Rép.centrafricaine
Chad	10	7	-0.8	-26.1	-21.4	-21.4	-40.8	-21.0	-13.6	-2.8	-27.7	-23.0	-23.1	-42.1	-22.8	-15.6	Tchad
Comoros	73	32	-1.0	-1.9	27.2	46.4	-16.7	1.3	11.7	-4.6	-5.0	22.5	41.1	-19.4	-1.8	8.3	Comores
Dem. Yemen	..	25	-1.4	15.0	68.8	44.9	10.5	36.3	0.9	-7.9	10.9	57.3	36.9	5.7	31.8	-2.1	Yémen démocratique
Djibouti	162	12[e]	-15.8	0.5	15.4	-2.2	5.3	3.6	-6.9	-17.4	-1.6	13.0	-4.2	3.2	1.3	-8.9	Djibouti
Equat. Guinea	22[e]	11[e]	-11.1	4.4	23.6	19.8	9.2	9.2	0.7	-3.4	1.4	20.7	17.3	6.1	6.1	-2.2	Guinée équatoriale
Ethiopia	(15)	42	17.8	2.8	42.0	6.0	-3.7	9.7	2.8	13.7	0.5	36.6	1.9	-5.8	7.3	0.6	Éthiopie
Gambia	131	16	1.4	2.3	8.3	3.8	5.7	-1.3	2.8	-0.7	0.0	6.0	1.5	3.3	-3.5	0.4	Gambie
Guinea	68	19	-1.8	3.9	6.5	-0.8	4.4	3.3	4.1	-6.0	1.7	6.0	-4.6	1.5	1.2	2.5	Guinée
Guinea-Bissau	37	15	13.8	-4.2	16.5	3.1	-2.2	-21.3	14.2	11.9	-6.0	14.4	1.3	-4.1	-22.7	12.1	Guinée-Bissau
Haiti	51	15	-15.2	-1.0	-23.5	9.8	6.8	2.5	-3.3	-17.4	-3.5	-25.4	7.0	4.1	-0.0	-4.1	Haïti
Lao P.D.R.	(8)[e]	(6)[d]	23.3	-1.0	14.6	2.9	2.5	-3.3	-2.3	20.5	-3.5	11.9	0.4	-0.0	-5.7	-4.7	Rép.dém.pop.lao
Lesotho	88	34	23.3	-1.0	14.6	2.9	2.5	-3.3	-2.3	20.5	-0.1	11.9	0.4	-0.0	1.7	8.1	Lesotho
Malawi	47	23	5.5	2.5	-9.8	-11.3	-6.9	4.3	10.9	2.9	-0.1	-12.1	-13.5	-9.3	1.7	8.1	Malawi
Maldives	..	..	..	-6.3	-10.6	-15.4	-11.7	-12.0	5.9	..	-8.6	-12.8	-17.4	-13.9	-14.2	3.2	Maldives
Mali	23	15	2.8	..	..	..	..	..	..	0.8	..	..	..	..	..	3.2	Mali
Nepal	33	21	..	-18.3	21.9	3.6	-36.7	-7.1	-7.3	..	-20.5	18.8	0.8	-38.4	-9.6	-9.9	Népal
Niger	61	19	23.1	4.3	10.2	6.8	-6.1	5.6	14.4	20.1	0.8	6.6	3.2	-9.2	2.0	10.5	Niger
Rwanda	56	21	14.3	..	..	..	..	..	..	10.7	..	..	..	..	..	..	Rwanda
Samoa	..	22[e]	..	..	..	..	..	..	..	..	..	..	..	..	..	..	Samoa
Sao Tome & Pr.	(67)	13	15.8	2.5	39.5	33.3	-44.7	0.7	..	14.2	0.7	37.8	31.7	-46.0	-1.6	..	Sao Tomé-et-Pr.
Sierra Leone	56	23	-0.5	2.5	-1.3	30.0	11.9	-1.3	-2.5	-2.0	0.7	-2.9	27.8	10.0	-3.0	-4.2	Sierra Leone
Somalia	66	16[e]	10.8	..	-17.0	36.4	-4.2	0.9	..	7.6	..	-19.5	32.4	-7.0	-2.0	..	Somalie
Sudan	(60)	22	13.2	..	6.9	-25.2	37.0	-24.3	-21.0	10.5	-30.1	4.3	-27.0	34.2	-26.7	-23.5	Soudan
Togo	58	8[e]	-11.1	-27.7	-17.1	..	..	..	..	-13.7	-30.1	-19.8	-13.0	..	..	..	Togo
Uganda	(17)	19	..	1.0	6.1	0.9	22.3	27.5	..	-0.8	-2.5	2.5	..	18.2	23.1	..	Ouganda
U.R. of Tanzania	45	19	2.5	1.0	9.0	6.6	-1.5	9.3	-3.7	-0.8	-1.8	5.8	3.4	-4.4	6.1	-6.5	R.-U. de Tanzanie
Yemen	183[e]	43[e]	24.6	1.2	..	..	..	..	..	21.0	-1.8	..	..	..	..	..	Yémen
All LDCs[c]	37	18	5.5	-2.3	1.5	11.2	-2.4	-5.0	2.5	2.8	-4.8	-1.0	8.4	-4.9	-7.5	-0.1	**Ensemble des PMA[c]**
All developing countries	222[e]	25[e]	9.9	2.5[f]	0.0	4.5	5.7	-0.7	..	7.1	-0.2[f]	-2.6	1.8	3.0	-3.2	..	**Ensemble des pays en développement**

Source: UNCTAD secretariat calculations based on data from the United Nations Statistical Office, the Economic Commission for Africa the World Bank and other international and national sources.

Source: Chiffres calculés par le secrétariat de la CNUCED d'après des données du Bureau de statistique des Nations Unies, de la Commission économique pour l'Afrique, de la Banque mondiale et d'autres sources internationales et nationales.

a/ Gross fixed capital formation plus increase in stocks. b/ Exponential trend function. c/ Only includes countries for which data are shown above. d/ 1981. e/ 1980-1982. f/ 1980-1982.

a/ Formation brute de capital fixe plus variation des stocks. b/ Fonction exponentielle de tendance. c/ Ne comprend que les pays pour lesquels les données figurent ci-dessus. d/ 1981. e/ 1982. f/ 1980-1982.

Table 7

Exports and imports: basic comparisons

Tableau 7

Exportations et importations: comparaisons de base

Country	Exports in 1983 / Exportations en 1983			Annual average growth rates of purchasing power of exports per capita (%) / Taux moyens de croissance annuelle du pouvoir d'achat des exportations par hab. (%)				Imports in 1983 / Importations en 1983			Annual average growth rates of import volume per capita (%) / Taux moyens de croissance annuelle des importations par habitant (%)				Pays
	Value ($ million) / Valeur (millions de dollars)	% of GDP / En % du PIB	Exports per cap. ($) / Exportations par hab. (dollars)	1970–1980a	1980–1981	1981–1982	1982–1983	Value ($ million) / Valeur (millions de dollars)	% of GDP / En % du PIB	Imports per cap. ($) / Importations par hab. (dollars)	1970–1980a	1980–1981	1981–1982	1982–1983	
Afghanistan	680	18.9b	39.5	5.1	0.2	4.2	-2.1	700	19.4b	40.7	3.4	14.7	14.1	2.7	Afghanistan
Bangladesh	690	6.5	7.3	-8.9	-5.1	6.4	4.1	2165	20.3	22.9	-2.3	9.9	-3.6	-11.5	Bangladesh
Benin	45	4.5	11.8	-12.9	-31.3	-10.7	36.5	320	31.7	84.0	2.5	1.4	-6.0	1.9	Bénin
Bhoutan	..	..	..	..	..	..	..	..	..	..	..	..	..	..	Bhoutan
Botswana	636	69.5	631.2	11.2	-25.4	21.3	41.7	740	80.9	735.1	5.6	14.6	-13.4	9.6	Botswana
Burkina Faso	57	5.1	8.6	2.8	-16.0	-24.4	4.1	288	25.6	43.6	-5.1	-5.1	3.9	-14.9	Burkina Faso
Burundi	76	5.7	17.0	0.8	9.5	25.9	-12.1	194	14.5	43.4	5.2	-3.9	35.0	-7.7	Burundi
Cape Verde	4	5.1	10.8	-10.3	-24.9	38.9	5.9	82	104.3	261.1	-2.1	5.7	3.4	18.0	Cap-Vert
Central African Rep.	100	16.5	40.8	-0.9	-28.3	38.9	-7.7	117	19.2	47.6	-5.0	21.9	31.1	-4.9	Rép. centrafricaine
Chad	160	25.1	33.4	1.7	-5.1	-6.9	27.1	120	18.8	25.0	-6.9	44.9	1.2	13.7	Tchad
Comoros	18	19.0	42.7	-6.6	46.9	22.6	-6.7	34	25.0	78.9	-10.5		1.5	5.8	Comores
Democratic Yemen	700	68.6c	324.4	0.3	-22.1	-10.7	-10.5	1600	156.9c	741.5	5.4	11.2	4.3	-7.2	Yémen démocratique
Djibouti	25	11.1	72.5	-13.5	9.0	-3.8	27.0	197	87.3	570.6	-2.0	6.7	-3.2	1.6	Djibouti
Equatorial Guinea	20	29.0d	53.3	-17.6	15.5	8.5	30.4	30	43.5d	79.0	-19.6	17.9	38.3	-26.9	Guinée équatoriale
Ethiopia	403	8.5	11.9	-4.3	-18.1	8.8	3.7	875	18.5	25.8	-2.2	-4.7	7.4	15.5	Éthiopie
Gambia	49	22.2	69.6	-5.0	-12.9	64.7	13.1	115	52.9	165.6	6.5	-24.1	-20.7	22.2	Gambie
Guinea	431	19.9	83.3	5.2	7.6	-6.6	14.1	280	12.9	54.1	-1.0	-1.8	-14.0	-3.3	Guinée
Guinea Bissau	12	7.2	13.9	-0.5	28.4	2.9	13.3	55	33.0	63.5	-10.5	-9.3	2.1	13.5	Guinée-Bissau
Haiti	166	9.4	31.3	3.3	-31.1	7.8	5.2	449	25.4	84.7	6.2	24.1	-3.8	6.5	Haïti
Lao People's Dem. Rep.	53	16.2d	12.6	5.4	6.9	23.4	35.1	140	42.9d	33.3	-13.3	-4.2	5.9	9.8	Rép. dém. pop. lao
Lesotho	23	6.2	16.1	8.2	-15.2	-25.4	-34.3	586	156.2	405.9	12.2	11.0	4.8	13.4	Lesotho
Malawi	229	17.3	35.6	0.4	-6.1	-4.7	-24.3	312	48.5	48.5	0.9	-18.9	-13.8	2.7	Malawi
Maldives	10	15.1	59.5	-11.7	10.0	58.7	16.5	35	53.4	210.1	4.1	7.1	43.4	-8.8	Maldives
Mali	167	14.1	22.1	4.9	-24.2	-4.2	16.5	344	29.2	45.7	6.5	-12.0	-12.3	5.5	Mali
Nepal	94	3.8	5.9	-7.2	75.8	-36.3	9.1	464	19.0	29.5	1.0	8.5	9.3	19.9	Népal
Niger	340	18.6	58.9	15.3	-21.1	-26.3	3.6	350	19.1	60.6	9.9	-15.7	-12.7	-19.6	Niger
Rwanda	79	5.2	13.9	1.8	15.2	2.4	-12.1	279	18.3	48.9	8.3	4.9	11.9	-2.3	Rwanda
Samoa	19	27.9d	118.0	-1.5	-33.7	21.8	51.9	56	82.4d	347.8	3.1	8.9	-23.1	16.4	Samoa
Sao Tome and Principe	10	35.5	108.7	-2.7	-49.4	19.6	12.1	18	64.5	197.3	-4.9	-11.3	11.3	1.2	Sao Tomé-et-Principe
Sierra Leone	119	7.7	34.3	-8.2	-27.2	-25.5	5.8	171	11.1	49.3	-3.5	-26.9	-1.9	-40.0	Sierra Leone
Somalia	210	13.7	39.9	-3.9	54.1	-4.7	26.3	180	11.7	34.2	1.1	45.0	-35.8	-45.3	Somalie
Sudan	624	8.1	30.6	-8.8	23.2	-24.0	-7.4	1354	17.7	66.5	1.6	-21.4	-18.3	6.5	Soudan
Togo	162	21.7	56.9	3.8	-37.2	-16.9	9.1	282	37.8	99.2	8.8	-16.0	-10.9	-26.8	Togo
Uganda	367	11.9c	25.1	-10.1	-27.8	34.1	9.1	385	12.5c	26.3	-11.3	-16.0	41.2	9.8	Ouganda
United Rep. of Tanzania	363	7.3	17.3	-9.4	9.2	-22.8	-16.6	767	15.4	36.6	-3.7	-5.5	-5.9	-30.8	Rép. Unie de Tanzanie
Yemen	45	1.4d	5.8	-0.4	104.4	-15.9	17.2	1400	43.6d	181.9	32.5	-5.1	-12.3	-6.5	Yémen
All LDCs	7185	11.5	23.4	3.3	-8.0	-2.0	5.7	15483	24.8	50.4	1.6	1.6	-4.5	-4.7	Ensemble des PMA
All developing countries e/	24984	20.2d	128.7	2.0	-2.0	-2.1	8.8	298163	24.2d	154.0	2.3	1.6	-5.4	2.1	Ensemble des pays en développement e/

Source: UNCTAD secretariat mainly based on UNCTAD Handbook of International Trade and Development Statistics, Supplement 1985.

Source: Calculs du secrétariat de la CNUCED principalement d'après le Manuel de statistiques du commerce international et du développement, supplément 1985, de la CNUCED.

a/ Exponential trend function. b/ Per cent of GDP at constant prices. c/ Per cent of GNP. d/ Per cent of GDP in 1982. e/ Excluding major petroleum exporters.

a/ Fonction exponentielle de tendance. b/ En pourcentage du PIB aux prix constants. c/ En pourcentage du PNB. d/ En pourcentage du PIB en 1982. e/ Non compris les principaux pays exportateurs de pétrole.

Table 8

Tableau 8

Unit value indices of imports: tentative estimates, 1970-1984

Indices de la valeur unitaire des importations: estimations approximatives,1970-1984

(1980 = 100)

Country	1970	1971	1972	1973	1974	1975	1976	1977	1978	1979	1981	1982	1983	1984	Pays
Afghanistan	29.3	31.0	33.0	40.8	53.1	55.5	56.1	61.8	68.0	84.0	95.8	91.4	87.4		Afghanistan
Bangladesh	27.5	29.0	31.4	40.0	56.0	58.2	58.0	63.7	70.2	83.1	92.7	85.7	83.3		Bangladesh
Benin	27.2	28.7	31.2	38.9	51.1	55.6	56.2	61.7	68.5	83.0	98.2	95.2	90.5		Bénin
Burkina Faso	28.6	30.6	32.8	40.7	52.5	56.0	56.6	62.2	68.9	84.0	97.0	93.7	89.5		Burkina Faso
Central African Rep.	31.3	33.5	36.6	44.6	57.8	60.9	61.3	67.2	75.9	89.4	93.8	91.0	88.4		Rép. centrafricaine
Chad	28.1	30.2	31.6	39.2	50.4	53.6	54.5	60.0	65.8	82.5	99.2	96.4	91.2		Tchad
Ethiopia	21.8	23.4	25.4	31.4	44.7	48.4	49.9	54.0	58.2	74.8	104.3	100.6	94.0		Ethiopie
Gambia	26.9	28.3	30.7	38.8	52.0	56.0	56.5	62.0	68.8	83.0	97.0	93.1	88.8		Gambie
Malawi	28.3	30.3	32.7	40.3	51.4	55.6	56.4	62.0	68.9	84.3	98.4	96.1	91.5		Malawi
Mali	27.6	29.5	31.6	39.3	52.4	55.1	55.8	61.5	67.4	83.5	96.9	93.0	89.0		Mali
Niger	27.7	29.5	31.9	39.0	51.2	53.9	55.1	60.6	65.6	82.3	99.1	95.7	91.7		Niger
Rwanda	28.9	30.6	32.8	40.8	53.4	56.3	57.2	62.8	68.9	84.6	97.1	93.7	90.4		Rwanda
Sierra Leone	24.5	26.1	28.4	35.5	47.2	50.7	51.8	56.2	61.3	77.0	101.3	97.0	91.1		Sierra Leone
Somalia	27.6	29.2	31.5	40.0	53.8	57.4	57.8	63.4	70.4	84.4	96.2	92.4	88.9		Somalie
Sudan	27.8	29.6	32.0	40.0	54.6	59.1	59.4	65.1	73.4	86.3	95.5	92.5	89.0		Soudan
Togo	27.3	28.9	31.4	39.3	52.4	56.8	57.5	63.0	70.3	84.4	97.6	94.9	90.7		Togo
Uganda	29.6	31.7	34.0	41.4	56.4	60.2	61.0	66.8	75.4	89.6	95.3	93.6	90.8		Ouganda
U. Rep. of Tanzania	23.8	25.8	28.0	34.3	48.2	52.0	53.0	57.5	63.0	78.1	101.0	97.0	91.5		Rép.-Unie de Tanzanie
ALL LDCs a/	26.7	28.5	30.5	38.2	51.9	55.7	56.2	61.6	67.7	82.4	97.0	93.0	88.9	87.1	Ensemble des PMA a/
All developing countries b/	21.8	23.4	25.2	31.2	45.8	49.5	50.7	55.3	59.4	75.6	102.3	97.8	92.1	90.1	Ensemble des pays en développment b/
All developing countries c/	23.4	25.2	27.4	34.1	48.5	53.2	54.5	59.8	65.5	80.3	98.9	95.3	90.9	89.0	Ensemble des pays en développment c/

Source: UNCTAD secretariat estimates.

a/ This index is based on the indices for individual countries shown above. It has been applied to obtain the data on import volume, export purchasing power and aid in constant prices in the case of individual LDCs for which such an index was not available.

b/ Excluding major petroleum exporters.

c/ Including major petroleum exporters.

Source: Estimations du secrétariat de la CNUCED.

a/ Cet indice est basé sur les indices pour les pays individuels qui figurent ci-dessus. On l'a utilisé pour obtenir les données concernant le volume des importations, le pouvoir d'achat des exportations et l'aide en prix constants dans les cas des PMA pour lesquels un tel indice n'était pas disponible.

b/ Non compris les principaux pays exportateurs de pétrole.

c/ Y compris les principaux pays exportateurs de pétrole.

Table 9

Export value and purchasing power: growth 1970-1984

Tableau 9

Valeur et pouvoir d'achat des exportations : évolution 1970-1984

Country	Annual average growth rates of export value (per cent) — Taux moyens de croissance annuelle de la valeur des exportations (en pourcentage)							Annual average growth rates of purchasing power of exports (per cent) — Taux moyens de croissance annuelle du pouvoir d'achat des exportations (en pourcentage)							Pays
	1970-1980a	1978/1979	1979/1980	1980/1981	1981/1982	1982/1983	1983/1984b	1970-1980a	1978/1979	1979/1980	1980/1981	1981/1982	1982/1983	1983/1984b	
Afghanistan	21.4	53.4	42.7	-1.6	2.0	-4.0	10.3	7.7	24.3	19.8	2.8	6.9	0.4		Afghanistan
Bangladesh	6.3	16.1	15.1	-10.3	0.8	3.4	15.9	-6.4	-1.9	-4.4	-3.2	8.9	6.4		Bangladesh
Benin	1.7	-8.6	68.7	-30.4	-10.6	33.9	0.0	-10.6	-24.5	40.1	-29.1	-7.9	40.9		Bénin
Bhutan	..	..	..	..	..	..	..	..	..	..	..	..	..		Bhoutan
Botswana	31.4	96.4	15.4	-25.1	20.3	40.2	6.9	15.4	61.4	-4.9	-22.8	25.6	46.6		Botswana
Burkina Faso	18.4	79.1	16.9	-16.7	-25.3	1.8	5.3	4.8	46.9	-1.8	-14.1	-22.6	6.5		Burkina Faso
Burundi	17.3	50.7	-37.5	9.2	23.9	-13.6	19.3	3.1	23.8	-48.5	12.6	29.4	-9.7		Burundi
Cape Verde	4.0	38.9	68.0	-26.2	25.8	2.6	0.0	-8.7	14.1	38.5	-23.9	42.1	7.3		Cap-Vert
Central African Republic	13.5	9.7	45.6	-31.3	38.0	-8.3	0.0	1.1	-6.8	30.1	-26.7	-4.8	-5.6		République centrafricaine
Chad	17.3	12.9	4.3	-3.8	-7.5	23.1	6.2	3.8	-9.9	-14.0	-3.0	26.5	30.0		Tchad
Comoros	10.4	89.2	-36.4	47.3	21.2	-8.0	2.7	-3.1	55.5	-47.5	51.8	36.6	-3.8		Comores
Democratic Yemen	17.9	142.0	66.8	-22.0	30.9	-11.9	-3.6	3.5	98.8	37.5	-19.7	-0.6	-7.9		Yémen démocratique
Djibouti	5.4	-38.9	72.7	10.5	-4.8	25.0	4.0	-7.5	-49.8	42.4	13.9	13.9	30.8		Djibouti
Equatorial Guinea	-4.4	70.6	-51.7	-12.0	6.2	17.6	0.0	-16.0	40.1	-60.2	17.8	10.9	23.1		Guinée équatoriale
Ethiopia	13.3	36.1	0.7	-13.7	8.0	-0.2	7.9	-2.0	5.9	-55.1	-15.6	12.0	6.7		Ethiopie
Gambia	12.0	48.5	-45.9	61.8	-8.5	10.2	-6.6	-1.6	23.0	-0.7	68.4	-4.5	15.6		Gambie
Guinea	22.3	8.4	20.5	28.2	-14.9	11.7	-7.2	7.4	-11.0	-35.2	10.0	-11.2	16.8		Guinée
Guinea-Bissau	18.3	40.0	-21.4	6.8	5.2	0.0	8.3	3.9	15.0	25.9	32.1	10.0	4.6		Guinée-Bissau
Haiti	19.6	-6.9	52.7	-31.9	2.5	2.5	5.4	5.0	-23.5	25.9	-29.8	32.1	7.2		Haïti
Lao People's Dem. Republic	23.1	191.7	-11.4	-6.5	-21.2	32.5	0.0	8.1	139.6	-27.0	9.7	26.5	38.6		République dém. populaire lao
Lesotho	26.0	41.5	29.3	-15.6	-26.7	-35.6	10.3	10.7	16.3	6.6	-13.1	-23.5	-32.6		Lesotho
Malawi	16.5	25.9	22.3	-5.3	-8.9	-6.9	0.4	3.0	2.9	3.1	-3.7	-6.7	-2.2		Malawi
Maldives	3.6	12.2	69.6	10.3	55.8	-25.4	0.0	-9.0	-7.8	39.8	13.6	62.7	-21.9		Maldives
Mali	21.3	32.3	38.5	24.6	-5.7	14.4	1.9	7.0	6.7	15.7	-22.2	-1.8	19.5		Mali
Nepal	8.3	19.8	-26.1	74.6	-37.6	-6.8	6.9	-4.9	-1.6	-39.1	80.0	-34.8	11.7		Népal
Niger	33.8	58.3	26.3	-19.6	-26.8	2.1	2.9	18.2	26.1	4.0	-18.9	-24.2	6.6		Niger
Rwanda	18.8	62.9	-33.3	15.8	2.3	-12.2	6.3	5.1	32.7	-43.6	19.2	6.0	-9.0		Rwanda
Samoa	13.3	63.6	-5.6	-35.3	18.2	46.2	17.9	-0.5	34.4	-22.1	-33.3	23.4	52.9		Samoa
Sao Tome and Principe	12.3	26.1	-36.1	-49.8	17.2	0.0	10.0	-1.3	3.6	-47.4	-48.2	22.4	4.6		Sao Tomé-et-Principe
Sierra Leone	6.5	28.0	-1.0	-25.0	-27.5	7.2	-2.5	-6.8	1.8	-23.7	-26.0	-24.2	14.1		Sierra Leone
Somalia	7.0	4.7	18.7	56.4	-4.3	5.5	4.8	1.2	-12.6	0.2	62.6	-0.4	9.6		Somalie
Sudan	5.0	1.5	21.2	-24.2	25.1	-8.5	23.5	-6.0	-14.7	-12.4	-21.7	26.9	30.0		Soudan
Togo	21.1	-9.5	53.7	-36.7	-16.5	9.6	-7.4	-6.4	-24.7	29.8	-35.1	-21.7	-4.3		Togo
Uganda	4.9	25.1	-20.8	-28.8	36.5	-18.4	7.4	-7.4	5.3	-29.0	-25.3	38.9	13.0		Ouganda
United Republic of Tanzania	7.5	7.1	-0.6	14.2	-23.3			-6.3	-13.6	-22.4	13.0	-20.1	-13.6		République-Unie de Tanzanie
Yemen	16.7	100.0	64.3	104.3	-17.0	15.4	2.2	2.5	64.3	35.4	110.6	-13.4	20.7		Yémen
All LDCs	13.1	29.2	15.7	-8.4	-2.6	3.7	5.9	-0.7	6.2	-4.6	-5.6	1.7	8.5	8.0	**Ensemble des PMA**
All developing countries c/	21.1	27.8	23.2	2.8	-4.0	5.0	13.6	4.6	0.4	-6.9	0.5	0.4	11.5	16.1	**Ensemble des pays en développement c/**

Source : UNCTAD secretariat calculations, based on UNCTAD Handbook of International Trade and Development Statistics, Supplement 1985.

a/ Exponential trend function.

b/ Preliminary estimates.

c/ Excluding major petroleum exporters.

Source : Calculs du secrétariat de la CNUCED, d'après le Manuel de Statistiques du Commerce et du développement, Supplément 1985, de la CNUCED.

a/ Fonction exponentielle de tendance.

b/ Estimations préliminaires.

c/ Non compris les principaux pays exportateurs de pétrole.

Table 10 / Tableau 10

Import value and volume : growth 1970-1984
Valeur et volume des importations : évolution 1970-1984

Country	Annual average growth rates of import value (per cent) — Taux moyens de croissance annuelle de la valeur des importations (en pourcentage)							Annual average growth rates of import volume (per cent) — Taux moyens de croissance annuelle du volume des importations (en pourcentage)							Pays
	1970-1980a	1978-1979	1979-1980	1980-1981	1981-1982	1982-1983	1983-1984b	1970-1980a	1978-1979	1979-1980	1980-1981	1981-1982	1982-1983	1983-1984b	
Afghanistan	19.4	16.1	-19.5	12.7	11.7	0.7	1.4	5.9	-6.0	-32.4	17.7	17.1	5.3		Afghanistan
Bangladesh	14.0	26.2	36.2	3.9	-8.7	-12.1	21.0	0.4	6.6	13.1	12.1	-1.3	-9.6		Bangladesh
Benin	19.7	2.6	3.4	2.7	-5.9	0.0	-3.1	5.2	-15.3	-14.1	4.6	-2.9	5.2		Bénin
Bhutan	..	..	..	..	..	..	..	..	..	..	..	..	..		Bhoutan
Botswana	24.9	47.4	32.7	15.1	-14.2	8.5	-9.3	9.7	21.1	9.4	18.6	-10.4	13.4		Botswana
Burkina Faso	21.9	32.2	19.2	-5.9	2.6	-16.8	-6.3	7.9	8.5	0.1	-3.0	6.2	-12.9		Burkina Faso
Burundi	22.4	55.1	10.5	-4.2	32.9	-9.3	1.0	7.5	27.4	-8.9	-1.3	38.8	-5.2		Burundi
Cape Verde	13.5	4.4	21.7	4.0	0.7	14.3	-6.3	-0.4	-14.3	0.4	7.1	5.1	19.5		Cap-Vert
Central African Republic	8.8	27.0	16.5	16.8	30.2	10.1	-9.0	-3.1	7.9	4.1	24.6	34.1	-2.7		République centrafricaine
Chad	7.4	-60.8	-13.8	46.9	0.6	10.1	-4.2	-5.0	-68.7	-28.9	48.1	3.5	16.3		Tchad
Comoros	12.1	59.4	18.3	-10.2	0.3	4.3	2.1	-1.5	30.9	-2.5	-7.5	4.7	9.1		Comores
Democratic Yemen	23.9	60.9	65.1	11.3	3.0	-8.6	0.0	8.8	32.2	36.1	14.6	7.5	-4.4		Yémen démocratique
Djibouti	19.4	12.0	37.4	16.7	-4.2	0.0	-4.3	4.9	-8.0	11.7	11.6	0.0	-4.3		Djibouti
Equatorial Guinea	-6.7	105.7	27.2	2.4	35.4	-28.6	0.0	-18.1	69.0	13.2	20.3	41.4	-25.3		Guinée équatoriale
Ethiopia	15.7	8.6	17.1	-24.8	6.6	19.1	-12.0	0.1	-15.5	-4.9	-1.9	10.6	19.0		Ethiopie
Gambia	25.6	40.6	68.2	-2.5	-15.7	-5.4	-15.3	10.3	-35.4	-2.8	-22.4	-18.9	24.9		Gambie
Guinea	15.2	-21.3	-9.4	-9.5	-0.2	10.3	-3.6	1.1	1.2	38.7	0.5	-12.0	-1.1		Guinée
Guinea-Bissau	6.5	23.2	-9.5	-0.2	3.7	-5.4	-6.0	-6.4	-25.3	-25.3	-6.7	4.1	15.3		Guinée-Bissau
Haiti	23.0	16.7	38.0	22.7	-6.1	3.7	1.9	8.0	-4.1	13.7	26.5	-1.9	8.5		Haïti
Lao People's Dem. Republic	1.3	31.3	39.4	-4.6	6.1	7.7	3.6	11.1	7.9	14.9	-1.7	8.6	12.6		République dém. populaire lao
Lesotho	30.7	32.3	28.5	10.5	3.0	11.2	-48.1	14.8	8.7	5.9	13.8	7.5	16.3		Lesotho
Malawi	17.1	17.8	10.6	-18.2	-13.6	-0.3	-3.8	3.5	-3.8	-6.8	-16.8	-11.6	5.4		Malawi
Maldives	22.1	58.5	33.3	40.9	7.2...										
Maldives	22.1	58.5	33.3	40.9	-0.3	3.6	0.0	7.3	30.2	9.9	10.6	47.0	-6.0		Maldives
Mali	23.2	26.0	22.6	-12.5	-13.8	3.6	-4.1	8.6	1.6	2.4	-9.7	-10.1	8.2		Mali
Nepal	17.8	15.1	34.4	7.8	7.2	17.3	-22.0	3.5	-5.4	10.8	11.1	11.9	22.7		Népal
Niger	27.5	51.0	28.6	-14.1	-13.3	-20.8	-5.7	12.6	20.3	5.8	-13.4	-10.3	-17.3		Niger
Rwanda	26.4	7.3	26.6	6.3	11.7	-2.4	-1.8	11.8	7.1	7.1	8.5	15.8	1.2		Rwanda
Samoa	18.5	37.7	-13.7	5.3	-25.4	12.0	-0.3	4.1	13.2	-28.9	9.6	-22.1	17.2		Samoa
Sao Tome and Principe	9.9	11.1	-5.0	-11.9	9.1	0.0	-0.3	-3.5	-8.8	-21.7	-9.2	13.9	4.6		Sao Tomé-et-Principe
Sierra Leone	11.9	14.2	39.4	-24.6	-4.5	-42.6	-5.6	-2.0	-9.1	7.3	-25.6	-0.2	-38.9		Sierra Leone
Somalia	21.0	2.1	41.5	47.1	-35.5	-45.5	-5.6	6.5	-14.8	19.4	53.0	-32.9	-43.3		Somalie
Sudan	19.1	-7.3	42.0	0.1	-18.6	5.4	-12.9	4.7	-21.2	22.6	4.9	-16.0	9.5		Soudan
Togo	26.9	-15.9	6.2	-20.8	-10.4	-27.7	34.5	11.5	-3.6	-10.3	-18.8	-7.9	-24.3		Togo
Uganda	3.4	-22.5	49.1	-17.1	43.6	10.3	0.0	8.7	-34.8	33.6	-13.0	46.2	13.8		Ouganda
United Republic of Tanzania	14.2	-5.8	13.8	-1.1	-6.4	-32.4	42.1	-0.5	-24.0	-11.1	-2.1	-2.6	-28.3		République-Unie de Tanzanie
Yemen	55.3	16.3	24.2	-5.1	-13.5	-8.0	-10.0	36.4	-4.5	2.4	-2.2	-9.7	-3.7		Yémen
All LDCs	18.8	14.5	27.2	1.1	-6.0	-6.4	-0.8	4.4	-5.9	4.9	4.2	-1.9	-2.1	1.2	**Ensemble des PMA**
All developing countries c/	21.4	25.8	29.8	6.5	-7.2	-1.4	4.2	4.9	-1.1	-1.8	4.1	-3.0	4.7	6.5	**Ensemble des pays en développement c/**

Source : UNCTAD secretariat calculations, based on UNCTAD *Handbook of International Trade and Development Statistics, Supplement 1985.*

a/ Exponential trend function.
b/ Preliminary estimates.
c/ Excluding major petroleum exporters.

Source : Calculs du secrétariat de la CNUCED, d'après le *Manuel de Statistiques du Commerce et du Développement, Supplément 1985,* de la CNUCED.

a/ Fonction exponentielle de tendance.
b/ Estimations préliminaires.
c/ Non compris les principaux pays exportateurs de pétrole.

Table 11

Commodity structure of exports of LDCs by main category (1983 or latest year available)

Tableau 11

Composition des exportations des PMA, par principales catégories de produits (1983 ou année disponible la plus récente)

Country / SITC	Year / Année	Total value ($ million) / Valeur totale (million de $)	All food items / Produits alimentaires (0+1+22+4)	Agricultural raw materials / Matières premières d'origine agricole (2-22-27-28)	Fuels / Combustibles (3)	Ores and metals / Minéraux et métaux (27+28+ 67+68)	Manufactured goods / Produits manufacturés (5+6+7+8 -67-68)	Un-allocated / Non-distribués (9)	Memo item / Pour mémoire — Textiles fibres, yarn and clothing / Fibres textiles, filés, tissus et vêtements (26+65+84)	Pays / CTCI
Afghanistan	1982	708	29.6	10.5	40.1	-	14.8a/	5.0	15.6	Afghanistan
Bangladesh	1982	667	20.0	15.6	2.2	0.1	61.5b/	0.6	62.3	Bangladesh
Benin	1982	34	70.3	14.4	0.2	2.5	12.5	0.1	17.5	Bénin
Bhutan	1981/82	22	28.8	13.8	-	-	39.3	18.1	-	Bhoutan
Botswana	1982	453	20.0	1.8	0.1	14.0	63.3c/	0.8	6.9	Botswana
Burkina Faso	1983	57	33.5	56.0	-	0.4	10.1	-	56.8	Burkina Faso
Burundi	1982	88	70.5	6.4	-	5.5	3.8	13.8	1.8	Burundi
Cape Verde	1982	4	63.3	1.4	-	22.3	2.9	10.1	0.1	Cap-Vert
Central African Rep.	1983	100	37.2	26.5	-	3.1	32.6	0.5	9.2	Rép. centrafricaine
Chad	1983	160	(26.6)	(37.5)	-	-	..	(35.9)	(37.5)	Tchad
Comoros	1983	18	79.2	0.6	0.0	1.4	16.9d/	1.8	0.1	Comores
Democratic Yemen	1982	795	13.4	4.2	76.9e/	-	1.6	4.0	2.3	Yémen démocratique
Djibouti	1980	2f/	57.2	-	-	-	42.7	-	-	Djibouti
Equatorial Guinea	1983	20	90.0	10.0	-	-	-	-	0.4	Guinée équatoriale
Ethiopia	1982	404	74.0	17.5	7.6	0.1	0.7	0.1	2.8	Ethiopie
Gambia	1981	27	89.4	4.1	-	0.8	3.3	2.4	3.4	Gambie
Guinea	1983	431	3.4	0.4	-	95.0g/	0.5	0.7	0.0	Guinée
Guinea-Bissau	1983	12	73.0	2.0	0.1	7.8	4.9	12.2	0.1	Guinée-Bissau
Haiti	1981	154	31.2	1.1	-	4.4	62.4i/	0.9	23.0	Haïti
Lao P.D.R.	1978	12	(16.2)	(47.2)	(15.9)h/	(6.8)	(1.4)	(12.5)	(0.0)	Rép. dém. pop. lao
Lesotho	1981	49	10.4	18.5	0.1	-	69.7	1.3	..	Lesotho
Malawi	1982	246	92.4	2.5	-	0.1	4.9	0.1	4.3	Malawi
Maldives	1981	9	85.8	4.7	0.7	0.3	8.4	0.0	1.2	Maldives
Mali	1981	155	32.7	48.3	-	0.4	6.1	12.5	47.7	Mali
Nepal	1982	88	22.8	14.4	-	1.1	60.6	1.1	37.7	Népal
Niger	1981	455	16.3	0.8	0.9	79.8	2.1	0.1	1.2	Niger
Rwanda	1983	79	80.6	2.0	0.1	15.3	1.0	1.0	-	Rwanda
Samoa	1983	19	91.5	4.0	-	0.4	3.7	0.5	0.2	Samoa
Sao Tome & Principe	1982	10	91.1	1.9	-	-	5.0	2.0	0.7	Sao Tomé-et-Principe
Sierra Leone	1981	153	24.1	1.5	0.0	33.7	40.3c/	0.3	0.1	Sierra Leone
Somalia	1980	133	86.7	7.7	4.8	0.0	0.5	0.3	0.0	Somalie
Sudan	1983	624	53.7	40.6	1.6	0.3	2.7	1.1	26.3	Soudan
Togo	1981	212	26.1	6.4	1.3	51.5	14.6	0.0	7.6	Togo
Uganda	1983	367	94.5	4.4	0.4	0.0	0.6	0.1	2.9	Ouganda
U.R. of Tanzania	1982	445	62.7	20.1	2.3	5.7	8.0	1.2	21.9	R.-U. de Tanzanie
Yemen	1981	47	21.4	2.3	0.0	1.1	73.0	2.1	0.4	Yémen
All LDCs	1982	277592	40.0	12.2	14.4	13.1	18.3	2.0	15.4	Ensemble des PMA
All developing countries i/	1982		21.9	4.8	25.0	8.2	38.5	1.6	..	Ensemble des pays en développement j/

Source : UNCTAD Handbook of International Trade and Development Statistics, Supplement 1985; and other international and national sources.

Source : CNUCED, Manuel de statistiques du commerce international et du développement, Supplément 1985, et autres sources internationales et nationales.

a/ Mainly carpets, etc. (SITC 657.5).
b/ Mainly jute fabrics woven (SITC 653.4) and textile products n.e.s. (SITC 656).
c/ Mainly diamonds.
e/ Petroleum products.
g/ Bauxite and concentrate of aluminium (SITC 287.31) and alumina (SITC 287.32).
i/ Mainly sporting goods.

d/ Essential oils (SITC 551.1) and textile products n.e.s.
f/ Excluding re-exports.
h/ Electricity.
i/ Excluding OPEC countries.

a/ Principalement les tapis, etc. (CTCI 657.5).
b/ Principalement les tissus de jute (CTCI 653.4) et les produits textiles etc. non classés ailleurs (CTCI 656).
c/ Principalement les diamants.
e/ Produits pétroliers.
g/ Bauxite et concentrés d'aluminium (CTCI 287.31) et alumina (CTCI 287.32).
i/ Principalement les articles de sport.

d/ Essences (CTCI 551.1).
f/ non-compris les ré-exportations.
h/ Electricité.
i/ Non compris les pays de l'OPEP.

Table 12

Commodity structure of imports of LDCs by main category (1983 or latest year available)

Tableau 12

Composition des importations des PMA, par principales catégories de produits (1983 ou année disponible la plus récente)

Country / Pays	Year / Année	Total value ($mill.) / Valeur totale (mill. de $)	Main category of imports (in %) / Principales catégories de produits importés (en %)						Selected commodity groups (in %) / Quelques groupes de produits (en %)		
			All food items / Produits alimentaires	Agricultural raw materials / Matières premières d'origine agricole	Fuels / Combustibles	Ores and metals / Minerais et métaux	Manufactured goods / Produits manufacturés	Un-allocated / Non-distribués	Cereals / Céréales	Crude and manufactured fertilizers / Engrais bruts et manufacturés	Transport equipment / Matériel de transport
SITC / CTCI			0+1+22+4	2-22-27-28	3	27+28+67+68	5+6+7+8-67-68	9	04	271+56	73
Afghanistan	1982	695	17.1	-	14.2	-	52.0	16.6	2.5	0.8	27.7
Bangladesh	1982	2463	26.0	5.3	12.2	8.3	47.9	0.3	15.7	6.0	5.6
Benin	1983	320	14.8	2.5	5.2	1.8	75.5	0.3	3.6	0.5	5.0
Bhutan	1981/82	52	11.5	..	14.0	7.5	51.5	15.5	5.1	0.0	11.3
Botswana	1982	682	16.2	4.3	14.2	8.3a/	51.3	5.6	5.1	0.2	11.7
Burkina Faso	1983	288	25.5	2.1	17.1	4.1	51.2	-	10.9	2.0	11.3
Burundi	1981	161	12.6	2.3	18.9	5.6	57.7	2.9	5.9	0.6	12.5
Cape Verde	1983	82	32.6	0.8	13.9	2.2	50.3	0.2	8.5	0.0	8.4
Central African Rep.	1981	95	17.8	0.6	0.2	1.6	78.9	0.8	4.2	0.2	18.4
Chad	1981	108	(23.0)	(2.1)	(1.6)	(2.9)	(70.1)	(0.3)	(11.0)	(1.8)	(8.3)
Comoros	1983	34	22.2	1.0	7.2	3.1	61.8	4.7	14.7	0.0	13.4
Democratic Yemen	1981	1699	(14.3)	(1.2)	(59.1)	(1.4)	(23.7)	(0.3)	(5.2)	(0.0)	(5.3)
Djibouti	1981	205	33.4	5.5	25.7	0.9	34.1	0.5	9.0	-	6.7
Equatorial Guinea	1981	31	..	..	..	..	..	..	..	..	..
Ethiopia	1982	787	9.8	2.7	24.6	4.2	58.7	-	5.6	0.8	12.2
Gambia	1981	124	24.1	2.0	9.3	3.5	61.0	0.2	6.6	2.7	9.7
Guinea	1983	280	12.8	0.7	29.2	2.9	53.9	0.5	5.3	0.3	7.8
Guinea-Bissau	1981	50	15.0	0.4	17.3	2.1	65.0	0.2	7.9	6.6	13.4
Haiti	1981	461	22.6	1.2	8.6	4.1	61.4	2.1	9.5	0.4	8.2
Lao P.D.R.	1981	125	20.8	0.1	18.9	3.6	53.5	3.3	16.2	3.3	14.1
Lesotho	1981	512	24.6	0.4	9.6	2.7	59.0	3.7	5.9	1.5	9.8
Malawi	1982	311	5.5	0.4	11.4	1.3	80.2	1.3	0.8	2.7	27.6
Maldives	1980	26	43.7	(1.6)b/	16.0	(2.1)	36.6	-	16.0	-	9.4d/
Mali	1983	344	15.4	0.7	17.6	2.6	63.1	0.4	5.4	7.0	10.0
Nepal	1981	369	9.6	0.6	19.1	7.2	62.9	0.5	3.7	7.0	7.7
Niger	1982	442	10.2	0.6	4.4	5.4	78.8	0.6	2.2	0.3	11.1
Rwanda	1983	279	11.9	4.1	18.4	..	62.1c/	3.4	5.4	0.1	9.5
Samoa	1983	56	25.2	0.7	13.1	3.1	54.9	3.0	4.0	0.8	18.3
Sao Tome & Principe	1977	14	46.0	0.5	1.8	3.0	45.7	3.0	15.1	0.3	6.0
Sierra Leone	1981	312	23.4	1.4	2.2	4.3	67.7	1.0	6.7	0.3	16.0
Somalia	1982	330	33.3	0.8	1.2	1.8	59.5	3.4	17.4	0.0	26.8
Sudan	1983	1354	13.0	1.2	21.4	3.1	60.9	0.4	5.1	2.7	12.6
Togo	1981	436	25.7	1.7	8.4	3.1	61.1	0.3	5.2	0.2	7.3
Uganda	1983	385	(13.1)	(0.3)	(27.7)	(2.5)	(56.1)	(0.3)	(3.1)	(0.0)	(11.1)
U.R. of Tanzania	1982	1134	12.1	1.2	8.5	5.7	72.1	0.4	8.6	1.1	22.2
Yemen	1981	1758	32.0	0.2	8.3	4.7	53.9	0.8	7.7	0.6	10.3
All LDCs / Ensemble des PMA	1982		19.5	1.9	17.6	4.3	55.1	1.6	7.8	1.9	11.6
All developing countries e/ / Ensemble des pays en développement e/	1982	334321	10.5	2.8	25.8	5.7	51.4	3.8	..	..	..

Source : UNCTAD Handbook of International Trade and Development Statistics, Supplement 1985, and other international and national sources.

Source : CNUCED, Manuel de statistiques du commerce international et du développement, Supplément 1985, et autres sources internationales et nationales.

a/ Including metal products. — Y compris les produits métalliques.
b/ SITC 2. — CTCI 2.
c/ SITC 5+6+7+8. — CTCI 5+6+7+8.
d/ SITC 7. — CTCI 7.
e/ Excluding OPEC countries. — Non compris les pays de l'OPEP.

Table 13

Tableau 13

Main markets for exports of LDCs : relative shares in 1983 (or latest year available)

Principaux marchés aux exportations des PMA : Parts relatives en 1983 (ou année disponible la plus récente)

Percentages

En pourcentage

Country	Year	Developed market economy countries — Pays développés à économie de marché					Socialist countries — Pays socialistes		Developing Countries — Pays en développement			Un-allocated	Pays
	Année	Total	EEC — CEE	Japan — Japon	USA and Canada — Etats-Unis et Canada	Other a/ — Autres a/	Eastern Europe — Europe orientale	Asia — Asie	Total	OPEC — OPEP	Other — Autres	Non-distribués	
Afghanistan	1982	16.8	12.7	0.0	1.1	3.0	(50.8)	(0.4)	32.0	3.1	28.9	-	Afghanistan
Bangladesh	1982	39.1	16.0	6.1	11.9	5.1	10.3	4.1	46.6	8.6	38.0	-	Bangladesh
Benin	1983	93.5	45.8	0.8	36.1	10.8	0.0	0.0	4.8	-	4.8	1.7	Bénin
Bhutan	1981/82	-	-	-	-	-	-	-	100.0	-	-	-	Bhoutan
Botswana	1982	85.5	13.8	0.1	11.9	59.7b/	-	-	12.9	0.1	12.8	1.6	Botswana
Burkina Faso	1983	34.6	27.7	4.4	1.1	1.4	-	11.4	53.7	1.4	52.3	0.3	Burkina Faso
Burundi	1983	90.6	71.2	7.2	2.1	10.1	-	-	5.6	-	5.6	3.8	Burundi
Cape Verde	1981	82.8	13.8	0.2	-	69.0	-	-	17.2	-	17.2	-	Cap-Vert
Central African Rep.	1982	94.1	72.2	-	4.8	16.9	-	0.7	5.2	0.4	4.8	-	Rép. centrafricaine
Chad	1982	65.4	30.7	1.6	0.2	32.9	-	-	27.5	-	27.5	7.1	Tchad
Comores	1983	94.7	66.1	0.5	24.3	3.8	-	-	2.6	-	2.6	2.7	Comores
Democratic Yemen	..	..	..	..	..	..	..	..	..	..	..	..	Yémen démocratique
Djibouti	1983	25.6	25.3	..	..	0.3	..	..	72.6	5.4	67.2	1.8	Djibouti
Equatorial Guinea	1983	94.1	68.1	-	0.4	25.6	-	-	5.5	-	5.5	0.4	Guinée équatoriale
Ethiopia	1983	64.6	33.7	4.9	21.9	4.1	1.5	-	32.5	6.2	26.3	1.4	Ethiopie
Gambia	1982	86.5	53.1	-	1.0	32.4	-	-	6.3	-	6.3	7.2	Gambie
Guinea	1983	93.7	36.3	-	36.7	20.7	-	-	5.1	0.1	5.0	1.2	Guinée
Guinea-Bissau	1981	82.6	17.9	-	-	64.7	-	9.5	7.9	-	7.9	-	Guinée-Bissau
Haiti	1982/83	(87.2)	33.4	0.5	53.3	..	(47.0)	-	(7.4)	..	(7.4)	(5.4)	Haïti
Lao People's Dem.Rep.	1983	10.4	1.4	4.1	4.8	0.1	-	7.9	27.1	..	27.1	7.6	Rép.dém.populaire lao
Lesotho	1981	99.1	10.3	-	0.2	88.6b/	-	-	0.9	-	0.9	-	Lesotho
Malawi	1983	72.1	46.4	4.7	6.8	14.2	-	-	26.6	-	26.6	1.3	Malawi
Maldives	1983	38.2	4.0	4.5	29.1	0.6	-	-	61.8	-	61.8	-	Maldives
Mali	1983	47.2	39.6	4.1	0.4	3.1	1.0	2.6	11.8	0.5	11.3	37.4	Mali
Nepal	1983/84	24.4	20.5	0.5	1.8	1.6	3.1	2.4	70.1	0.0	70.1	0.0	Népal
Niger	1981	64.4	41.5	17.7	0.0	5.2	-	-	34.9	34.1	0.8	0.7	Niger
Rwanda	1982	20.6	19.8	-	0.3	0.5	-	-	79.4	-	79.4	-	Rwanda
Samoa	1982	87.5	11.9	25.0	20.0	30.6	-	-	6.3	-	6.3	6.2	Samoa
Sao Tome & Principe	1980	96.9	86.2	-	-	10.7	-	-	0.4	-	0.4	2.7	Sao Tomé-et-Principe
Sierra Leone	1982	96.4	62.7	0.7	30.9	2.1	-	1.6	2.0	0.0	2.0	-	Sierra Leone
Somalia	1980	16.2	15.2	0.0	0.2	0.8	-	0.5	83.3	79.2	4.1	-	Somalie
Sudan	1983	37.0	24.4	5.4	2.0	5.3	8.6	9.2	44.1	19.7	24.4	1.1	Soudan
Togo	1982	67.5	54.2	0.7	0.1	12.5	4.8	0.0	27.3	1.0	26.3	0.4	Togo
Uganda	1982	94.3	34.6	6.3	43.9	9.5	-	0.0	3.7	0.2	3.5	1.9	Ouganda
U.R. of Tanzania	1981	58.7	45.1	2.8	4.1	6.7	2.8	0.2	36.9	11.6	25.3	1.4	R.-U. de Tanzanie
Yemen	1982	19.5	18.9	0.6	0.0	-	-	0.2	73.6	19.2	54.4	6.7	Yémen
All LDCs	1982	58.3	29.5	3.5	12.1	13.2	8.1	1.7	29.7	8.8	20.9	2.2	Ensemble des PMA
All developing countriesC/	1982	60.6	18.7	9.6	26.0	6.3	5.8	1.7	30.5	8.3	22.2	1.4	Ensemble des pays en développement c/

Source : UNCTAD Handbook of International Trade and Development Statistics, Supplement 1985; IMF, Direction of Trade (tapes and Yearbook 1984) and other international and national souces.

a/ Including EFTA.
b/ Including the South African Customs Union.
c/ Excluding OPEC countries.

Source : CNUCED Manuel de statistiques du commerce international et du développement, Supplément 1985; FMI, Direction of Trade (bandes magnétiques et Yearbook 1984) et autres sources internationales et nationales.

a/ Y compris l'AELE.
b/ Y compris l'Union douanière de l'Afrique du sud.
c/ Non compris les pays de l'OPEP.

Table 14

Tableau 14

Main sources of imports of LDCs : relative shares in 1983
(or latest year available)

Principales sources d'importation des PMA : parts relatives en 1983
(ou année disponible la plus récente)

Percentages / En pourcentage

Country / Pays	Year / Année	Developed market economy countries / Pays développés à économie de marché					Socialist countries / Pays socialistes		Developing Countries / Pays en développement			Un-allocated / Non-distribués
		Total	EEC / CEE	Japan / Japon	USA and Canada / Etats-Unis et Canada	Other / Autres [a]	Eastern Europe / Europe orientale	Asia / Asie	Total	OPEC / OPEP	Other / Autres	
Afghanistan	1982	19.1	3.0	12.0	0.6	3.5	(60.3)	(1.1)	19.5	0.0	19.5	-
Bangladesh	1983	44.8	15.5	7.3	16.1	5.9	5.2	2.8	44.5	18.3	26.2	2.7
Benin	1983	86.8	52.6	2.9	0.5	30.8	-	3.8	9.5	-	9.5	-
Bhutan	1981/82	(2.7)	-	-	-	(2.7)	-	-	(97.3)	-	(97.3)	-
Botswana	1982	92.0	3.5	0.3	1.7	86.5 [b]	-	-	6.5	0.0	6.5	1.4
Burkina Faso	1983	61.2	43.6	4.3	10.8	2.5	0.3	2.2	36.0	2.4	33.6	0.3
Burundi	1983	58.1	45.9	6.4	3.5	2.3	2.4	3.2	31.1	14.4	16.7	5.1
Cape Verde	1983	88.7	39.3	-	-	49.4	-	2.8	7.8	-	7.8	0.7
Central African Rep.	1982	66.8	56.3	4.2	3.9	2.4	0.2	0.5	25.0	0.9	24.1	7.5
Chad	1983	69.0	58.1	0.1	9.6	1.2	-	0.3	26.6	0.8	25.8	4.1
Comoros	1980	82.0	53.6	4.4	23.3	0.7	-	-	16.3	-	16.3	1.7
Democratic Yemen	1983	24.3	13.7	5.7	2.2	2.7	0.2	-	75.5	50.8	24.7	-
Djibouti	1983	56.8	44.7	8.4	2.5	1.2	-	-	27.2	1.3	25.9	16.0
Equatorial Guinea	1982	92.8	25.4	0.3	1.0	66.1	-	-	4.9	0.8	4.1	2.3
Ethiopia	1982	58.7	37.1	9.0	4.9	7.7	31.5	0.5	8.3	1.2	7.1	1.0
Gambia	1980	59.8	51.4	2.8	2.8	2.7	7.9	15.9	7.6	-	7.6	8.8
Guinea	1983	65.3	49.1	1.3	9.2	5.7	-	-	28.7	0.1	28.6	6.0
Guinea-Bissau	1983	75.5	42.8	2.2	-	30.5	-	4.2	20.3	-	20.3	-
Haiti	1983	91.7	11.6	4.9	73.8	1.4	..	..	7.2	-	7.2	(1.1)
Lao People's Dem.Rep.	1982	32.8	18.2	12.4	0.4	1.8	..	..	66.0	-	66.0	1.2
Lesotho	1981	99.1	1.5	0.0	0.3	97.3 [b]	-	-	0.9	-	0.9	-
Malawi	1983	82.5	27.9	6.9	3.9	43.8	-	-	17.2	-	17.2	0.3
Maldives	1981	30.9	18.7	10.7	0.9	0.6	0.3	-	67.0	1.5	65.5	1.8
Mali	1983/84	61.6	51.9	3.1	3.1	3.5	-	1.2	36.4	0.3	36.1	0.8
Nepal	1983	21.7	6.8	10.9	2.4	1.6	9.3	6.0	63.0	0.3	62.7	0.0
Niger	1983	54.1	45.6	4.4	0.7	3.4	0.3	1.2	38.4	15.1	23.3	6.0
Rwanda	1982	60.4	40.4	13.0	5.0	2.0	0.7	7.0	31.9	0.1	31.8	0.1
Samoa	1982	78.4	4.0	11.8	9.8	52.8	0.1	6.9	14.5	-	14.5	-
Sao Tome & Principe	1980	96.3	35.7	8.8	-	51.8	-	-	0.4	-	0.4	3.3
Sierra Leone	1977	54.5	36.5	6.8	8.7	2.5	4.5	3.8	35.4	23.8	11.6	1.8
Somalia	1980	72.7	57.1	1.3	12.1	2.2	1.2	2.2	23.9	7.8	16.1	-
Sudan	1983	53.9	37.3	3.2	9.6	3.7	5.1	2.4	36.5	18.8	17.7	2.1
Togo	1982	75.8	60.9	6.4	5.3	3.2	1.6	3.0	18.8	5.5	13.3	0.8
Uganda	1983	46.6	36.6	5.0	2.2	2.8	0.0	0.4	46.9	3.0	43.9	6.0
U.R. of Tanzania	1983	67.2	39.6	10.4	6.5	10.7	1.5	1.8	26.1	0.9	25.2	3.4
Yemen	1982	52.6	30.3	13.3	2.1	6.9	1.5	4.3	36.4	17.4	19.0	5.2
All LDCs / Ensemble des PMA		55.4	27.1	6.6	7.8	14.0	6.4	2.0	33.9	12.3	21.6	2.3
All developing countries [c] / Ensemble des pays en développement [c]	1982	54.5	18.0	12.1	18.0	6.4	6.4	3.3	35.9	18.3	17.6	-

Source : UNCTAD Handbook of International Trade and Development Statistics, Supplement 1985; IMF, Direction of Trade (tapes and Yearbook 1984) and other international and national souces.

Source : CNUCED Manuel de statistiques du commerce international et du développement, Supplément 1985; FMI, Direction of Trade (bandes magnétiques et Yearbook 1984) et autres sources internationales et nationales.

a/ Including EFTA.
b/ Including the South African Customs Union.
c/ Excluding OPEC countries.

a/ Y compris l'AELE.
b/ Y compris l'Union douanière de l'Afrique du sud.
c/ Non compris les pays de l'OPEP.

Table 15

Leading exports of individual LDCs, 1982
(or latest year available)

Tableau 15

Principales exportations des PMA, par pays individuels, 1982
(ou année disponible la plus récente)

SITC / CTCI	Country and leading export commodity[a]	Value of exports in $ million / Valeur des exportations en millions de dollars	As % of country total / En % du total du pays	As % of all developing countries / En % de l'ensemble des pays en développement	As % of World / En % du Monde	Pays et principaux produits exportés[a]
		(1)	(2)	(3)	(4)	
	Afghanistan					**Afghanistan**
	All commodities	757.0	100.00	0.16	0.04	Ensemble des produits
341	Gas, natural	283.6	35.47	2.37	0.80	Gaz, naturel
051	Fresh fruit	154.0	20.34	3.97	1.63	Fruits frais
657	Floor coverings, tapestries	80.8	10.67	4.45	1.75	Tapis et tapisseries
	Bangladesh					**Bangladesh**
	All commodities	671.1	100.00	0.14	0.04	Ensemble des produits
656	Textiles, etc. products	163.3	24.33	12.28	4.77	Articles en textiles, etc.
653	Woven textiles, non-cotton	125.1	18.64	4.04	0.89	Tissus autres que les tissus de coton
264	Jute	100.1	14.92	82.26	78.89	Jute
031	Fresh fish, simply preserved	66.4	9.90	1.40	0.60	Poisson frais,conservé de façon simple
611	Leather	56.5	8.41	5.06	1.70	Cuirs
074	Tea and mate	50.4	7.51	4.12	3.54	Thé et maté
	Benin					**Bénin**
	All commodities	22.0	100.00	0.00	0.00	Ensemble des produits
072	Cocoa	7.5	34.05	0.30	0.23	Cacao
422	Fixed vegetable oil, non-soft	5.1	23.03	0.20	0.17	Huiles végétales fixes, non fluides
263	Cotton	2.9	13.38	0.11	0.04	Coton
221	Oil seeds, nuts, kernels	1.4	6.34	0.12	0.02	Graines, noix, amandes oléagineuses
661	Cement, etc. building products	1.3	5.74	0.09	0.03	Ciment,etc., produits de construction
	Burkina Faso					**Burkina Faso**
	All commodities	56.2	100.00	0.01	0.00	Ensemble des produits
263	Cotton	23.6	41.92	0.89	0.36	Coton
221	Oil seeds, nuts, kernels	9.0	16.01	0.75	0.10	Graines, noix, amandes oléagineuses
001	Live animals	7.1	12.66	0.80	0.14	Animaux vivants
629	Articles of rubber, n.e.s.	2.9	5.10	0.39	0.03	Articles en caoutchouc, n.d.a.
	Burundi					**Burundi**
	All commodities	88.0	100.00	0.02	0.00	Ensemble des produits
071	Coffee	60.1	68.29	0.66	0.60	Café
	Cape Verde					**Cap-Vert**
	All commodities	5.0	100.00	0.00	0.00	Ensemble des produits
031	Fresh fish, simply preserved	2.1	42.14	0.04	0.02	Poisson frais,conservé de façon simple
276	Other crude minerals	1.1	21.91	0.13	0.03	Autres minéraux bruts
032	Fish etc. tinned, prepared	0.7	14.40	0.08	0.03	Préparation et conserves de poissons
051	Fresh fruit	0.3	5.40	0.01	0.00	Fruits frais
	Central African Republic					**République centrafricaine**
	All commodities	107.9	100.00	0.02	0.01	Ensemble des produits
071	Coffee	35.8	33.17	0.39	0.36	Café
667	Pearls, precious and semi-precious stones (diamonds)	26.3	24.39	1.82	0.26	Perles fines, pierres gemmes et similaires (diamants)
242	Wood rough	14.0	12.98	0.53	0.25	Bois bruts
243	Wood shaped	7.7	7.16	0.45	0.08	Bois équarris
263	Cotton	6.9	6.36	0.26	0.10	Coton
291	Crude animal materials, n.e.s.	6.3	5.84	1.53	0.50	Matières brutes d'origine animale, n.d.a.
	Chad					**Tchad**
	All commodities	58.0	100.00	0.01	0.00	Ensemble des produits
263	Cotton	43.2	74.46	1.74	0.70	Coton
652	Cotton fabrics, woven	10.0	17.16	0.47	0.15	Tissus de coton
	Comoros					**Comores**
	All commodities	11.0	100.00	0.00	0.00	Ensemble des produits
075	Spices	5.5	49.94	0.65	0.55	Epices
551	Essential oils, perfumes, etc.	2.2	19.65	1.06	0.14	Huiles essentielles, produits utilisés en parfumerie, etc.
283	Non-ferrous metal ores	1.6	14.15	0.03	0.02	Minerais de métaux communs non-ferreux
221	Oil seeds, nuts, kernels	0.6	5.28	0.05	0.01	Graines, noix, amandes oléagineuses
	Democratic Yemen					**Yémen démocratique**
	All commodities	737.0	100.00	0.16	0.04	Ensemble des produits
332	Petroleum products	507.5	68.86	1.25	0.53	Produits dérivés du pétrole
031	Fresh fish, simply preserved	80.6	10.94	1.70	0.73	Poisson frais, conservé de façon simple
331	Crude petroleum, etc.	55.9	7.58	0.03	0.02	Pétrole brut, etc.
	Equatorial Guinea					**Guinée équatoriale**
	All commodities	25.3	100.00	0.01	0.00	Ensemble des produits
072	Cocoa	13.6	53.61	0.55	0.42	Cacao
242	Wood rough	7.3	28.96	0.28	0.13	Bois bruts
283	Non-ferrous metal ores	1.3	5.15	0.02	0.01	Minerais de métaux communs non-ferreux

Table 15 (continued)　　　　　　　　　　Tableau 15 (suite)　　　　TD/B/AC.17/25/Add.5
　　　　　　　　　　　　　　　　　　　　　　　　　　　　　　　　　page 17

Leading exports of individual LDCs, 1982　　　Principales exportations des PMA, par pays individuels, 1982
(or latest year available)　　　　　　　　　(ou année disponible la plus récente)

		(1)	(2)	(3)	(4)	
	Ethiopia					**Ethiopie**
	All commodities	404.3	100.00	0.09	0.02	Ensemble des produits
071	Coffee	248.7	61.53	2.73	2.47	Café
211	Hides, skins, undressed	41.2	10.19	11.81	1.55	Cuirs et peaux non apprêtés
332	Petroleum products	30.9	7.65	0.08	0.03	Produits dérivés du pétrole
	Gambia					**Gambie**
	All commodities	44.0	100.00	0.01	0.00	Ensemble des produits
221	Oil seeds, nuts, kernels	18.6	42.32	1.56	0.20	Graines, noix, amandes oléagineuses
421	Fixed vegetable oils, soft	13.6	31.00	1.29	0.41	Huiles végétales fixes, fluides
081	Animal feeding stuff	5.4	12.24	0.16	0.05	Nourriture destinée aux animaux
	Guinea					**Guinée**
	All commodities	420.5	100.00	0.09	0.02	Ensemble des produits
283	Non-ferrous metal ores	399.3	94.96	6.98	4.29	Minerais de métaux communs non-ferreux
	Guinea-Bissau					**Guinée-Bissau**
	All commodities	12.0	100.00	0.00	0.00	Ensemble des produits
221	Oil seeds, nuts, kernels	5.2	43.52	0.44	0.06	Graines, noix, amandes oléagineuses
031	Fresh fish, simply preserved	2.9	24.56	0.06	0.03	Poisson frais, conservé de façon simple
276	Other crude minerals	1.0	8.69	0.12	0.03	Autres minéraux bruts
263	Cotton	0.6	5.19	0.02	0.01	Coton
243	Wood shaped	0.6	5.12	0.04	0.01	Bois équarris
	Haiti					**Haïti**
	All commodities	162.0	100.00	0.03	0.01	Ensemble des produits
071	Coffee	36.4	22.47	0.40	0.36	Café
841	Clothing (except fur clothing)	29.5	18.23	0.18	0.08	Vêtements (à l'exclusion des vêtements de fourrure)
894	Toys, sporting goods, etc.	19.1	11.77	0.51	0.22	Jouets, articles pour divertissements, etc.
722	Electric power machinery, etc.	8.7	5.39	0.37	0.03	Machines électriques génératrices, etc.
	Lao People's Democratic Republic					**République démocratique populaire lao**
	All commodities	18.0	100.00	0.00	0.00	Ensemble des produits
242	Wood rough	5.4	30.07	0.20	0.10	Bois bruts
673	Iron and steel shapes	2.8	15.78	0.22	0.02	Profilés, en fer ou en acier
071	Coffee	1.5	8.15	0.02	0.01	Café
243	Wood shaped	1.4	7.66	0.08	0.01	Bois équarris
	Malawi					**Malawi**
	All commodities	259.0	100.00	0.05	0.01	Ensemble des produits
121	Tobacco, unmanufactured	128.2	49.51	6.50	3.01	Tabacs bruts
074	Tea and mate	48.9	18.88	4.00	3.43	Thé et maté
061	Sugar and honey	40.5	15.65	0.53	0.36	Sucre et miel
	Maldives					**Maldives**
	All commodities	10.0	100.00	0.00	0.00	Ensemble des produits
031	Fresh fish, simply preserved	5.4	54.52	0.12	0.15	Poisson frais, conservé de façon simple
032	Fish etc. tinned, prepared	2.6	25.74	0.27	0.10	Préparation et conserves de poisson
074	Tea and mate	0.5	5.40	0.04	0.04	Thé et maté
	Mali					**Mali**
	All commodities	146.0	100.00	0.03	0.01	Ensemble des produits
263	Cotton	66.9	45.80	2.52	1.01	Coton
221	Oil seeds, nuts, kernels	23.7	16.26	1.99	0.26	Graines, noix, amandes oléagineuses
001	Live animals	9.7	6.66	1.09	0.19	Animaux vivants
	Nepal					**Nepal**
	All commodities	87.0	100.00	0.02	0.00	Ensemble des produits
611	Leather	16.5	18.91	1.47	0.49	Cuirs
657	Floor coverings, tapestries	14.1	16.23	0.78	0.31	Tapis et tapisseries
042	Rice	9.6	11.03	0.54	0.27	Riz
653	Woven textiles, non-cotton	6.8	7.81	0.22	0.05	Tissus autres que les tissus de coton
291	Crude animal materials, n.e.s.	6.4	7.38	1.56	0.51	Matières brutes d'origine animale, n.d.a.
054	Vegetables, fresh, frozen or simple preserved	6.4	7.31	0.24	0.08	Légumes frais, congelés ou simplement en conserve
656	Textiles, etc. products	4.8	5.51	0.36	0.14	Articles en textiles, etc.
264	Jute	4.6	5.32	3.80	3.65	Jute
	Niger					**Niger**
	All commodities	333.0	100.00	0.07	0.02	Ensemble des produits
515	Radioactive and associated materials	299.3	89.89	91.16	7.56	Matières radioactives, produits associés
331	Crude petroleum, etc.	19.6	5.88	0.01	0.01	Pétrole brut, etc.
	Rwanda					**Rwanda**
	All commodities	89.0	100.00	0.02	0.00	Ensemble des produits
071	Coffee	65.9	74.01	0.72	0.65	Café
283	Non-ferrous metal ores (tin and tungsten)	9.0	10.11	0.16	0.10	Minerais de métaux communs non-ferreux (étain et tungstène)
074	Tea and mate	6.2	6.98	0.51	0.44	Thé et maté

Table 15 (continued)

Leading exports of individual LDCs, 1982
(or latest year available)

Tableau 15 (suite)

Principales exportations des PMA, par pays individuels, 1982
(ou année disponible la plus récente)

SITC / CTCI	Country and leading export commodity[a/]	Value of exports in $ million / Valeur des exportations en millions de dollars	As % of country total / En % du total du pays	As % of all developing countries / En % de l'ensemble des pays en développement	As % of World / En % du Monde	Pays et principaux produits exportés[a/]
		(1)	(2)	(3)	(4)	
	Samoa					Samoa
	All commodities	13.0	100.00	0.00	0.00	Ensemble des produits
221	Oil seeds, nuts, kernels	7.0	53.71	0.58	0.08	Graines, noix, amandes oléagineuses
072	Cocoa	2.4	18.41	0.10	0.07	Cacao
054	Vegetables, fresh, frozen or simply preserved	1.1	8.35	0.04	0.01	Légumes frais, congelés ou simplement en conserve
	Sao Tome and Principe					Sao Tomé-et-Principe
	All commodities	7.4	100.00	0.00	0.00	Ensemble des produits
072	Cocoa	5.1	69.20	0.21	0.16	Cacao
221	Oil seeds, nuts, kernels	1.5	19.66	0.12	0.02	Graines, noix, amandes oléagineuses
	Sierra Leone					Sierra Leone
	All commodities	125.0	100.00	0.03	0.01	Ensemble des produits
667	Pearls, precious and semi-precious stones	48.4	38.70	3.35	0.47	Perles fines, pierres gemmes et similaires
275	Natural abrasives	28.3	22.67	34.39	5.75	Abrasifs naturels
283	Non-ferrous metal ores	13.1	10.48	0.23	0.14	Minerais de métaux communs non-ferreux
072	Cocoa	11.2	8.98	0.45	0.35	Cacao
071	Coffee	11.2	8.96	0.12	0.11	Café
	Somalia					Somalie
	All commodities	212.0	100.00	0.04	0.01	Ensemble des produits
001	Live animals	162.0	76.42	18.23	3.17	Animaux vivants
051	Fresh fruit (bananas)	12.0	5.66	0.31	0.13	Fruits frais (bananes)
211	Hides, skins, undressed	11.4	5.36	3.26	0.43	Cuirs et peaux non apprêtés
	Sudan					Soudan
	All commodities	499.0	100.00	0.11	0.03	Ensemble des produits
263	Cotton	130.0	26.06	4.90	1.96	Coton
044	Maize (corn), unmilled	75.0	15.03	6.10	0.85	Maïs non moulu
001	Live animals	64.0	12.83	7.20	1.25	Animaux vivants
292	Crude vegetable materials, n.e.s.	40.3	8.07	3.45	0.88	Matières brutes d'origine végétale, n.d.a.
221	Oil seeds, nuts, kernels	35.4	7.09	2.96	0.38	Graines, noix, amandes oléagineuses
081	Animal feeding stuff	26.2	5.26	0.80	0.26	Nourriture destinée aux animaux
	Togo					Togo
	All commodities	126.0	100.00	0.03	0.01	Ensemble des produits
271	Fertilizers, crude	64.6	51.25	5.67	3.15	Engrais bruts
332	Petroleum products	20.5	16.30	0.05	0.02	Produits dérivés du pétrole
072	Cocoa	15.4	12.21	0.62	0.47	Cacao
071	Coffee	12.2	9.66	0.13	0.12	Café
	Uganda					Ouganda
	All commodities	354.2	100.00	0.07	0.02	Ensemble des produits
071	Coffee	340.3	96.09	3.73	3.38	Café
	United Republic of Tanzania					République-Unie de Tanzanie
	All commodities	427.0	100.00	0.09	0.02	Ensemble des produits
071	Coffee	131.3	30.76	1.44	1.30	Café
263	Cotton	56.4	13.21	2.12	0.85	Coton
075	Spices	50.5	11.82	5.99	5.11	Epices
074	Tea and mate	22.6	5.28	1.84	1.58	Thé et maté
	Yemen					Yémen
	All commodities	18.0	100.00	0.00	0.00	Ensemble des produits
276	Other crude minerals	3.6	19.98	0.42	0.09	Autres minéraux bruts
211	Hides, skins, undressed	3.1	17.00	0.88	0.12	Cuirs et peaux non apprêtés
332	Petroleum products	2.4	13.15	0.01	0.00	Produits dérivés du pétrole
071	Coffee	2.2	12.16	0.02	0.02	Café

Source : UNCTAD Handbook of International Trade and Development Statistics, Supplement 1985.

Source : CNUCED Manuel de statistiques du commerce international et du développement, Supplément 1985.

Note : Column (1) shows export values f.o.b. in millions of dollars. Column (2) shows for each commodity presented its percentage share in the individual country export total, while columns (3) and (4) show the relative importance of each commodity shown expressed as a percentage of the relevant total group for that commodity (i.e. "all developing countries" and "world" respectively).

Note : La colonne (1) montre la valeur des exportations f.o.b. en millions de dollars. La colonne (2) montre, pour chaque produit indiqué, sa part en pourcentage dans le total des exportations du pays concerné, alors que les colonnes (3) et (4) montrent l'importance relative de chaque produit indiqué présenté comme part en pourcentage du total du groupe de produits auquel il se rapporte (total se référant respectivement à "l'ensemble des pays en développement" et au "monde").

a/ A "leading export commodity" is one which accounts for at least 5 per cent of the country's total exports.

a/ Par "principaux produits exportés" on entend les produits équivalent chacun à 5 pour cent au moins du total des exportations du pays concerné.

Table 16
Leading exports of LDCs as a group (Ranked according to 1982 value in $ million)a/

Tableau 16
Principales exportations de l'ensemble des PMA (Classées selon leur valeur en millions de dollars en 1982)a/

SITC CTCI	Item	Value of exports in $ million / Valeur des exportations en millions de dollars	As % of total exports of LDCs / En % du total des exportations des PMA	As % of all developing countries, exports of products shown / En % du total des exportations des produits indiqués effectuées par l'ensemble des pays en développement	As % of world exports of products shown / En % du total des exportations des produits indiqués effectuées par le monde	Produit
	All commodities	6349.9	100.00	1.34	0.34	Ensemble des produits
071	Coffee	967.2	15.23	10.60	9.61	Café
332	Petroleum products	604.3	9.52	1.49	0.63	Produits dérivés du pétrole
283	Ores & concentrates of non-ferrous base metals	432.7	6.81	7.56	4.65	Minerais de métaux communs non-ferreux & concentrés
263	Cotton	389.7	6.14	14.68	5.88	Coton
515	Radioactive and associated materials	299.3	4.71	91.16	7.56	Matières radioactives et produits associés
341	Gas, natural and manufactured	286.7	4.52	2.39	0.81	Gaz naturel et gaz manufacturé
001	Live animals	252.8	3.98	28.45	4.94	Animaux vivants
051	Fruit, fresh and nuts, fresh or dried	191.7	3.02	4.94	2.03	Fruits frais et noix fraîches ou sèches
656	Made-up articles, of textile materials,n.e.s.	176.4	2.78	13.26	5.15	Articles façonnés en textiles, n.d.a.
031	Fish, fresh and simply preserved	172.4	2.71	3.64	1.55	Poisson frais ou conservé de façon simple
121	Tobacco, unmanufactured	154.4	2.43	7.83	3.63	Tabacs bruts
221	Oil seeds, nuts and kernels	147.4	2.32	12.33	1.59	Graines, noix et amandes oléagineuses
653	Textile fabrics, other than cotton fabrics	134.3	2.12	4.34	0.96	Tissus autres que les tissus de coton
074	Tea and Mate	133.2	2.10	10.89	9.34	Thé et maté
264	Jute	105.4	1.66	86.60	83.04	Jute
211	Hides and skins, undressed	105.3	1.66	30.20	3.98	Cuirs et peaux, non-apprêtés
667	Pearls, precious and semi-precious stones	98.1	1.55	6.79	0.96	Perles fines, pierres gemmes et similaires
657	Floor coverings, tapestries, etc.	97.8	1.54	5.39	2.12	Tapis et tapisseries, etc.
292	Crude vegetable materials, n.e.s.	96.3	1.52	8.25	2.11	Matières brutes d'origine végétale, n.d.a.
611	Leather	92.8	1.46	8.31	2.79	Cuirs
044	Maize (corn.), unmilled	77.4	1.22	6.29	0.87	Maïs, non moulu
331	Crude petroleum, etc.	75.5	1.19	0.04	0.03	Pétrole brut, etc.
841	Clothing (except fur clothing)	75.3	1.19	0.46	0.21	Vêtements(à l'exclusion des vêtements de fourrure)
054	Vegetables, fresh, frozen or simply preserved	74.4	1.17	2.76	0.96	Légumes frais, congelés ou simplement en conserve
075	Spices	70.5	1.11	8.36	7.13	Epices
061	Sugar and honey	66.3	1.04	0.86	0.59	Sucre et miel
271	Fertilizers, crude	64.6	1.02	5.67	3.15	Engrais bruts
072	Cocoa	61.8	0.97	2.48	1.90	Cacao
081	Feeding-stuff for animals	59.8	0.94	1.82	0.60	Nourriture destinée aux animaux
291	Crude animal materials, n.e.s.	50.6	0.80	12.26	4.01	Matières brutes d'origine animale, n.d.a.
242	Wood, rough	38.0	0.60	1.43	0.69	Bois bruts
275	Natural abrasives	34.6	0.54	41.97	7.01	Abrasifs naturels
042	Rice	26.5	0.42	1.49	0.74	Riz
655	Special textile fabrics and related products	22.6	0.36	3.91	0.52	Textiles spéciaux et produits connexes
212	Fur skins, undressed	21.9	0.35	49.93	1.52	Pelleteries, non-apprêtées
718	Machines for special industries	21.9	0.34	2.46	0.07	Machines pour industries spécialisées
421	Fixed vegetable oils, soft	21.8	0.34	2.06	0.65	Huiles végétales fixes, fluides
652	Cotton fabrics, woven	21.3	0.34	1.02	0.33	Tissus de coton
894	Toys, sporting goods, etc.	20.8	0.33	0.55	0.24	Jouets, articles pour divertissements, etc.
265	Vegetable fibres, except cotton and jute	20.7	0.33	14.48	6.98	Fibres végétales autres que le coton et le jute
651	Textile yarn and thread	19.4	0.31	0.75	0.17	Filés et fils textiles
243	Wood, shaped or simply worked	19.1	0.30	1.11	0.21	Bois équarris ou dégrossis
422	Other fixed vegetable oils	13.6	0.21	0.55	0.46	Autres huiles végétales fixes
722	Electric power machinery, etc.	13.3	0.21	0.57	0.05	Machines électriques génératrices, etc.
276	Other crude minerals	11.4	0.18	1.32	0.30	Autres minéraux bruts
724	Telecommunications apparatus	11.2	0.18	0.19	0.04	Appareils de télécommunications
732	Road motor vehicles	10.3	0.16	0.35	0.01	Véhicules automobiles routiers

Source : UNCTAD secretariat computations based on data of the United Nations Statistical Office.

a/ Data for 34 LDCs (i.e., excluding Botswana and Lesotho) accounting for over 90 per cent of the total exports of LDCs. "Leading exports" refer to exports exceeding $ 10 million in 1982.

Source : Calculs du secrétariat de la CNUCED basés sur des données du Bureau de statistique des Nations Unies.

a/ Les données se rapportent à 34 PMA (c.à.d. à l'exclusion du Botswana et du Lesotho) dont les exportations représentent plus de 90 pour cent du total des exportations des PMA. Par "principales exportations", on entend les exportations de produits atteignant plus de 10 millions de $ en 1982.

Table 17

Tableau 17

Foreign exchange receipts and import volume expressed in constant 1980 dollars a/ per capita, 1970-1983

Rentrées de devises et volume des importations, en dollars constants de 1980 a/ par habitant, 1970-1983

A. Export purchasing power per capita

A. Pouvoir d'achat des exportations, par habitant

Country	1970	1971	1972	1973	1974	1975	1976	1977	1978	1979	1980	1981	1982	1983	Pays
Afghanistan	23.6	25.3	29.0	29.1	31.7	28.6	37.0	34.4	31.2	37.8	44.2	44.3	46.1	45.2	Afghanistan
Bangladesh	27.7	16.6	14.1	10.9	8.9	6.6	9.2	8.6	9.3	8.9	8.3	7.9	8.4	8.7	Bangladesh
Benin	38.7	53.6	41.2	39.3	28.5	19.0	21.7	20.8	15.6	11.5	15.6	10.7	9.6	13.1	Bénin
Bhutan	..	..	..	..	..	..	..	..	..	..	..	..	..	..	Bhoutan
Botswana	156.4	228.1	282.5	318.5	321.3	338.7	400.3	359.2	388.4	603.7	554.0	413.0	501.2	710.1	Botswana
Burkina Faso	12.4	10.1	11.6	11.4	12.5	14.1	16.8	15.3	10.6	15.2	14.6	12.2	9.3	9.6	Burkina Faso
Burundi	26.9	19.8	25.0	22.0	15.9	15.4	28.6	37.3	25.8	31.4	15.8	17.3	21.8	19.1	Burundi
Cape Verde	29.6	27.2	24.9	19.5	14.1	12.9	12.5	11.3	9.1	10.2	14.0	10.5	13.6	14.4	Cap-Vert
Central African Republic	51.1	49.9	54.8	41.8	41.1	37.5	45.8	56.9	43.3	39.5	50.2	36.0	50.0	46.2	République centrafricaine
Chad	35.1	32.9	39.2	36.2	27.6	31.5	36.0	57.9	43.9	38.7	32.6	30.9	28.8	36.6	Tchad
Comoros	69.2	75.3	67.7	43.7	55.8	55.8	49.4	41.8	37.7	56.5	28.6	42.0	51.5	48.0	Comores
Democratic Yemen	351.4	228.7	208.1	164.7	268.0	182.8	180.6	163.4	153.8	296.6	395.6	308.3	408.6	365.0	Yémen démocratique
Djibouti	257.7	206.7	200.0	274.3	171.8	134.3	122.6	244.6	97.3	45.5	61.3	66.8	64.2	81.5	Djibouti
Equatorial Guinea	322.0	332.4	205.9	161.6	208.8	146.0	54.7	68.6	74.3	102.0	39.8	45.9	49.8	60.0	Guinée équatoriale
Ethiopia	22.8	21.4	25.5	29.3	22.5	18.1	20.8	17.9	17.9	18.5	13.7	11.2	12.2	12.6	Ethiopie
Gambia	135.9	96.8	127.6	114.7	175.5	159.8	111.3	132.3	94.5	111.8	48.3	42.1	69.3	78.4	Gambie
Guinea	70.5	65.3	58.2	48.0	52.3	80.1	105.3	107.5	96.6	84.1	81.7	87.9	82.1	93.7	Guinée
Guinea-Bissau	26.4	15.5	17.4	16.9	12.4	20.3	47.6	48.9	19.9	21.8	13.6	17.5	15.2	15.6	Guinée-Bissau
Haiti	36.3	38.4	31.5	30.7	30.8	31.7	47.6	48.1	48.6	36.5	45.1	31.1	33.5	35.2	Haïti
Lao People's Dem. Republic	4.2	6.8	4.1	4.0	6.3	5.8	6.1	4.5	4.8	11.2	7.9	8.5	10.5	14.2	République dém. populaire lao
Lesotho	20.8	13.6	23.3	29.3	23.9	19.1	24.6	18.3	36.8	41.8	43.5	36.8	27.5	18.1	Lesotho
Malawi	46.0	49.6	49.0	49.0	46.1	47.7	54.7	58.5	47.6	47.6	47.9	44.9	40.8	38.9	Malawi
Maldives	128.2	128.0	86.6	83.8	59.8	35.1	38.9	40.3	41.7	37.2	50.6	55.7	88.4	67.0	Maldives
Mali	21.0	16.9	18.2	22.3	19.8	15.6	24.1	31.3	25.0	26.0	29.4	22.3	21.4	24.9	Mali
Nepal	13.7	14.3	15.7	13.3	10.0	13.8	13.1	9.6	9.6	9.2	5.5	9.6	6.1	6.7	Népal
Niger	27.9	30.3	39.0	35.7	22.7	36.2	50.9	53.8	85.7	105.3	106.6	84.1	62.0	64.2	Niger
Rwanda	23.3	18.7	14.7	19.8	16.4	17.1	31.4	32.1	21.1	27.1	14.8	17.0	17.4	15.3	Rwanda
Samoa	132.0	146.4	112.9	124.7	169.3	83.8	82.4	159.1	105.5	140.0	108.3	71.7	87.4	132.8	Samoa
Sao Tome and Principe	405.2	327.9	301.5	436.5	414.9	157.1	175.5	455.0	375.2	384.0	199.8	101.0	120.9	122.3	Sao Tomé-et-Principe
Sierra Leone	145.3	133.5	141.8	126.4	104.3	78.4	69.4	68.5	82.4	82.5	61.9	45.0	33.6	37.6	Sierra Leone
Somalia	40.2	42.3	47.3	46.2	38.8	49.6	48.9	27.2	38.1	30.8	28.8	44.4	42.4	44.8	Somalie
Sudan	77.4	77.6	75.9	72.3	41.3	46.2	56.5	59.6	41.3	34.2	29.1	35.8	27.2	34.4	Soudan
Togo	99.8	82.0	75.1	71.5	162.0	97.1	78.2	105.3	139.6	102.6	129.9	81.6	67.7	62.7	Togo
Uganda	97.2	81.4	80.5	65.9	51.2	38.1	51.7	73.9	37.5	38.1	26.2	18.9	25.3	27.6	Ouganda
United Republic of Tanzania	80.4	77.3	79.1	72.1	53.9	45.0	56.3	55.5	43.0	35.9	26.9	29.4	22.7	18.9	République-Unie de Tanzanie
Yemen	2.1	2.6	2.4	3.7	4.2	3.3	2.3	2.8	1.6	2.5	3.3	6.7	5.6	6.6	Yémen
All LDCs	42.1	36.4	36.4	33.4	28.8	25.8	31.2	32.9	28.5	29.5	27.4	25.2	24.9	26.3	Ensemble des PMA
All developing countries b/	122.0	113.1	122.2	142.2	134.3	118.5	137.7	145.5	150.6	147.4	133.9	131.2	128.5	139.8	Ensemble des pays en développement b/

Source : UNCTAD secretariat estimates mainly based on UNCTAD Handbook of International Trade and Development Statistics, Supplement 1985.

a/ Exports, external assistance and total receipts in all years are expressed in terms of their command over imports at 1980 prices. (For the deflators used, see table 8).

b/ Excluding major petroleum exporters.

Source : Estimations du secrétariat de la CNUCED principalement d'après le Manuel de statistiques du Commerce International et du Développement, Supplément 1985, de la CNUCED.

a/ Les recettes d'exportations, les rentrées au titre de l'aide extérieure et le total des rentrées de devises pour toutes les années sont exprimés en pouvoir d'achat à l'importation aux prix de 1980. (Pour les déflateurs utilisés, se reporter au tableau 8).

b/ Non compris les principaux pays exportateurs de pétrole.

Table 17 (continued)

Foreign exchange receipts and import volume, expressed in constant 1980 dollars a/ per capita, 1970-1983

Tableau 17 (suite)

Rentrées de devises et volume des importations, en dollars constants de 1980 a/ par habitant, 1970-1983

B. External assistance per capita b/ — B. Aide extérieure, par habitant b/

Country	1970	1971	1972	1973	1974	1975	1976	1977	1978	1979	1980	1981	1982	1983	Pays
Afghanistan	14.1	20.8	20.8	14.1	12.5	13.6	14.8	13.8	13.2	12.9	21.0	17.6	11.1	17.4	Afghanistan
Bangladesh	13.6	10.0	12.3	16.8	14.2	24.6	12.2	12.4	17.1	16.4	14.0	13.0	17.7	16.4	Bangladesh
Benin	20.8	37.6	21.5	24.9	24.0	35.5	32.8	33.0	34.4	35.6	113.4	35.5	55.1	33.1	Bénin
Bhutan	0.7	0.3	0.6	1.2	1.7	3.3	4.8	3.9	5.7	5.7	6.5	7.7	9.1	10.7	Bhoutan
Botswana	86.0	96.7	344.4	504.3	24.2	204.9	122.8	79.4	37.3	194.3	58.8	121.3	131.0	144.5	Botswana
Burkina Faso	15.2	18.6	20.3	26.3	34.7	28.5	27.4	31.7	39.7	43.3	38.0	36.1	41.9	34.2	Burkina Faso
Burundi	19.7	23.1	24.8	21.8	20.1	25.5	21.9	25.7	28.2	31.4	32.2	33.3	39.8	46.5	Burundi
Cape Verde	-	-	-	2.0	-0.7	55.4	165.3	149.8	178.5	140.6	208.3	176.0	233.5	232.2	Cap-Vert
Central African Republic	22.8	23.7	37.9	30.6	33.8	46.2	30.8	29.9	30.8	42.9	55.7	47.8	46.5	46.1	République centrafricaine
Chad	21.9	26.9	26.0	29.9	41.1	35.9	28.7	35.5	49.0	23.4	7.6	11.9	13.2	19.4	Tchad
Comoros	109.3	110.4	115.1	153.7	170.5	111.6	135.9	150.6	51.5	55.2	108.9	127.6	94.8	114.1	Comores
Democratic Yemen	67.1	39.6	61.8	43.8	76.5	88.5	222.9	124.3	79.6	67.0	125.7	72.4	99.2	84.3	Yémen démocratique
Djibouti	295.2	231.5	267.3	227.6	272.0	281.1	217.7	351.5	516.5	90.7	229.7	208.6	188.2	222.7	Djibouti
Equatorial Guinea	-	48.7	47.7	28.1	118.5	2.3	-7.7	-14.2	5.7	6.7	28.4	31.9	35.8	66.6	Guinée équatoriale
Ethiopia	9.7	7.7	8.5	9.9	10.1	10.3	10.3	7.6	5.7	10.7	8.4	8.5	7.2	10.4	Ethiopie
Gambia	12.0	28.3	34.2	34.4	44.4	27.3	39.4	74.7	94.0	88.1	132.4	132.1	72.0	61.4	Gambie
Guinea	42.4	40.8	68.1	60.6	33.5	10.3	8.5	16.4	29.9	17.8	31.4	25.0	16.5	18.4	Guinée
Guinea-Bissau	11.4	18.7	2.9	-	7.6	56.6	70.0	93.7	108.6	90.3	88.4	91.2	82.6	82.1	Guinée-Bissau
Haiti	6.3	5.8	4.3	5.1	7.3	23.4	27.8	30.0	28.4	31.1	23.5	22.8	27.0	25.5	Haïti
Lao People's Dem. Republic	86.3	82.9	70.2	56.8	36.4	25.6	28.0	26.5	44.7	30.2	22.5	23.7	25.7	22.7	République dém. populaire lao
Lesotho	35.2	54.3	41.8	32.7	34.7	46.0	44.1	51.0	60.0	57.7	67.7	71.4	71.6	80.6	Lesotho
Malawi	32.9	24.6	34.3	16.8	18.2	30.6	26.0	33.5	31.3	42.8	31.6	32.0	22.3	17.9	Malawi
Maldives	6.6	23.8	18.9	12.6	14.9	72.9	75.3	57.5	97.8	55.0	146.8	111.5	13.9	108.5	Maldives
Mali	23.5	23.8	23.6	30.5	41.2	42.1	26.6	31.7	40.7	39.0	38.5	35.3	29.7	31.8	Mali
Nepal	8.0	7.4	8.2	7.9	5.1	6.4	6.7	13.8	8.2	11.9	11.0	12.5	14.1	14.1	Népal
Niger	40.4	41.5	31.5	42.7	57.8	60.2	63.5	46.7	66.6	62.4	47.4	68.6	54.5	38.2	Niger
Rwanda	21.1	22.2	23.1	23.1	20.7	37.1	33.9	33.7	37.8	38.3	30.2	29.7	29.8	29.9	Rwanda
Samoa	39.6	48.8	106.1	64.1	75.6	164.0	137.8	259.8	72.9	259.7	159.2	161.3	160.4	220.1	Samoa
Sao Tome and Principe	-3.3	-	-	-	13.3	17.5	24.1	25.2	43.3	24.9	45.9	72.2	119.6	149.2	Sao Tomé-et-Principe
Sierra Leone	41.8	49.0	7.0	14.6	58.1	108.6	68.6	179.3	84.4	71.6	115.0	77.7	132.0	21.3	Sierra Leone
Somalia	6.9	7.1	40.6	34.6	28.0	62.0	56.2	36.2	38.3	41.9	45.8	37.6	44.3	94.8	Somalie
Sudan	29.2	37.1	11.9	15.8	41.3	42.9	52.9	79.9	156.0	99.7	68.8	19.3	36.8	60.8	Soudan
Togo	14.9	12.6	40.9	28.0	4.9	7.5	7.0	4.0	-14.9	3.5	10.3	11.8	13.0	42.6	Togo
Uganda	21.6	23.7	12.4	35.3	35.6	52.1	39.5	44.5	46.5	51.3	44.4	42.5	38.1	14.5	Ouganda
United Republic of Tanzania	21.6	23.7	35.9	35.3	35.6	52.1	39.5	44.5	46.5	51.3	44.4	42.5	38.1	32.0	République-Unie de Tanzanie
Yemen	12.0	19.4	13.2	20.7	47.6	56.7	75.5	91.0	71.2	62.1	77.1	58.8	72.2	56.4	Yémen
All LDCs	17.5	17.7	20.0	21.1	21.4	30.3	25.4	26.5	27.5	27.6	28.4	25.0	27.4	27.1	Ensemble des PMA
All developing countries c/	46.1	45.7	47.2	55.8	49.8	53.1	54.5	51.2	59.9	46.4	41.9	42.2	39.5	42.8	Ensemble des pays en développement c/

Source : UNCTAD secretariat estimates mainly based on data from the OECD secretariat and the UNCTAD secretariat.

a/ Exports, external assistance, and total receipts in all years are expressed in terms of their command over imports at 1980 prices. (For the deflators used, see table 8).

b/ Total financial flows as in table 22A.

c/ Excluding major petroleum exporters.

Source : Estimations du secrétariat de la CNUCED principalement d'après des données de l'OCDE et de la CNUCED.

a/ Les recettes d'exportations, les rentrées au titre de l'aide extérieure et le total des rentrées de devises pour toutes les années sont exprimés en pouvoir d'achat à l'importation aux prix de 1980. (Pour les déflateurs utilisés, se reporter au tableau 8).

b/ Total des apports financiers comme au tableau 22A.

c/ Non compris les principaux pays exportateurs de pétrole.

Table 17 (continued)

Foreign exchange receipts and import volume, expressed in constant 1980 dollars a/ per capita, 1970-1983

Tableau 17 (suite)

Rentrées de devises et volume des importations, en dollars constants de 1980 a/ par habitant, 1970-1983

C. Total receipts b/, per capita

C. Total des rentrées de devises b/, par habitant

Country	1970	1971	1972	1973	1974	1975	1976	1977	1978	1979	1980	1981	1982	1983	Pays
Afghanistan	37.7	46.0	49.8	43.2	44.2	42.2	51.7	48.2	44.5	50.7	65.2	61.9	57.2	62.6	Afghanistan
Bangladesh	41.3	26.6	26.5	27.8	23.1	31.2	21.5	20.9	26.4	25.3	22.3	20.9	26.1	25.1	Bangladesh
Benin	59.5	91.2	62.8	64.3	52.5	54.5	54.6	53.8	50.0	47.1	128.9	46.2	64.7	46.1	Bénin
Bhutan	..	..	..	..	..	..	..	..	..	..	..	..	..	..	Bhoutan
Botswana	242.5	324.8	626.9	822.8	345.5	543.6	523.1	438.6	425.6	798.0	612.6	534.4	632.2	854.6	Botswana
Burkina Faso	27.6	28.7	31.9	37.8	47.2	42.6	44.2	46.9	50.3	58.4	52.6	48.3	51.2	43.8	Burkina Faso
Burundi	46.5	42.9	49.8	43.8	36.0	41.0	50.5	63.0	54.0	62.7	48.0	50.6	61.6	65.7	Burundi
Cape Verde	..	..	..	21.5	13.4	68.2	177.8	161.1	187.6	150.8	222.3	186.5	247.0	246.6	Cap-Vert
Central African Republic	73.9	73.6	92.7	72.4	74.9	83.7	76.6	86.9	74.1	82.3	105.9	83.8	96.5	92.2	République centrafricaine
Chad	57.0	59.8	65.2	66.1	68.7	67.4	65.2	93.4	92.9	62.1	40.2	42.8	42.0	56.0	Tchad
Comoros	178.5	185.7	182.9	197.3	226.3	167.3	185.3	192.4	89.2	111.6	137.5	169.6	146.2	162.1	Comores
Democratic Yemen	418.5	268.3	269.9	208.5	344.5	271.3	403.5	287.7	233.4	363.6	521.3	380.7	507.7	449.2	Yémen démocratique
Djibouti	552.8	438.2	467.4	501.9	443.8	415.4	340.4	596.1	613.8	136.2	291.0	275.4	252.4	304.3	Djibouti
Equatorial Guinea	..	..	253.6	189.6	327.3	148.6	47.1	54.4	79.9	108.6	68.2	77.8	85.6	126.6	Guinée équatoriale
Ethiopia	32.4	31.8	33.1	37.8	32.3	28.2	31.0	29.2	26.5	29.2	21.3	19.7	19.4	23.1	Ethiopie
Gambia	147.9	125.2	161.8	149.1	220.3	187.1	150.7	207.0	188.5	199.9	180.7	174.1	141.2	139.8	Gambie
Guinea	112.9	106.1	126.2	108.6	85.8	90.4	113.8	123.8	126.4	102.0	113.1	112.9	98.6	112.0	Guinée
Guinea-Bissau	37.8	34.2	20.3	..	20.0	76.9	86.6	116.8	128.5	102.0	108.6	108.6	97.8	97.8	Guinée-Bissau
Haiti	42.6	44.2	35.8	35.7	38.1	55.1	75.5	78.9	76.9	67.6	68.6	53.9	60.5	60.7	Haïti
Lao People's Dem. Republic	90.5	89.7	74.4	60.8	42.7	31.3	34.0	31.0	49.5	41.4	30.5	32.2	36.2	36.9	République dém. populaire lao
Lesotho	56.0	67.9	65.1	62.0	58.6	65.1	68.6	69.2	96.8	99.5	111.2	114.3	98.9	98.6	Lesotho
Malawi	78.8	74.2	84.2	65.8	64.3	78.3	80.7	92.0	78.8	90.5	79.5	76.9	63.1	56.9	Malawi
Maldives	134.8	151.9	105.5	96.4	74.7	108.0	114.2	97.8	139.5	92.2	197.4	167.2	102.3	175.5	Maldives
Mali	44.5	40.7	41.8	52.9	61.1	57.7	50.7	63.0	65.7	65.1	67.9	57.6	51.0	56.7	Mali
Nepal	21.7	21.8	24.0	21.3	15.2	20.2	19.8	23.3	17.8	21.1	16.5	22.2	20.2	20.8	Népal
Niger	68.2	71.8	70.5	78.4	80.5	96.4	114.4	100.5	152.3	167.1	154.0	152.7	116.5	102.4	Niger
Rwanda	44.4	41.0	37.7	42.9	37.1	54.3	65.3	65.9	58.9	65.4	45.0	46.7	47.2	45.2	Rwanda
Samoa	171.6	195.2	219.0	188.9	244.9	247.8	220.2	418.8	328.8	399.7	267.5	233.0	247.8	352.9	Samoa
Sao Tome and Principe	..	..	..	..	..	177.4	432.5	516.4	448.1	427.3	245.6	173.0	240.5	271.5	Sao Tomé-et-Principe
Sierra Leone	142.0	161.2	148.7	140.9	117.5	95.9	93.4	93.7	109.5	107.4	89.5	64.5	61.3	58.9	Sierra Leone
Somalia	82.0	91.3	88.0	80.8	96.9	158.2	117.6	206.5	122.5	102.4	143.8	122.2	174.4	139.7	Somalie
Sudan	84.3	84.8	87.9	88.1	69.3	108.2	112.7	95.8	79.7	76.1	74.8	73.4	71.5	95.2	Soudan
Togo	129.0	119.1	116.0	99.5	203.3	140.1	131.1	185.3	295.6	202.3	198.7	100.9	104.5	105.3	Togo
Uganda	112.1	94.1	92.8	68.7	56.0	45.6	58.7	77.9	22.6	41.6	36.5	30.7	38.3	42.1	Ouganda
United Republic of Tanzania	102.0	101.0	114.9	107.4	89.5	97.1	95.8	100.0	89.5	87.2	71.3	71.9	60.8	50.9	République-Unie de Tanzanie
Yemen	14.1	21.9	15.6	24.4	51.9	60.0	77.7	93.7	72.8	64.6	80.3	65.4	77.8	62.9	Yémen
All LDCs	59.3	53.9	56.2	54.3	50.1	55.9	56.5	59.3	55.8	56.9	55.6	50.1	52.2	53.3	**Ensemble des PMA**
All developing countries	168.1	158.8	169.4	198.0	184.1	171.6	192.1	196.7	210.4	193.8	175.8	173.4	168.0	182.6	**Ensemble des pays en développement**

Source : Table 17, pp. 20 and 21.

a/ Exports, external assistance and total receipts in all years are expressed in terms of their command over imports at 1980 prices. (For the deflators used, see table 8).

b/ Export purchasing power plus external assistance.

c/ Excluding major petroleum exporters.

Source : Tableau 17, pages 20 et 21.

a/ Les recettes d'exportations, les rentrées au titre de l'aide extérieure et le total des rentrées de devises pour toutes les années sont exprimés en pouvoir d'achat à l'importation aux prix de 1980. (Pour les déflateurs utilisés, se reporter au tableau 8).

b/ Pouvoir d'achat des exportations plus aide extérieure.

c/ Non compris les principaux pays exportateurs de pétrole.

Table 17 (end)

Foreign exchange receipts and import volume, expressed in constant 1980 dollars[a]/ per capita, 1970-1982

Tableau 17 (fin)

Rentrées de devises et volume des importations, en dollars constants de 1980[a]/ par habitant, 1970-1983

D. Import volume per capita

D. Volume des importations par habitant

Country	1970	1971	1972	1973	1974	1975	1976	1977	1978	1979	1980	1981	1982	1983	Pays
Afghanistan	30.7	41.9	42.0	33.5	33.4	44.8	41.4	54.6	57.3	52.5	34.6	39.7	45.3	46.5	Afghanistan
Bangladesh	40.5	22.6	30.1	33.1	25.2	28.7	20.3	22.1	25.4	26.5	29.3	32.2	31.0	27.5	Bangladesh
Benin	88.6	97.1	106.6	100.1	98.0	116.9	125.3	136.1	138.9	114.6	95.6	96.9	91.1	92.8	Bénin
Bhutan	..	..	..	..	..	..	..	..	..	..	..	..	..	..	Bhoutan
Botswana	344.7	448.0	530.9	622.0	491.3	514.0	474.4	549.6	617.7	720.6	760.8	871.7	754.5	827.0	Botswana
Burkina Faso	33.7	35.3	40.0	44.9	50.5	48.4	44.8	58.1	55.8	59.3	58.1	55.1	57.2	48.7	Burkina Faso
Burundi	24.6	31.3	29.8	22.7	22.7	29.9	30.5	31.0	36.6	45.8	40.8	39.2	53.0	48.9	Burundi
Cape Verde	237.0	272.4	298.7	332.3	239.2	257.5	187.9	212.6	271.6	229.9	227.7	240.7	248.9	293.8	Cap-Vert
Central African Republic	57.9	51.5	47.8	58.7	39.4	55.1	41.9	43.9	33.0	34.8	35.4	43.2	56.6	53.8	République centrafricaine
Chad	60.5	56.0	50.8	53.9	43.7	61.6	51.7	75.0	77.0	23.6	16.4	23.8	24.1	27.4	Tchad
Comoros	124.5	125.5	124.2	131.0	161.2	128.3	69.5	46.1	77.9	98.2	92.3	82.7	83.9	88.8	Comores
Democratic Yemen	520.6	376.4	323.0	281.7	492.6	343.3	420.4	491.1	458.2	587.4	775.5	862.4	899.3	834.2	Yémen démocratique
Djibouti	726.2	806.1	891.1	932.5	1116.7	1225.3	919.9	670.2	855.0	733.2	611.9	653.2	632.0	641.9	Djibouti
Equatorial Guinea	309.1	332.4	292.6	229.6	92.1	112.6	21.9	46.7	40.6	67.2	74.6	87.9	121.6	88.9	Guinée équatoriale
Ethiopia	32.1	31.9	28.9	26.2	23.8	22.3	21.9	24.9	30.2	24.9	23.8	22.1	23.8	27.4	Ethiopie
Gambia	143.9	163.9	167.8	161.6	164.3	199.8	235.3	216.2	242.0	271.3	253.7	192.4	152.6	186.5	Gambie
Guinea	74.6	70.3	85.9	116.4	72.6	89.5	113.7	88.6	86.9	54.9	74.5	73.2	63.0	60.9	Guinée
Guinea-Bissau	194.5	199.9	186.0	193.9	137.1	107.8	98.2	84.9	91.2	94.7	68.0	61.7	62.9	71.4	Guinée-Bissau
Haiti	46.0	49.0	44.9	43.6	46.6	56.0	78.9	72.6	67.1	74.9	74.9	93.0	89.5	95.3	Haïti
Lao People's Dem. Republic	141.5	93.0	57.7	45.8	37.5	22.1	22.9	22.9	28.5	30.0	33.6	32.2	34.1	37.4	République dém. populaire lao
Lesotho	112.7	126.1	165.0	200.6	199.6	239.8	302.3	299.0	315.7	334.9	346.0	384.1	402.6	456.7	Lesotho
Malawi	65.9	76.2	80.9	70.4	71.6	86.2	67.9	68.2	86.8	81.4	73.9	59.9	51.6	53.0	Malawi
Maldives	78.9	101.2	146.1	125.7	101.6	90.5	71.4	104.7	125.2	157.7	168.8	180.8	259.3	236.4	Maldives
Mali	29.9	36.7	37.4	46.3	55.5	51.1	42.5	39.9	63.7	63.1	63.0	55.5	48.7	51.3	Mali
Nepal	27.4	19.1	21.4	17.1	12.6	23.6	28.6	20.0	23.3	21.5	23.3	25.3	27.7	33.2	Népal
Niger	50.5	43.1	47.6	49.5	41.6	40.2	48.2	65.9	92.7	108.6	111.8	94.3	82.3	66.1	Niger
Rwanda	27.0	28.1	27.0	18.6	25.7	39.1	40.0	39.0	54.0	45.6	47.2	49.5	55.4	54.2	Rwanda
Samoa	369.5	317.2	428.9	427.6	338.7	443.0	353.3	434.7	508.1	567.6	401.3	436.9	336.1	391.3	Samoa
Sao Tome and Principe	455.9	374.8	344.6	335.8	244.0	246.9	197.6	279.0	318.4	287.1	222.1	197.1	219.4	222.0	Sao Tomé-et-Principe
Sierra Leone	166.9	150.9	146.6	151.3	159.9	119.8	95.6	102.5	133.1	119.0	125.6	91.9	90.1	54.1	Sierra Leone
Somalia	58.4	76.1	82.6	87.2	80.8	86.4	80.4	98.4	85.9	67.6	75.5	109.4	70.3	38.4	Somalie
Sudan	74.8	78.4	72.1	72.1	83.8	109.1	99.9	97.5	92.9	70.9	84.4	85.9	70.1	74.7	Soudan
Togo	117.9	117.1	127.7	118.3	102.0	134.1	138.5	188.3	259.1	243.8	213.4	167.7	149.5	109.4	Togo
Uganda	59.3	78.3	46.1	36.9	34.1	29.5	24.3	31.1	27.3	17.2	22.3	18.7	26.4	29.0	Ouganda
United Republic of Tanzania	98.7	106.2	102.6	97.4	99.2	93.5	74.2	76.4	103.1	75.7	65.0	61.4	57.8	40.0	République-Unie de Tanzanie
Yemen	22.8	24.0	47.0	56.2	62.1	86.9	116.6	261.9	285.5	264.9	263.2	249.8	219.0	204.7	Yémen
All LDCs	56.6	52.1	53.2	53.2	50.9	55.4	51.8	58.4	65.5	60.0	61.3	62.3	59.5	56.7	Ensemble des PMA
All developing countries[b]/	144.3	145.6	144.8	158.4	173.8	165.8	166.1	173.1	184.6	178.0	170.4	173.0	163.7	167.2	Ensemble des pays en développement[b]/

For source and notes see table 17 p. 20.

Pour la source et les notes se référer au tableau 17 p. 20.

Table 18

External assistance (net disbursements), exports and imports, 1982

$ million

Tableau 18

Aide extérieure (versements nets), exportations et importations 1982

Millions de dollars

Country	Technical assistance DAC / Assistance technique CAD	Total concessional assistance[a] / Total de l'aide concessionnelle[a] — All sources / Toutes provenances	Of which: / Of which: DAC / CAD	Of which: / OPEC / OPEP	Non-concessional[b] assistance / Aide non-concessionnelle[b] — All sources / Toutes provenances	Exports / Exportations (f.o.b.)	Imports / Importations (c.i.f.)	Total concessional assistance from all sources as % of imports / Total de l'aide concessionnelle de toutes provenances en % des importations	Pays
Afghanistan	13.9	167.2	9.0	0.4	3.0	708.0	695.0	24.1	Afghanistan
Bangladesh	133.1	1388.1	1197.8	149.4	17.4	667.0	2463.1	56.4	Bangladesh
Benin	27.9	80.9	76.0	1.6	112.6	33.6	320.0	25.3	Bénin
Bhutan	6.2	11.3	11.3	-	-	-	-	-	Bhutan
Botswana	42.8	101.4	92.9	8.5	17.1	453.4	682.5	14.9	Botswana
Burkina Faso	73.7	209.7	201.0	8.7	43.7	56.0	346.2	60.6	Burkina Faso
Burundi	46.8	130.4	120.6	5.9	30.4	88.0	214.0	60.9	Burundi
Cape Verde	20.6	59.5	53.2	0.2	7.6	3.9	71.5	83.2	Cap-Vert
Central African Rep.	31.2	89.8	88.7	1.1	11.5	109.0	123.4	72.8	Rép. centrafricaine
Chad	15.3	61.4	60.9	0.5	-1.7	130.0	108.6	56.5	Tchad
Comoros	9.6	36.4	26.1	10.3	0.4	20.0	32.6	111.7	Comores
Democratic Yemen	14.8	164.6	57.4	84.2	28.4	795.0	1750.0	9.4	Yémen démocratique
Djibouti	30.8	58.3	54.8	3.5	0.3	20.0	196.8	29.6	Djibouti
Equatorial Guinea	4.1	17.1	13.0	1.0	-4.9	17.0	41.5	41.2	Guinée équatoriale
Ethiopia	53.1	216.7	199.8	0.1	21.4	404.0	787.0	27.5	Ethiopie
Gambia	17.4	50.6	43.0	3.6	-4.9	44.0	96.9	52.2	Gambie
Guinea	20.5	64.0	60.2	2.5	13.5	385.8	296.0	21.6	Guinée
Guinea-Bissau	15.2	64.4	59.7	3.7	0.8	12.0	49.7	129.7	Guinée-Bissau
Haiti	34.1	127.7	125.7	2.0	2.9	162.0	432.7	29.5	Haïti
Lao P.D.R.	11.3	98.3	37.9	0.4	-0.2	40.0	130.0	75.6	Rép. dém. pop. lao
Lesotho	32.3	89.6	86.8	2.8	3.9	36.0	527.0	17.0	Lesotho
Malawi	37.2	121.2	121.2	0.0	13.0	246.0	311.0	39.0	Malawi
Maldives	3.6	5.5	3.0	2.5	-3.4	13.4	39.3	14.0	Maldives
Mali	55.0	193.6	159.3	31.0	8.9	145.8	332.0	58.3	Mali
Nepal	63.8	202.7	195.3	5.4	-1.2	87.6	395.4	51.3	Népal
Niger	68.2	251.8	167.6	82.6	41.2	333.0	442.0	57.0	Niger
Rwanda	49.6	150.6	148.9	1.7	3.1	90.0	286.0	52.7	Rwanda
Samoa	7.6	24.1	21.9	1.0	-0.2	90.0	286.0	48.1	Samoa
Sao Tome & Principe	2.8	9.9	9.4	0.5	1.3	10.0	18.1	54.5	Sao Tomé-et-Principe
Sierra Leone	21.3	90.6	80.8	0.9		111.0	298.0	30.4	Sierra Leone
Somalia	92.0	467.9	279.0	182.9	152.0	199.0	330.0	141.8	Somalie
Sudan	117.9	746.4	554.4	157.2	64.7	499.0	1285.0	58.1	Soudan
Togo	30.3	76.1	73.4	2.7	20.0	177.0	390.6	19.5	Togo
Uganda	29.5	135.6	127.4	6.2	36.3	335.0	349.0	38.9	Uganda
U. R. of Tanzania	180.7	688.3	656.6	29.0	59.7	445.0	1134.0	60.7	Rép.-Unie de Tanzanie
Yemen	64.7	427.6	136.6	285.6	73.9	39.0	1521.0	28.1	Yémen
All LDCs	1478.9	6881.5	5410.6	1081.8	772.4	6928.5	16546.1	41.6	Ensemble des PMA
All developing countries[c]	6757.2	28784.6	22276.0	4581.8	44254.3	237468.0	302531.9	9.5	Ensemble des pays en développement[c]

Source: UNCTAD secretariat estimates mainly based on data from the OECD/DAC secretariat, the World Bank and UNCTAD, Handbook of International Trade and Development, Statistics, Supplement 1985.

a/ Including technical assistance. b/ Including private flows from DAC member countries. c/ Excluding major petroleum exporters.

Source: Estimations du secrétariat de la CNUCED principalement d'après des données du secrétariat de l'OCDE/CAD et de la Banque mondiale et du Manuel de statistiques du commerce international et du développement, Supplément 1985, de la CNUCED.

a/ Y compris l'assistance technique. b/ Y compris les apports privés en provenance des pays membres du CAD. c/ Non compris les principaux pays exportateurs de pétrole.

Table 18 (continued)   Tableau 18 (suite)

External assistance (net disbursements), exports and imports, 1983

Aide extérieure (versements nets), exportations et importations, 1983

$ million   Millions de dollars

Country	Technical assistance Assistance technique DAC/CAD	Total concessional assistance / Total de l'aide concessionnelle, All sources Toutes provenances	Of which: DAC/CAD	Of which: OPEC/OPEP	Non-concessional assistance / Aide non-concessionnelle, All sources Toutes provenances	Exports Exportations (f.o.b.)	Imports Importations (c.i.f.)	Total concessional assistance from all sources as % of imports / Total de l'aide concessionnelle de toutes provenances en % des importations	Pays
Afghanistan	15.2	262.5	15.7	-2.1	-0.2	680.0	700.0	37.5	Afghanistan
Bangladesh	176.3	1097.8	957.4	123.8	193.7	690.0	2164.8	50.7	Bangladesh
Benin	25.8	108.7	80.4	6.4	5.3	45.0	320.0	34.0	Bénin
Bhutan	7.2	12.9	12.9	-	-	-	-	-	Bhutan
Botswana	40.5	103.4	91.2	12.2	25.9	635.6	740.2	14.0	Botswana
Burkina Faso	65.2	190.3	187.5	2.8	11.8	57.0	288.0	66.1	Burkina Faso
Burundi	45.4	149.2	132.4	3.8	35.5	76.0	194.0	76.9	Burundi
Cape Verde	17.8	60.4	56.3	0.2	4.2	4.0	81.7	73.9	Cap-Vert
Central African Rep.	29.3	94.9	93.0	0.3	4.9	100.0	116.6	81.4	Rép. centrafricaine
Chad	21.7	86.4	86.2	0.2	-1.6	160.0	119.6	72.2	Tchad
Comoros	10.1	42.3	29.5	9.8	1.4	18.4	34.0	124.4	Comores
Democratic Yemen	13.9	117.5	56.9	36.3	44.1	700.0	1600.0	7.3	Yémen démocratique
Djibouti	29.3	66.8	51.3	14.8	1.5	25.0	196.8	33.9	Djibouti
Equatorial Guinea	3.9	21.3	12.0	0.5	0.9	20.0	29.6	71.9	Guinée équatoriale
Ethiopia	61.9	305.1	257.7	-	26.9	403.0	875.0	34.9	Ethiopie
Gambia	15.8	42.3	40.9	1.4	-4.3	48.5	115.4	36.6	Gambie
Guinea	14.7	76.3	68.3	0.9	8.2	431.0	280.0	27.2	Guinée
Guinea-Bissau	16.2	60.5	52.7	6.8	2.5	12.0	54.8	110.5	Guinée-Bissau
Haiti	32.2	130.0	128.5	1.5	-10.0	166.0	448.9	29.0	Haïti
Lao P.D.R.	10.7	84.7	29.3	0.4	0.3	53.0	140.0	60.5	Rép. dém. pop. lao
Lesotho	32.0	101.4	93.3	7.6	2.0	23.2	586.1	17.3	Lesotho
Malawi	34.8	117.0	117.0	-	-11.6	229.0	312.0	37.5	Malawi
Maldives	3.8	11.4	6.9	4.5	4.8	10.0	35.3	32.3	Maldives
Mali	53.5	212.7	166.7	43.2	0.2	166.8	344.0	61.8	Mali
Nepal	68.0	201.1	199.3	1.3	-3.4	93.6	463.8	43.4	Népal
Niger	60.9	169.6	150.3	18.2	32.5	340.0	350.0	48.5	Niger
Rwanda	53.8	153.4	147.9	1.6	0.7	79.0	279.0	55.0	Rwanda
Samoa	7.4	27.1	27.1	-	4.4	19.0	56.0	48.4	Samoa
Sao Tome & Principe	1.7	12.2	11.2	0.5	-	10.0	18.1	67.2	Sao Tomé-et-Principe
Sierra Leone	19.3	66.3	63.6	1.6	1.0	119.0	171.0	38.8	Sierra Leone
Somalia	120.2	343.9	292.6	48.0	100.4	210.0	180.0	191.1	Somalie
Sudan	127.4	962.8	602.9	353.4	138.8	624.0	1354.0	71.1	Soudan
Togo	27.8	110.7	105.7	5.0	-0.8	162.0	282.5	39.2	Togo
Uganda	33.6	136.4	123.9	11.5	56.0	367.0	385.0	35.4	Uganda
U. R. of Tanzania	172.2	608.3	572.2	32.4	5.6	363.0	767.0	79.3	Rép.-Unie de Tanzanie
Yemen	60.1	317.3	124.3	193.3	68.2	45.0	1400.0	22.7	Yémen
All LDCs	1529.6	6667.5	5245.0	944.7	749.5	7185.0	15483.4	43.1	Ensemble des PMA
All developing countries[c]	7131.4	28122.6	22034.4	4154.5	48165.6	249283.9	298163.0	9.4	Ensemble des pays en développement[c]

For sources and notes, see Table 18 p.24.   Pour les sources et les notes, se référer au Tableau 18 p.24.

Table 19

External assistance (net disbursements), exports and imports per capita, 1982

Tableau 19

Aide extérieure (versements nets), exportations et importations par habitant, 1982

$ — Dollars

Country / Pays	Technical assistance / Assistance technique DAC / CAD	Total concessional assistance / Total de l'aide concessionnelle All sources / Toutes provenances	Of which: DAC / CAD	Of which: OPEC / OPEP	Non-concessional assistance / Aide non-concessionnelle All sources / Toutes provenances	Exports / Exportations (f.o.b.)	Imports / Importations (c.i.f.)
Afghanistan	0.8	10.0	0.5	0.0	0.2	42.2	41.4
Bangladesh	1.4	15.0	12.9	1.6	0.2	7.2	26.6
Bénin	7.6	21.9	20.6	0.4	30.5	9.1	86.7
Bhutan / Bhoutan	4.7	8.5	8.5	-	-	-	-
Botswana	44.0	104.2	95.5	8.7	17.6	466.0	701.4
Burkina Faso	11.4	32.5	31.1	1.3	6.8	8.7	53.6
Burundi	10.8	30.0	27.7	1.4	7.0	20.2	49.2
Cape Verde / Cap-Vert	66.7	192.5	172.2	0.6	24.6	12.6	231.4
Central African Rep. / Rép. centrafricaine	13.0	37.5	37.0	0.5	4.8	45.5	51.5
Chad / Tchad	3.3	13.1	13.0	0.1	-0.4	27.8	23.2
Comoros / Comores	23.0	87.2	62.4	24.6	1.0	47.8	78.0
Democratic Yemen / Yémen démocratique	7.1	78.6	27.4	40.2	13.6	379.8	836.1
Djibouti	91.9	174.0	163.6	10.4	0.9	59.7	587.6
Equatorial Guinea / Guinée équatoriale	11.2	46.6	35.4	2.7	-13.4	46.3	113.1
Ethiopia / Ethiopie	1.6	6.6	6.1	-	0.6	12.3	23.9
Gambia / Gambie	25.5	74.2	63.0	5.3	-7.2	64.5	142.1
Guinea / Guinée	4.1	12.7	11.9	0.5	2.7	76.3	58.5
Guinea-Bissau / Guinée-Bissau	17.9	75.9	70.3	4.4	0.9	14.1	58.5
Haiti / Haïti	6.6	24.6	24.2	0.4	0.6	31.1	83.2
Lao P.D.R. / Rép. dém. pop. lao	2.8	24.0	9.2	0.1	-0.0	9.7	31.7
Lesotho	22.9	63.6	61.6	2.0	2.8	25.6	374.3
Malawi	5.9	19.3	19.3	0.0	2.1	39.3	49.6
Maldives	22.1	33.7	18.4	15.3	-20.9	82.2	241.1
Mali	7.5	26.4	21.7	4.2	1.2	19.9	45.2
Nepal / Népal	4.1	13.2	12.7	0.4	0.1	5.7	25.7
Niger	12.2	44.9	29.9	14.7	7.3	59.3	78.8
Rwanda	9.0	27.3	27.0	0.3	0.6	16.3	51.9
Samoa	47.5	150.4	136.9	6.3	-1.3	81.3	312.5
Sao Tome & Principe / Sao Tomé-et-Principe	31.5	111.2	105.6	5.6	-	112.4	203.9
Sierra Leone	6.2	26.6	23.7	0.3	0.4	32.5	87.4
Somalia / Somalie	18.1	92.0	54.9	36.0	29.9	39.1	64.9
Sudan / Soudan	6.0	37.7	28.0	7.9	3.3	25.2	64.9
Togo	11.0	27.6	26.7	1.0	7.3	64.3	141.8
Uganda / Ouganda	2.1	9.6	9.0	0.4	2.6	23.7	24.7
U. R. of Tanzania / Rép.-Unie de Tanzanie	8.9	34.0	32.5	1.4	3.0	22.0	56.1
Yemen / Yémen	8.7	57.2	18.3	38.2	9.9	5.2	203.6
All LDCs / Ensemble des PMA	4.9	22.9	18.0	3.6	2.6	23.2	55.3
All developing countries / Ensemble des pays en développement	3.6	15.2	11.8	2.4	23.4	125.7	160.2

For sources and notes, see table 18 p 24.

Pour les sources et les notes, se référer au tableau 18 p.24.

Table 19 (continued)

External assistance (net disbursements), exports and imports per capita, 1983

$

Tableau 19 (suite)

Aide extérieure (versements nets), exportations et importations par habitant, 1983

Dollars

Country	Technical assistance / Assistance technique DAC CAD	Total concessional assistance / Total de l'aide concessionnelle All sources Toutes provenances	Of which: DAC CAD	Of which: OPEC OPEP	Non-concessional assistance / Aide non-concessionnelle All sources Toutes provenances	Exports Exportations (f.o.b.)	Imports Importations (c.i.f.)	Pays
Afghanistan	0.9	15.2	0.9	-0.1	0.0	39.5	40.7	Afghanistan
Bangladesh	1.9	11.6	10.1	1.3	2.0	7.3	22.9	Bangladesh
Benin	6.8	28.5	21.1	1.7	1.4	11.8	84.0	Bénin
Bhutan	5.3	9.5	9.5	-	-	-	-	Bhutan
Botswana	40.2	102.7	90.6	12.1	25.7	631.2	735.1	Botswana
Burkina Faso	9.9	28.8	28.4	0.4	1.8	8.6	43.6	Burkina Faso
Burundi	10.2	33.4	29.6	0.9	7.9	17.0	43.4	Burundi
Cape Verde	56.9	193.0	179.9	0.6	13.4	12.8	261.1	Cap-Vert
Central African Rep.	12.0	38.7	38.0	0.1	2.0	40.8	47.6	Rép. centrafricaine
Chad	4.5	18.0	18.0	0.0	-0.3	33.4	25.0	Tchad
Comoros	23.4	98.1	68.4	22.7	3.2	42.7	78.9	Comores
Democratic Yemen	6.4	54.4	26.4	16.8	20.4	324.4	741.4	Yémen démocratique
Djibouti	84.9	193.6	148.7	42.9	4.3	72.5	570.6	Djibouti
Equatorial Guinea	10.4	56.8	32.0	1.3	2.4	53.3	79.0	Guinée équatoriale
Ethiopia	1.8	9.0	7.6	-	0.8	11.9	25.8	Ethiopie
Gambia	22.7	60.7	58.7	2.0	-6.2	69.6	165.6	Gambie
Guinea	2.8	14.7	13.2	0.2	1.6	83.3	54.1	Guinée
Guinea-Bissau	18.8	70.1	61.1	7.9	2.9	13.9	63.5	Guinée-Bissau
Haiti	6.1	24.5	24.2	0.3	-1.9	31.3	84.7	Haïti
Lao P.D.R.	2.5	20.1	7.0	0.1	0.1	12.6	33.3	Rép. dém. pop. lao
Lesotho	22.2	70.2	64.6	5.3	1.4	16.1	405.9	Lesotho
Malawi	5.4	18.2	18.2	-	-1.8	35.6	48.5	Malawi
Maldives	22.6	67.9	41.1	26.8	28.6	59.5	210.1	Maldives
Mali	7.1	28.2	22.1	5.7	0.0	22.1	45.7	Mali
Nepal	4.3	12.8	12.7	0.1	-0.2	5.9	29.5	Népal
Niger	10.6	29.4	26.0	3.2	5.6	58.9	60.6	Niger
Rwanda	9.4	26.9	25.9	0.3	0.1	13.9	48.9	Rwanda
Samoa	46.0	168.3	168.3	-	27.3	118.0	347.8	Samoa
Sao Tome & Principe	18.5	132.6	121.7	5.4	-	108.7	197.3	Sao Tomé-et-Principe
Sierra Leone	5.6	19.1	18.3	0.5	0.3	34.3	49.3	Sierra Leone
Somalia	22.8	65.3	55.5	9.1	19.1	39.9	34.2	Somalie
Sudan	6.3	47.3	29.6	17.4	6.8	30.6	66.5	Soudan
Togo	9.8	38.9	37.1	1.8	-0.3	56.9	99.2	Togo
Uganda	2.3	9.3	8.5	0.8	3.8	25.1	26.3	Ouganda
U. R. of Tanzania	8.2	29.0	27.3	1.5	0.3	17.3	36.6	Rép.-Unie de Tanzanie
Yemen	7.8	41.2	16.2	25.1	8.9	5.8	181.9	Yémen
All LDCs	5.0	21.6	17.0	3.1	2.4	23.4	50.4	Ensemble des PMA
All developing countries[c]	3.7	14.5	11.4	2.1	24.9	128.7	154.0	Ensemble des pays en développement[c]

For sources and notes, see table 18 p 24.

Pour les sources et les notes, se référer au tableau 18 p.24.

Table 20A — Tableau 20A

Composition of total financial flows in current dollars, 1970-1983 : all LDCs
Composition des courants financiers en dollars courants : 1970-1983 : ensemble des PMA

Net disbursements in $ million — Versements nets en millions de dollars

	1970	1971	1972	1973	1974	1975	1976	1977	1978	1979	1980	1981	1982	1983
I. Concessional loans and grants / Prêts concessionnels et dons	(918)	(1004)	1228	1667	2515	3646	3265	3782	4679	5525	6893	6511	6881	6667
Of which / Dont : DAC / CAD	(817)	(889)	1003	1426	1819	2743	2292	2593	3736	4513	5348	5194	5411	5245
– Bilateral / Apports bilatéraux a/	(631)	(671)	760	1001	1237	1815	1409	1622	2307	2847	3366	3218	3448	3145
– Multilateral a/ / Apports multilatéraux a/	(186)	(218)	243	425	582	928	883	971	1429	1666	1982	1976	1962	2100
– Grants / Dons	(533)	(605)	910	1049	1346	1693	1483	1704	2848	3406	4736	4107	4013	3866
– Loans / Prêts	(284)	(284)	93	376	472	1050	809	889	888	1107	612	1087	1398	1379
– Technical assistance / Assistance technique	(281)	(324)	357	412	475	619	627	653	886	1112	1431	1505	1479	1530
– Other / Autres	(536)	(565)	646	1013	1344	2124	1665	1941	2850	3401	3917	3689	3932	3715
OPEC / OPEP	(6)	(15)	25	23	439	656	760	959	736	791	1028	870	1082	945
– Bilateral / Apports bilatéraux	(6)	(15)	25	23	345	576	677	852	647	695	895	666	919	803
– Multilateral b/ / Apports multilatéraux b/	(–)	(–)	–	–	94	81	83	108	90	96	132	204	163	141
– Grants / Dons	(–)	(2)	6	24	260	436	396	705	380	233	429	247	571	610
– Loans / Prêts	(6)	(13)	19	–1	180	220	364	255	356	558	599	624	510	334
II. Non-concessional flows / Courants financiers non-concessionnels	(103)	(129)	181	238	177	565	401	517	360	795	1194	582	772	749
Of which / Dont : DAC / CAD	(103)	(129)	181	238	18	435	359	514	401	774	1144	559	847	402
– Bilateral official a/ / Apports publics bilatéraux a/	(–2)	(13)	55	65	1	6	35	33	18	122	228	151	188	184
– Multilateral a/ / Apports multilatéraux a/	(54)	(54)	59	40	14	107	23	41	67	90	89	64	65	81
– Export credits c/ / Crédits à l'exportation c/	(34)	(44)	50	43	35	211	215	329	248	403	873	201	178	66
– Direct investment / Investissements directs	(12)	(16)	16	30	9	53	63	114	51	35	52	103	161	81
– Other d/ e/ / Autres d/ e/	(4)	(2)	–	60	–40	58	23	–3	17	124	–98	40	256	–10
TOTAL FINANCIAL FLOWS / TOTAL DES APPORTS FINANCIERS	(1021)	(1133)	1409	1906	2693	4216	3666	4299	5039	6319	8087	7093	7654	7417

Source : UNCTAD secretariat calculations mainly based on OECD/DAC and UNCTAD data.

a/ From multilateral agencies mainly financed by DAC member countries.
b/ From multilateral agencies mainly financed by OPEC member countries.
c/ Guaranteed private.
d/ Bilateral financial flows originating in DAC countries and their capital markets in the form of bond lending and bank lending (either directly or through syndicated "Eurocurrency credits").
e/ Only flows allocated by individual recipient country.

Source : Chiffres calculés par le secrétariat de la CNUCED principalement d'après des données de l'OCDE/CAD et de la CNUCED.

a/ En provenance des institutions multilatérales essentiellement financées par les pays membres du CAD.
b/ En provenance des institutions multilatérales essentiellement financées par les pays membres de l'OPEP.
c/ Privés garantis.
d/ Apports financiers bilatéraux provenant des pays du CAD ou passant par leurs marchés de capitaux, sous forme d'émissions d'obligations et de prêts bancaires (soit directement, soit comme crédits consortiaux en euromonnaies).
e/ Uniquement les apports alloués par pays bénéficiaires.

Table 20B
Composition of total financial flows in current dollars : 1970-1983 :
all developing countries
Net disbursements in $ million

Tableau 20B
Composition des courants financiers en dollars courants, 1970-1983 :
ensemble des pays en développement
Versements nets en millions de dollars

	1970	1971	1972	1973	1974	1975	1976	1977	1978	1979	1980	1981	1982	1983
I. Concessional loans and grants / Prêts concessionnels et dons	7937	8853	9405	11895	15939	20155	19071	18482	25814	29535	35664	34631	31926	30833
Of which: / Dont: DAC / CAD	6697	7530	7860	8691	10732	12851	12046	12626	16783	20622	24257	24122	23949	23583
– Bilateral / – Apports bilatéraux a/	5632	6236	6490	6739	8038	9222	8629	8973	11917	14809	16896	17161	16941	16542
– Multilateral a/ / – Apports multilatéraux a/	1065	1294	1370	1952	2694	3670	3417	3653	4866	5813	7360	6960	7008	7041
– Grants / – Dons	4000	4405	5149	5359	6693	7892	7529	8218	10919	13756	16518	16080	15933	16218
– Loans / – Prêts	2697	3125	2711	3332	4039	5000	4518	4408	5863	6866	7739	8041	8016	7364
– Technical assistance / – Assistance technique	1907	2098	2311	2809	3214	3967	3803	4070	4991	6241	7242	7370	7350	7711
– Other / – Autres	4790	5432	5549	5881	7518	8924	8243	8556	11791	14382	17014	16751	16599	15872
OPEC / OPEP	391	441	660	2031	4265	5797	5579	4470	7549	7157	9202	8295	5893	5190
– Bilateral / – Apports bilatéraux	391	441	660	2031	4148	5638	5160	4249	7248	6906	8917	7922	5542	4865
– Multilateral b/ / – Apports multilatéraux b/	–	–	–	–	117	159	418	221	301	250	285	372	351	324
– Grants / – Dons	364	369	480	1586	2727	3166	2602	3017	2262	3751	4015	3473	2986	2401
– Loans / – Prêts	27	73	180	446	1538	2631	2977	1453	5287	3406	5187	4822	2907	2789
II. Non-concessional flows / Courants financiers non-concessionnels	8917	9527	10893	17117	17392	32885	35120	39671	51651	45826	51605	62934	56503	59677
Of which: / Dont: DAC / CAD	8597	9237	10783	16877	14673	29676	32815	37730	49866	43591	48277	61983	53827	57600
– Bilateral official / – Apports publics bilatéraux	690	799	994	1881	1482	1743	1922	1799	2858	2645	4425	4091	5211	3479
– Multilateral a/ / – Apports multilatéraux a/	659	868	940	1213	1666	2333	2324	2523	2731	3566	4373	5252	6144	6855
– Export credits c/ / – Crédits à l'exportation c/	1927	2306	1380	1146	2188	4087	5835	7777	9334	7470	10767	8768	6527	7110
– Direct investment / – Investissements directs	3390	3027	3755	4057	928	10589	7870	9285	10924	11605	10061	16119	11695	7919
– Other d/ / – Autres d/	(1930)	(2237)	(3714)	(8580)	(8408)	(10925)	(14864)	(16346)	(24019)	(18305)	(18651)	(27753)	(24250)	(32237)
TOTAL FINANCIAL FLOWS / TOTAL DES APPORTS FINANCIERS	16853	18380	20298	29013	33331	53040	54190	58154	77465	75360	87269	97565	88429	90510

For sources and notes, see table 20A.

Pour les sources et les notes, se référer au tableau 20A.

Table 21A

Composition of total financial flows in constant dollars, 1970-1983 : all LDCs

Net disbursements in millions of 1980 dollars

Tableau 21A

Composition des courants financiers en dollars constants, 1970-1983 : ensemble des PMA

Versements nets en millions de dollars de 1980

	1970	1971	1972	1973	1974	1975	1976	1977	1978	1979	1980	1981	1982	1983
I. Concessional loans and grants / I. Prêts concessionnels et dons	(3441)	(3528)	4020	4367	4849	6548	5807	6136	6908	6701	6893	6709	7402	7502
Of which : / Dont :														
DAC / CAD	(3061)	(3125)	3283	3734	3507	4926	4076	4207	5517	5474	5348	5352	5820	5901
– Bilateral a/ / – Apports bilatéraux a/	(2364)	(2358)	2487	2621	2386	3259	2505	2632	3407	3453	3366	3316	3709	3539
– Multilateral a/ / – Apports multilatéraux a/	(697)	(768)	796	1113	1121	1667	1571	1576	2110	2021	1982	2036	2111	2363
– Grants / – Dons	(1996)	(2126)	2980	2748	2596	3041	2637	2765	4205	4132	4736	4231	4316	4350
– Loans / – Prêts	(1065)	(999)	303	986	911	1865	1439	1442	1312	1342	612	1120	1504	1551
– Technical assistance / – Assistance technique	(1052)	(1138)	1169	1080	916	1112	1116	1059	1309	1349	1431	1551	1591	1721
– Other / – Autres	(2005)	(1987)	2114	2654	2591	3814	2960	3148	4208	4125	3917	3801	4229	4180
OPEC / OPEP	(22)	(52)	82	61	847	1179	1352	1557	1087	960	1028	897	1164	1063
– Bilateral / – Apports bilatéraux	(22)	(52)	82	61	665	1034	1205	1382	955	843	895	686	989	904
– Multilateral b/ / – Apports multilatéraux b/	(–)	(–)	–	–	182	145	148	174	133	117	132	211	175	159
– Grants / – Dons	(1)	(8)	19	63	501	783	704	1143	562	283	429	254	615	687
– Loans / – Prêts	(21)	(45)	63	-2	347	395	648	413	526	677	599	643	549	376
II. Non-concessional flows / II. Courants financiers non-concessionnels	(335)	(455)	594	624	342	1023	713	839	531	964	1194	600	831	843
Of which : / Dont :														
DAC / CAD	(385)	(455)	594	624	35	782	638	834	592	939	1144	576	911	453
– Bilateral official c/ / – Apports publics bilatéraux	(-6)	(47)	181	170	3	10	62	54	27	148	228	156	202	207
– Multilateral a/ / – Apports multilatéraux a/	(201)	(189)	194	103	26	191	39	66	98	110	89	66	69	92
– Export credits c/ / – Crédits à l'exportation c/	(127)	(155)	165	113	67	380	383	534	367	488	873	208	191	74
– Direct investment / – Investissements directs	(45)	(57)	53	80	17	96	113	184	76	42	52	106	174	91
– Other d/ e/ / – Autres d/ e/	(16)	(6)	–	158	-77	104	42	-5	25	150	-98	41	275	-11
TOTAL FINANCIAL FLOWS / TOTAL DES APPORTS FINANCIERS	(3826)	(3983)	4613	4992	5191	7571	6519	6975	7440	7666	8087	7309	8233	8345

For sources and notes, see table 20A.

Pour les sources et les notes, se référer au tableau 20A.

Table 21B

Composition of total financial flows in constant dollars, 1970-1983 :
all developing countries

Net disbursements in millions of 1980 dollars

Tableau 21B

Composition des courants financiers en dollars constants : 1970-1983 :
ensemble des pays en développement

Versements nets en millions de dollars de 1980

	1970	1971	1972	1973	1974	1975	1976	1977	1978	1979	1980	1981	1982	1983	
I. Concessional loans and grants	33975	35173	34375	34843	32891	37892	35018	30881	39411	36794	35664	35031	33518	33904	**I. Prêts concessionels et dons**
Of which: DAC	23065	29917	28729	25457	22146	24236	22119	21096	25622	25691	24257	24400	25143	25932	Dont: CAD
– Bilateral a/	24110	24776	23720	19738	16586	17337	15844	14992	18193	18449	16896	17359	17786	18190	– Apports bilatéraux a/
– Multilateral a/	4560	5141	5008	5719	5560	6899	6275	6103	7429	7242	7360	7041	7357	7743	– Apports multilatéraux a/
– Grants	17122	17499	18820	15697	13811	14837	13824	13730	16671	17137	16518	16266	16727	17834	– Dons
– Loans	11547	12418	9909	9760	8335	9400	8295	7365	8952	8554	7739	8134	8416	8098	– Prêts
– Technical assistance	8165	8334	8446	8229	6632	7458	6983	6800	7620	7775	7242	7455	7716	8479	– Assistance technique
– Other	20504	21583	20283	17227	15514	16778	15136	14295	18002	17917	17014	16944	17427	17454	– Autres
OPEC	1672	1753	2413	5950	8801	10899	10243	7469	11525	8916	9202	8390	6187	5707	OPEP
– Bilateral b/	1672	1753	2413	5950	8560	10600	9476	7100	11066	8604	8917	8014	5818	5350	– Apports bilatéraux
– Multilateral b/	–	–	–	–	241	298	768	369	459	312	285	377	369	357	– Apports multilatéraux b/
– Grants	1557	1464	1756	4645	5628	5952	4777	5041	3453	4673	4015	3513	3135	2640	– Dons
– Loans	115	288	658	1306	3173	4947	5466	2428	8072	4243	5187	4877	3052	3067	– Prêts
II. Non-concessional flows	38171	37849	39814	50139	35890	61826	64487	66285	78856	57090	51605	63660	59321	65623	**II. Courants financiers non-concessionnels**
Of which: DAC	36801	36697	39412	49436	30279	55793	60255	63041	76131	54306	48277	62698	56512	63339	Dont: CAD
– Bilateral official a/	2955	3174	3633	5510	3058	3277	3529	3007	4363	3295	4425	4138	5471	3826	– Apports publics bilatéraux
– Multilateral a/	2821	3448	3434	3554	3438	4386	4267	4215	4169	4442	4373	5313	6450	7538	– Apports multilatéraux a/
– Export credits c/	8249	9162	5044	5356	4516	7683	10715	12994	14251	9306	10767	8869	6852	7818	– Crédits à l'exportation c/
– Direct investment	14512	12027	13725	11885	1915	19907	14451	15514	16678	14457	10061	16305	12278	8708	– Investissements directs
– Other d/	(8264)	(8886)	(13576)	(25132)	(17351)	(20540)	(27294)	(27312)	(36670)	(22805)	(18651)	(28073)	(25460)	(35448)	– Autres d/
TOTAL FINANCIAL FLOWS	72146	73022	74189	84982	68781	99715	99505	97166	118267	93884	87269	98690	92839	99527	**TOTAL DES APPORTS FINANCIERS**

For sources and notes, see table 20A.

Pour les sources et les notes, se référer au tableau 20A.

Table 22A

Composition of total financial flows in constant dollars per capita, 1970-1983: all LDCs

Net disbursements in 1980 dollars

Tableau 22A

Composition des courants financiers en dollars constants par habitant, 1970-1983: ensemble des PMA

Versements nets en dollars de 1980

	1970	1971	1972	1973	1974	1975	1976	1977	1978	1979	1980	1981	1982	1983
I. Concessional loans and grants / I. Prêts concessionnels et dons	(15.7)	(15.7)	17.4	18.4	20.0	26.2	22.7	23.3	25.5	24.1	24.2	22.9	24.6	24.3
Of which: DAC / Dont: CAD	(14.0)	(13.9)	14.2	15.8	14.4	19.7	15.9	16.0	20.4	19.7	18.8	18.3	19.4	19.1
– Bilateral / – Apports bilatéraux a/	(10.8)	(10.5)	10.8	11.1	9.8	13.0	9.8	10.0	12.6	12.4	11.8	11.3	12.3	11.5
– Multilateral a/ / – Apports multilatéraux a/	(3.2)	(3.4)	3.4	4.7	4.6	6.7	6.1	6.0	7.8	7.3	7.0	7.0	7.0	7.7
– Grants / – Dons	(9.1)	(9.5)	12.9	11.6	10.7	12.2	10.3	10.5	15.5	14.9	16.6	14.5	14.4	14.1
– Loans / – Prêts	(4.9)	(4.4)	1.3	4.2	3.8	7.5	5.6	5.5	4.8	4.8	2.1	3.8	5.0	5.0
– Technical assistance / – Assistance technique	(4.8)	(5.1)	5.1	4.6	3.8	4.5	4.4	4.0	4.8	4.9	5.0	5.3	5.3	5.6
– Other / – Autres	(9.2)	(8.8)	9.2	11.2	10.7	15.3	11.5	12.0	15.6	14.9	13.7	13.0	14.1	13.6
OPEC / OPEP	(0.1)	(0.2)	0.4	0.3	3.5	4.7	5.3	5.9	4.0	3.5	3.6	3.1	3.9	3.4
– Bilateral / – Apports bilatéraux	(0.1)	(0.2)	0.4	0.3	2.7	4.1	4.7	5.2	3.5	3.0	3.1	2.3	3.3	2.9
– Multilateral b/ / – Apports multilatéraux b/	(–)	(–)	–	–	0.7	0.6	0.6	0.7	0.5	0.4	0.5	0.7	0.6	0.5
– Grants / – Dons	(–)	(–)	0.1	0.3	2.1	3.1	2.7	4.3	2.1	1.0	1.5	0.9	2.0	2.2
– Loans / – Prêts	(0.1)	(0.2)	0.3	–	1.4	1.6	2.5	1.6	1.9	2.4	2.1	2.2	1.8	1.2
II. Non-concessional flows / II. Courants financiers non-concessionnels	(1.8)	(2.0)	2.6	2.6	1.4	4.1	2.8	3.2	2.0	3.5	4.2	2.1	2.8	2.7
Of which: DAC / Dont: CAD	(1.8)	(2.0)	2.6	2.6	0.1	3.1	2.5	3.2	2.2	3.4	4.0	2.0	3.0	1.5
– Bilateral official / – Apports publics bilatéraux	(–)	(0.2)	0.8	0.7	–	–	0.2	0.2	0.1	0.5	0.8	0.5	0.7	0.7
– Multilateral a/ / – Apports multilatéraux a/	(0.9)	(0.8)	0.8	0.4	0.1	0.8	0.2	0.3	0.4	0.4	0.3	0.2	0.2	0.3
– Export credits c/ / – Crédits à l'exportation c/	(0.6)	(0.7)	0.7	0.5	0.3	1.5	1.5	2.0	1.4	1.8	3.1	0.7	0.6	0.2
– Direct Investment / – Investissements directs	(0.2)	(0.3)	0.2	0.3	-0.1	0.4	0.4	0.7	0.3	0.2	0.2	0.4	0.6	0.3
– Other d/e/ / – Autres d/e/	(0.1)	(–)	–	0.7	-0.3	0.4	0.2	–	0.1	0.5	-0.3	0.1	0.9	–
TOTAL FINANCIAL FLOWS / TOTAL DES APPORTS FINANCIERS	(17.5)	(17.7)	20.0	21.1	21.4	30.3	25.4	26.5	27.5	27.6	28.4	25.0	27.4	27.1

For sources and notes, see table 20A.

Pour les sources et les notes, se référer au tableau 20A.

Table 22B

Composition of total financial flows in constant dollars per capita, 1970-1983:
all developing countries

Net disbursements in 1980 dollars

Tableau 22B

Composition des courants financiers en dollars constants par habitant, 1970-1983:
ensemble des pays en développement

Versements nets en dollars de 1980

Item	Élément	1970	1971	1972	1973	1974	1975	1976	1977	1978	1979	1980	1981	1982	1983
I. Concessional loans and grants	I. Prêts concessionnels et dons	19.8	19.9	19.0	18.8	17.3	19.4	17.5	15.0	18.7	17.0	16.1	15.4	14.3	14.1
Of which: DAC	Dont: CAD	16.7	17.0	15.9	13.7	11.7	12.4	11.0	10.3	12.1	11.9	10.9	10.7	10.7	10.8
– Bilateral	– Apports bilatéraux	14.0	14.1	13.1	10.7	8.7	8.9	7.9	7.3	8.6	8.5	7.6	7.6	7.6	7.6
– Multilateral a/	– Apports multilatéraux a/	2.7	2.9	2.8	3.1	2.9	3.5	3.1	3.0	3.5	3.3	3.3	3.1	3.1	3.2
– Grants	– Dons	10.0	9.9	10.4	8.5	7.3	7.6	6.9	6.7	7.9	7.9	7.4	7.1	7.1	7.4
– Loans	– Prêts	6.7	7.0	5.5	5.3	4.4	4.8	4.1	3.6	4.2	4.0	3.5	3.6	3.6	3.4
– Technical assistance	– Assistance technique	4.7	4.7	4.7	4.4	3.5	3.8	3.5	3.3	3.6	3.6	3.3	3.3	3.3	3.5
– Other	– Autres	11.9	12.2	11.2	9.3	8.2	8.6	7.6	7.0	8.5	8.3	7.7	7.4	7.4	7.3
OPEC	OPEP	1.0	1.0	1.3	3.2	4.6	5.6	5.1	3.6	5.5	4.1	4.1	3.7	2.6	2.4
– Bilateral	– Apports bilatéraux	1.0	1.0	1.3	3.2	4.5	5.4	4.7	3.5	5.2	4.0	4.0	3.5	2.5	2.2
– Multilateral b/	– Apports multilatéraux b/	–	–	–	–	0.1	0.2	0.4	0.2	0.2	0.1	0.1	0.2	0.2	0.1
– Grants	– Dons	0.9	0.8	1.0	2.5	3.0	3.0	2.4	2.5	1.6	2.2	1.8	1.5	1.3	1.1
– Loans	– Prêts	0.1	0.2	0.4	0.7	1.7	2.5	2.7	1.2	3.8	2.0	2.3	2.1	1.3	1.3
II. Non-concessional flows	II. Courants financiers non-concessionnels	22.2	21.5	22.0	27.1	18.9	31.7	32.2	32.3	37.4	26.4	23.2	27.9	25.3	27.3
Of which: DAC	Dont: CAD	21.4	20.8	21.8	26.7	15.9	28.6	30.1	30.7	36.1	25.1	21.7	27.5	24.1	26.4
– Bilateral official	– Apports publics bilatéraux	1.7	1.8	2.0	3.0	1.6	1.7	1.8	1.5	2.1	1.5	2.0	1.8	2.3	1.6
– Multilateral a/	– Apports multilatéraux a/	1.6	2.0	1.9	1.9	1.8	2.2	2.1	2.1	2.0	2.1	2.0	2.3	2.8	3.1
– Export credits c/	– Crédits à l'exportation c/	4.8	5.2	2.8	1.8	2.4	3.5	5.4	6.3	6.8	4.3	4.8	3.9	2.9	3.3
– Direct Investment	– Investissements directs	8.4	6.8	7.6	6.4	1.0	10.2	7.2	7.5	7.9	6.7	4.5	7.2	5.2	3.6
– Other d/	– Autres d/	(4.8)	(5.0)	(7.5)	(13.6)	(9.1)	(10.5)	(13.6)	(13.3)	(17.4)	(10.5)	(8.4)	(12.3)	(10.9)	(14.8)
TOTAL FINANCIAL FLOWS	TOTAL DES APPORTS FINANCIERS	41.9	41.4	41.1	45.9	36.2	51.1	49.7	47.3	56.1	43.4	39.3	43.3	39.7	41.4

For sources and notes, see table 20A.

Pour les sources et les notes, se référer au tableau 20A.

Table 23

Tableau 23

Percentage distribution of financial flows to all LDCs and to all developing countries by type of flow, 1970, 1975 and 1979-1983

Répartition en pourcentage des apports financiers à l'ensemble des PMA et à l'ensemble des pays en développement, par catégorie d'apports, 1970, 1975 et 1979-1983

Percentages — En pourcentage

	Least developed countries — Pays les moins avancés							All developing countries — Ensemble des pays en développement						
	1970	1975	1979	1980	1981	1982	1983	1970	1975	1979	1980	1981	1982	1983
I. Concessional loans and grants — I. Prêts concessionnels et dons	89.9	86.5	87.4	85.2	91.8	89.9	89.9	47.1	38.0	39.2	40.9	35.5	36.1	34.1
Of which: — Dont: DAC — CAD	80.0	65.1	71.4	66.1	73.2	70.7	70.7	39.7	24.3	27.4	27.8	24.7	27.1	26.1
– Bilateral — Apports bilatéraux	61.8	43.0	45.0	41.6	45.4	45.1	42.4	33.4	17.4	19.7	19.4	17.6	19.2	18.3
– Multilaterala/ — Apports multilatérauxa/	18.2	22.0	26.4	24.5	27.8	25.6	28.3	6.3	6.9	7.7	8.4	7.1	7.9	7.8
– Grants — Dons	52.2	40.2	53.9	58.6	57.9	52.4	52.1	23.7	14.9	18.3	18.9	16.5	18.0	17.9
– Loans — Prêts	27.8	24.9	17.5	7.6	15.3	18.3	18.6	16.0	9.4	9.1	8.9	8.2	9.1	8.1
– Technical Assistance — Assistance technique	27.5	14.7	17.6	17.7	21.2	19.3	20.6	11.3	7.5	8.3	8.3	7.5	8.3	8.5
– Other — Autres	52.5	50.4	52.8	48.4	52.0	51.4	50.1	28.4	16.8	19.1	19.5	17.2	18.8	17.5
OPEC — OPEP	0.6	15.6	12.5	12.7	12.3	14.1	12.7	2.3	10.9	9.5	10.5	8.5	6.7	5.7
– Bilateral — Apports bilatéraux	0.6	13.7	11.0	11.1	9.4	12.0	10.8	2.3	10.6	9.2	10.2	8.1	6.3	5.4
– Multilateralb/ — Apports multilatérauxb/	-	1.9	1.5	1.6	2.9	2.1	1.9	-	0.3	0.3	0.3	0.4	0.4	0.3
– Grants — Dons	0.0	10.3	3.7	5.3	3.5	7.5	8.2	2.2	6.0	5.0	4.6	3.6	3.4	2.6
– Loans — Prêts	0.5	5.2	8.8	7.4	8.8	6.7	4.5	0.2	5.0	4.5	5.9	4.9	3.3	3.1
II. Non-concessional flows — II. Courants financiers non-concessionnels	10.1	13.5	12.6	14.8	8.2	10.1	10.1	52.9	62.0	60.8	59.1	64.5	63.9	65.9
Of which: — Dont: DAC — CAD	10.1	10.3	12.2	14.1	7.9	11.1	5.4	51.0	56.0	57.8	55.3	63.5	60.9	63.6
– Bilateral official — Apports publics bilatéraux	-0.1	0.1	1.9	2.8	2.1	2.5	2.5	4.1	3.3	3.5	5.1	4.2	5.9	3.8
– Multilaterala/ — Apports multilatérauxa/	5.3	2.5	1.4	1.1	0.9	0.8	1.1	3.9	4.4	4.7	5.0	5.4	6.9	7.6
– Export creditsc/ — Crédits à l'exportationc/	3.3	5.0	6.4	10.8	2.8	2.3	0.9	11.4	7.7	9.9	12.3	9.0	7.4	7.9
– Direct investment — Investissements directs	1.2	1.3	0.6	0.6	1.4	2.1	1.1	20.1	20.0	15.4	11.5	16.5	13.2	8.7
– Other d/ — Autres d/	0.4e/	1.4e/	2.0e/	-1.2e/	0.6e/	3.3e/	-0.1e/	11.5	20.6	24.3	21.4	28.4	27.4	35.6
TOTAL FINANCIAL FLOWS — TOTAL DES APPORTS FINANCIERS	100.0	100.0	100.0	100.0	100.0	100.0	100.0	100.0	100.0	100.0	100.0	100.0	100.0	100.0

For source and notes see table 20A.

Pour les sources et les notes, se référer au tableau 20A.

Table 24 / Tableau 24

Share of LDCs in flows to all developing countries, by type of flow, 1970-1983

Part des PMA dans les apports financiers à l'ensemble des pays en développement, par catégories d'apports, 1970-1983

Percentages / En pourcentage

	1970	1971	1972	1973	1974	1975	1976	1977	1978	1979	1980	1981	1982	1983
I. Concessional loans and grants / **I. Prêts concessionels et dons**	(11.6)	(11.3)	13.1	14.0	15.8	18.1	17.1	20.5	18.1	18.7	19.3	18.8	21.6	21.6
Of which: / Dont :														
DAC / CAD	(12.2)	(11.8)	12.8	16.4	16.9	21.3	19.0	20.5	22.3	21.9	22.0	21.5	22.6	22.2
– Bilateral / – Apports bilatéraux	(11.2)	(10.8)	11.7	14.9	15.4	19.7	16.3	18.1	19.4	19.2	19.9	18.7	20.4	19.0
– Multilateral a/ / – Apports multilatérauxa/	(17.5)	(16.9)	17.7	21.8	21.6	25.3	25.8	26.6	29.4	28.7	26.9	28.4	28.0	29.8
– Grants / – Dons	(13.3)	(13.7)	17.7	19.6	20.1	21.5	19.7	20.7	26.1	24.8	28.7	25.6	25.2	23.8
– Loans / – Prêts	(10.5)	(9.1)	3.4	11.3	11.7	21.0	17.9	20.2	15.2	16.1	7.9	13.5	17.4	18.7
– Technical Assistance / – Assistance technique	(14.7)	(15.4)	15.5	14.7	14.8	15.6	16.5	16.0	17.8	17.8	19.8	20.4	20.1	19.8
– Other / – Autres	(11.2)	(10.4)	11.6	17.2	17.9	23.8	20.2	22.7	24.2	23.6	23.0	22.0	23.7	23.4
OPEC / OPEP	(1.5)	(3.4)	3.8	1.1	10.3	11.3	13.6	21.6	9.8	11.1	11.2	10.5	18.4	18.2
– Bilateral b/ / – Apports bilatéraux	(1.5)	(3.4)	3.8	1.1	8.3	10.2	13.1	20.1	8.9	10.1	10.0	8.4	16.6	16.5
– Multilateral b/ / – Apports multilatérauxb/	–	–	–	–	80.9	50.9	19.8	48.7	29.9	38.4	46.3	54.8	46.3	43.5
– Grants / – Dons	(0.1)	(0.6)	1.2	1.5	9.5	13.8	15.2	23.4	16.8	6.2	10.7	7.1	19.1	25.4
– Loans / – Prêts	(20.8)	(17.5)	10.6	..	11.7	8.4	12.2	17.5	6.7	16.4	11.6	12.9	17.6	12.0
II. Non-concessional flows / **II. Courants financiers non-concessionnels**	(1.2)	(1.4)	1.7	1.4	1.0	1.7	1.1	1.3	0.7	1.7	2.3	0.9	1.4	1.3
Of which: / Dont :														
DAC / CAD														
– Bilateral official / – Apports publics bilatéraux	(1.2)	(1.4)	1.7	1.4	0.1	1.5	1.1	1.4	0.8	1.8	2.4	0.9	1.6	0.7
– Multilateral a/ / – Apports multilatérauxa/	(..)	(1.7)	5.6	3.5	0.1	0.3	1.8	1.9	0.6	4.6	5.2	3.7	3.6	5.3
– Export credits c/ / – Crédits à l'exportationc/	(8.1)	(6.2)	6.3	3.3	0.8	4.6	0.9	1.6	2.4	2.5	2.0	1.2	1.0	1.2
– Direct Investment / – Investissements directs	(1.8)	(1.9)	3.6	3.8	1.6	5.2	3.7	4.2	2.7	2.4	8.1	2.3	2.7	0.9
– Other d/ / – Autres d/	(0.4)	(0.5)	0.4	0.8	0.9	0.5	0.8	1.2	0.5	0.3	0.5	0.5	1.4	1.0
– Other e/ / – Autres e/	(0.2)	(0.1)	(0.0)	(0.7)	..	(0.5)	(0.2)	..	(0.1)	(0.7)	..	(0.1)	(1.1)	..
TOTAL FINANCIAL FLOWS / **TOTAL DES APPORTS FINANCIERS**	(6.1)	(6.2)	6.9	6.6	8.1	7.9	6.8	7.4	6.5	8.4	9.3	7.3	8.7	8.2

Note : No percentage is shown when either the net flow to all LDCs or the net flow to all developing countries in a particular year is negative. For other notes and sources, see table 20A.

Note : Aucune donnée n'est indiquée dans le cas où dans une année quelconque, les versements nets, soit aux PMA, soit aux pays en développement dans leur ensemble, sont négatifs. Pour les autres notes et sources, se référer au tableau 20A.

Table 25A
Bilateral ODA from individual DAC member countries and total financial flows from individual multilateral agencies a/ to all LDCs, 1973-1983

Tableau 25A
APD bilatérale de chaque pays membre du CAD et apports financiers totaux de chaque institution multilatérale a/ à l'ensemble des PMA, 1973-1983

Net disbursements in $ million / Versements nets en millions de dollars	1973	1974	1975	1976	1977	1978	1979	1980	1981	1982	1983
A. Bilateral donors / A. Donneurs bilatéraux											
Australia / Australie	7.9	38.2	29.9	14.4	17.6	29.7	48.9	30.4	55.5	80.7	47.1
Austria / Autriche	0.6	0.4	0.6	1.5	2.4	3.1	2.9	5.7	9.0	7.1	7.1
Belgium / Belgique	34.2	39.5	52.5	54.1	58.9	75.1	101.5	96.2	85.4	69.3	61.4
Canada	101.8	126.5	166.1	125.4	110.3	170.0	185.9 b/	166.0 b/	168.2	224.7	227.7
Denmark / Danemark	23.1	38.0	48.7	47.2	60.9	77.3	94.4	116.0	74.6	84.1	97.2
Finland / Finlande	4.6	7.0	12.6	15.9	11.3	10.5	14.9 b/	22.1	23.9	21.6	32.7
France	155.5	220.9	251.7	226.8	219.1	257.7	350.3 b/	411.4	477.8	406.1	381.8
Germany, Federal Republic of / Allemagne, République fédérale d'	147.4	187.5	252.6	237.2	256.7	383.7	526.2	580.6	528.1	541.0	441.8
Italy / Italie	18.4	13.8	12.3	9.8	11.5	13.1	17.0	37.3	60.6	112.1	159.2
Japan / Japon	41.6	45.0	69.7	59.8	105.1	216.8	330.4	362.9	293.6	406.8	265.1
Netherlands / Pays-Bas	15.2	44.2	62.7	81.5	156.4	217.6	260.8	308.1	285.2	254.6	202.9
New Zealand / Nouvelle-Zélande	2.5	3.5	10.2	4.4	4.8	5.6	6.2	6.1	4.8	3.5	4.0
Norway / Norvège	11.1	31.3	38.2	39.1	61.8	77.4	90.5	94.6	90.4	121.9	120.2
Sweden / Suède	60.1	71.4	120.9	115.3	142.0	149.8	216.5	198.5	180.7	167.5	147.7
Switzerland / Suisse	7.5	8.2	13.5	11.6	20.0	42.1	28.8	57.3	55.7	58.7	66.0
United Kingdom / Royaume-Uni	54.5	72.0	108.5	98.5	119.7	198.2	266.7	334.0	294.9	250.7	206.8
United States / Etats-Unis	315.0	290.0	564.0	266.0	263.0	380.0	388.0	558.0	529.0	638.0	676.0
Total bilateral concessional / Total des apports bilatéraux concessionnels	1001.0	1237.4	1814.7	1408.7	1621.8	2307.7	2929.9	3385.2	3217.4	3448.4	3144.7
B. Multilateral donors / B. Donneurs multilatéraux											
1. Concessional / 1. Apports concessionnels											
AfDF / FAfD	-	-	3.9	10.5	22.3	34.1	52.8	80.6	76.1	82.9	113.6
AsDB / BAsD	5.3	4.8	26.6	15.6	24.0	56.2	58.7	75.4	64.5	58.9	80.9
EEC/EDF / CEE/FED	161.6	249.6	288.6	183.7	211.6	291.8	365.7	444.6	480.8	388.4	369.9
IBRD / BIRD	-	-	-	0.1	6.1	13.3	19.5	18.7	9.8	3.0	2.5
IDA / AID	125.1	158.0	270.8	352.5	358.6	372.9	472.6	493.8	572.4	696.3	739.4
IDB / BID	-0.0	0.8	14.6	15.7	21.3	16.9	15.9	8.9	10.0	12.5	14.9
IFAD / FIDA	-	-	-	-	-	-	1.1	12.9	22.6	27.8	50.3
IMF trust fund / Fonds fiduciaire du FMI	-	-	-	-	37.7	239.9	198.4	246.7	2.6	-	-
UN / ONU	133.0	168.4	323.1	305.0	289.4	404.0	481.3	600.7	737.0	692.6	728.3
of which: UNDP / dont: PNUD	56.3	59.4	92.6	95.1	90.4	113.7	141.6	175.8	260.9	228.3	197.1
UNHCR	14.1	8.8	9.0	10.0	7.6	18.0	35.8	96.9	100.9	88.6	111.1
UNICEF	11.1	20.1	26.6	23.9	32.7	49.4	66.8	71.9	65.5	62.1	77.9
UNTA / ATNU	11.4	12.6	14.7	16.7	16.7	26.5	23.3	6.7	30.4	27.9	40.8
WFP / PAM	33.4	51.1	120.5	95.6	116.3	151.9	172.1	168.2	217.2	217.9	229.5
Other UN / Autres ONU	6.7	16.4	59.7	63.7	21.8	44.5	41.7	81.2	62.1	67.8	71.9
Total multilateral concessional / Total des apports multilatéraux concessionnels	425.0	581.6	927.6	883.1	971.4	1429.1	1666.0	1982.3	1975.8	1962.4	2099.8
2. Non-concessional / 2. Apports non-concessionnels											
AfDB / BAfD	7.0	5.7	14.6	15.9	20.2	18.1	25.4	32.1	26.2	36.3	50.8
AsDB / BAsD	5.2	1.6	1.1	-	-0.2	-0.7	-0.7	0.2	-0.6	-1.0	-0.7
EEC/EDF / CEE/FED	-	-	-	-	-	12.4	15.2	19.0	4.7	5.7	10.9
IBRD / BIRD	25.9	7.0	91.8	0.3	14.1	19.8	37.7	31.8	31.2	15.9	13.1
IFC / SFI	1.2	-1.0	-1.0	5.6	0.6	16.2	13.2	6.4	2.5	7.7	7.5
Total multilateral non-concessional / Total des apports multilatéraux non-concessionnels	39.3	13.3	106.5	21.8	40.7	65.8	90.8	89.5	64.0	64.6	81.6
Total concessional (A+B.1) / Total des apports concessionnels (A+B.1)	1426.0	1819.0	2742.3	2291.8	2593.2	3736.8	4595.9	5367.5	5193.2	5410.8	5244.5
GRAND TOTAL / TOTAL GENERAL	1465.3	1832.3	2848.8	2313.6	2633.9	3802.6	4686.7	5457.0	5257.2	5475.4	5326.1

Source : UNCTAD secretariat based on information from the OECD/DAC secretariat.
a/ Multilateral agencies mainly financed by DAC member countries.
b/ Including flows to LDCs not allocated by recipient country.

Source : Secrétariat de la CNUCED, d'après des renseignements du secrétariat de l'OCDE/CAD.
a/ Institutions multilatérales essentiellement financées par les pays membres du CAD.
b/ Y compris les apports aux PMA non alloués par pays bénéficiaires.

Table 25A(continued)

Bilateral ODA from individual DAC member countries and total financial flows from individual multilateral agencies_a/ to all LDCS : main recipients in 1983_b/

	Main recipients in 1983_b/
A. Bilateral donors	
Australia	U.-R. of Tanzania, Bangladesh, Samoa.
Austria	Cape Verde, U.-R. of Tanzania, Ethiopia, Nepal, Afghanistan.
Belgium	Rwanda, Burundi.
Canada	Bangladesh, U.R. of Tanzania.
Denmark	U.-R. of Tanzania, Bangladesh, Sudan.
Finland	U.-R. of Tanzania, Sudan.
France	Central African Rep., Burkina Faso.
Germany, Fed.Rep. of	Sudan.
Italy	Somalia, Sudan, U.-R. of Tanzania.
Japan	Bangladesh, U.-R. of Tanzania, Nepal.
Netherlands	U.-R. of Tanzania, Sudan, Bangladesh, Burkina Faso
New Zealand	Samoa.
Norway	U.-R. of Tanzania, Bangladesh.
Sweden	U.-R. of Tanzania, Bangladesh, Ethiopia.
Switzerland	Nepal, Rwanda, Mali.
United Kingdom	Sudan, U.-R. of Tanzania, Bangladesh.
United States	Bangladesh, Sudan.
B. Multilateral donors	
1. Concessional flows	
AfDF	Mali, Ethiopia.
AsDB	Bangladesh, Nepal.
EEC/EDF	Ethiopia, Bangladesh.
IBRD	Sudan.
IDA	Bangladesh.
IDB	Haïti.
IFAD	Malawi, Ethiopia.
UN	Somalia, Bangladesh
of which: UNDP	Bangladesh.
UNHCR	Somalia, Sudan.
UNICEF	Bangladesh, Ethiopie.
UNTA	-
WFP	Bangladesh, Ethiopia, Somalia.
Other UN	Chad
2. Non-concessional flows	
AfDB	Niger, Uganda, Burundi, U.-R. of Tanzania.
AsDB	Bangladesh.
EEC/EDF	Niger, Botswana, Burkina-Faso.
IBRD	Botswana, U.-R. of Tanzania.
IFC	Burundi, Guinea, Mali.

Source : UNCTAD secretariat, based on information from the OECD/DAC secretariat.

a/ Multilateral agencies mainly financed by DAC member countries.

b/ Accounting each for 10 per cent or more of the total provided to all LDCs.

Tableau 25A (suite)

APD bilatérale de chaque pays membre du CAD et apports financiers totaux de chaque institution multilatérale_a/ à l'ensemble des PMA : principaux bénéficiaires en 1983_b/

	Principaux pays bénéficiaires en 1983_b/
A. Donneurs bilatéraux	
Australie	R.-U. de Tanzanie, Bangladesh, Samoa.
Autriche	Cap-Vert, R.U. de Tanzanie, Ethiopie, Népal, Afghanistan.
Belgique	Rwanda, Burundi.
Canada	Bangladesh, R.-U. de Tanzanie.
Danemark	R.-U. de Tanzanie, Bangladesh, Soudan.
Finlande	R.-U. de Tanzanie, Soudan.
France	Rép. centrafricaine, Burkina Faso.
Allemagne, Rép. féd.d'	Soudan.
Italie	Somalie, Soudan, R.-U. de Tanzanie.
Japon	Bangladesh, R.-U. de Tanzanie, Népal.
Pays-Bas	R.-U. de Tanzanie, Soudan, Bangladesh, Burkina Faso.
Nouvelle-Zélande	Samoa.
Norvège	R.-U. de Tanzanie, Bangladesh.
Suède	R.-U. de Tanzanie, Bangladesh, Ethiopie.
Suisse	Népal, Rwanda, Mali.
Royaume-Uni	Soudan, R.-U. de Tanzanie, Bangladesh.
Etats-Unis	Bangladesh, Soudan.
B. Donneurs multilatéraux	
1. Apports concessionnels	
FaFd	Mali, Ethiopie.
BAsD	Bangladesh, Népal.
CEE/FED	Ethiopie, Bangladesh.
BIRD	Soudan.
AID	Bangladesh.
BID	Haïti.
FIDA	Malawi, Ethiopie.
ONU	Somalie, Bangladesh.
dont : PNUD	Bangladesh.
UNHCR	Somalie, Soudan.
UNICEF	Bangladesh, Ethiopie.
ATNU	-
PAM	Bangladesh, Ethiopie, Somalie.
Autres ONU	Tchad.
2. Apports non-concessionnels	
BAfD	Niger, Ouganda, Burundi, R.-U. de Tanzanie.
BAsD	Bangladesh.
CEE/FED	Niger, Botswana, Burkina Faso.
BIRD	Botswana, R.-U. de Tanzanie.
SFI	Burundi, Guinée, Mali.

Source : Secrétariat de la CNUCED, d'après des renseignements du secrétariat de l'OCDE/CAD.

a/ Institutions multilatérales essentiellement financées par les pays membres du CAD.

b/ Recevant individuellement 10 pour cent ou davantage du total accordé à l'ensemble des PMA.

Table 25B
Bilateral ODA from individual DAC member countries and total financial flows from individual multilateral agencies a/ to all LDCs, 1973-1983

Tableau 25B
APD bilatérale de chaque pays membre du CAD et apports financiers totaux de chaque institution multilatérale a/ à l'ensemble des PMA, 1973-1983

Net disbursements in millions of constant 1980 dollars b/ — Versements nets en millions de dollars constants de 1980 b/

	1973	1974	1975	1976	1977	1978	1979	1980	1981	1982	1983
A. Bilateral donors / Donneurs bilatéraux											
Australia / Australie	20.7	73.6	53.7	25.6	28.6	43.9	59.3	30.4	57.2	86.8	53.0
Austria / Autriche	1.6	0.8	1.1	2.7	3.9	4.6	3.5	5.7	9.3	7.6	8.0
Belgium / Belgique	89.6	76.2	94.3	96.6	95.6	110.9	123.1	96.2 c/	88.0	74.5	69.1
Canada	266.6	243.9	298.3	223.0	178.9	251.0	225.5 c/	166.0 c/	173.3	241.7	256.2
Denmark / Danemark	60.5	73.3	87.5	83.9	98.8	114.5	116.0	116.0	76.9	90.5	109.4
Finland / Finlande	12.0	13.5	22.6	28.3	18.3	15.5	18.1	22.1	24.6	23.2	36.8
France	407.3	425.9	452.0	403.3	355.9	380.5	424.9 c/	411.4	492.3	436.8	429.6
Germany, Federal Republic of / Allemagne, République fédérale d'	386.1	361.5	453.7	421.8	416.5	566.5	638.3	580.6	544.2	581.9	497.1
Italy / Italie	48.2	26.6	22.1	17.4	18.7	19.3	20.6	37.3	62.4	120.6	179.1
Japan / Japon	109.0	86.8	125.2	106.3	170.5	320.1	400.8	362.9	302.5	437.6	298.3
Netherlands / Pays-Bas	39.8	85.2	112.6	144.9	253.7	321.3	316.4	308.1	293.9	273.9	228.3
New Zealand / Nouvelle-Zélande	6.5	6.7	18.3	7.8	7.8	8.3	7.5	6.1	4.9	3.8	4.5
Norway / Norvège	29.1	60.3	68.6	69.5	100.3	114.3	109.8	94.6	93.1	131.1	135.2
Sweden / Suède	157.4	137.7	217.1	205.1	230.4	221.2	262.6	198.5	186.2	180.2	166.2
Switzerland / Suisse	19.6	15.8	24.2	20.6	32.4	62.2	34.9	57.3	57.4	63.1	74.3
United Kingdom / Royaume-Uni	142.7	138.8	194.9	175.2	194.2	292.6	323.5	334.0	303.9	269.7	232.7
United States / Etats-Unis	825.0	559.1	1012.9	473.1	426.7	561.1	470.6	558.0	545.1	686.2	760.6
Total bilateral concessional / Total des apports bilatéraux concessionnels	2621.8	2385.6	3259.2	2505.2	2631.1	3407.2	3554.0	3385.2	3315.2	3709.2	3538.1
B. Multilateral donors / Donneurs multilatéraux											
1. Concessional / Apports concessionnels											
AfDF / FAfD	-	-	7.0	18.7	36.2	50.3	64.0	80.6	78.4	89.2	127.8
AsDB / BAsD	13.9	9.3	47.8	27.7	38.9	83.0	71.2	75.4	66.5	63.4	91.0
EEC/EDF / CEE/FED	423.3	481.2	518.3	326.7	343.3	430.8	443.6	444.6	495.4	417.8	416.2
IBRD / BIRD	-	-	-	0.2	9.9	19.6	23.7	18.7	10.1	3.2	2.8
IDA / AID	327.7	304.6	486.3	626.9	581.8	550.6	573.3	493.8	589.8	749.0	831.9
IDB / BID	-0.0	1.5	26.2	27.9	34.6	25.0	19.3	8.9	10.3	13.4	16.8
IFAD / FIDA	-	-	-	-	-	-	1.3	12.9	23.3	29.9	56.6
IMF trust fund / Fonds fiduciaire du FMI	-	-	-	-	61.2	354.2	240.7	246.7	2.7	-	-
UN / ONU	348.3	324.7	580.3	542.4	470.1	596.5	583.8	600.7	759.4	745.0	819.4
of which: UNDP / dont: PNUD	147.5	114.5	166.3	169.1	146.7	167.9	171.8	175.8	268.8	245.6	221.8
UNHCR	36.9	17.0	16.2	17.8	12.3	26.6	43.4	96.9	104.0	95.3	125.0
UNICEF	29.1	38.8	47.8	42.5	53.0	72.9	81.0	71.9	67.5	66.8	87.6
UNFPA / ATNU	29.9	24.3	26.4	29.7	34.1	39.1	28.3	6.7	31.3	30.0	45.9
WFP / PAM	87.5	98.5	216.4	170.0	188.7	224.3	208.8	168.2	223.8	234.4	258.2
Other UN / Autres ONU	17.5	31.6	107.2	113.3	35.4	65.7	50.6	81.2	64.0	72.9	80.9
Total multilateral concessional / Total des apports multilatéraux concessionnels	1113.1	1121.3	1665.9	1570.5	1575.9	2110.0	2020.9	1982.3	2035.9	2110.8	2362.5
2. Non-concessional / Apports non-concessionnels											
AfDB / BAfD	18.3	11.0	26.2	28.3	32.8	26.7	30.8	32.1	27.0	39.0	57.2
AsDB / BAsD	13.6	3.1	2.0	-	-0.3	-1.0	-0.8	0.2	-0.6	-1.1	-0.8
EEC/EDF / CEE/FED	-	-	-	-	-	18.3	18.4	19.0	4.8	6.1	12.3
IBRD / BIRD	67.8	13.5	164.9	0.5	22.9	29.2	45.7	31.8	32.1	17.1	14.7
IFC / SFI	3.1	-1.9	-1.8	10.0	10.7	23.9	16.0	6.4	2.6	8.3	8.4
Total multilateral non-concessional / Total des apports multilatéraux non-concessionnels	102.9	25.6	191.3	33.8	66.0	97.2	110.1	89.5	65.9	69.5	91.8
Total concessional (A+B.1) / Total des apports concessionnels (A+B.1)	3734.9	3506.8	4925.1	4075.8	4207.0	5517.2	5557.8	5367.5	5351.1	5819.9	5900.7
GRAND TOTAL / TOTAL GENERAL	3837.9	3532.5	5116.4	4114.5	4273.0	5614.3	5685.0	5457.0	5417.0	5889.4	5992.5

Source : Table 25A. — Tableau 25A.

a/ Multilateral agencies mainly financed by DAC member countries. — Institutions multilatérales essentiellement financées par les pays membres du CAD.

b/ Actual disbursements were converted to 1980 prices using the index for the LDCs in table 8. — Les versements effectifs ont été convertis aux prix de 1980 en utilisant l'indice pour les PMA qui figure au tableau 8.

c/ Including flows not allocated by recipient country. — Y compris les apports non alloués par pays bénéficiaires.

Table 26

Concessional assistance to LDCs from individual DAC member countries and multilateral agencies mainly financed by them:

Relative importance and relative shares as compared to all developing countries, 1970, 1975 and 1979-1983

Percentages

Table 26

Aide concessionnelle aux PMA en provenance des pays membres du CAD et des institutions multilatérales essentiellement financées par ceux-ci:

Importance relative et parts relatives par rapport à l'ensemble des pays en développement, 1970, 1975 et 1979-1983

En pourcentage

	Relative importance of individual DAC countries and multilateral agencies in all their ODA flows to LDCs — Importance relative des différents pays du CAD et institutions multilatérales dans l'ensemble de leurs apports concessionnels aux PMA							Share of LDCs in LDA flows to all developing countries — Parts des PMA dans le total des apports concessionnels aux pays en développement							
	1970	1975	1979	1980	1981	1982	1983	1970	1975	1979	1980	1981	1982	1983	
A. Bilateral donors															**A. Donneurs bilatéraux**
Australia	0.5	1.1	1.1	0.6	1.1	1.5	0.9	2.2	6.9	10.5	6.2	10.2	14.4	8.9	Australie
Austria	0.4	0.0	0.1	0.1	0.2	0.1	0.1	87.8	1.2	6.4	4.0	5.8	4.4	5.9	Autriche
Belgium	2.8	1.9	2.2	1.8	1.6	1.3	1.2	24.6	21.0	23.6	21.7	23.8	24.3	21.8	Belgique
Canada	4.3	6.1	4.0	3.1	3.2	4.2	4.3	13.1	27.1	31.4	25.3	25.3	27.3	27.0	Canada
Denmark	0.9	1.8	2.3	2.2	1.4	1.6	1.9	20.0	45.7	38.8	45.8	36.9	41.2	42.1	Danemark
Finland	-	0.5	0.3	0.4	0.5	0.4	0.6	-	51.4	39.2	40.0	35.9	27.9	38.5	Finlande
France	10.2	9.2	7.6	7.7	9.2	7.5	7.3	9.8	14.0	12.4	12.0	13.5	12.3	12.3	France
Germany, Federal Republic of	8.6	9.2	11.4	10.8	10.2	10.0	8.4	16.5	24.5	24.7	27.1	24.0	24.0	22.9	Allemagne, Rép. fédéral d'
Italy	3.6	0.4	0.4	0.7	1.2	2.1	3.0	34.7	21.4	53.1	42.0	35.2	37.4	38.7	Italie
Japan	3.6	2.5	7.2	6.8	5.7	7.5	5.1	7.9	8.2	17.1	18.1	13.1	20.3	12.8	Japon
Netherlands	0.7	2.3	5.7	5.7	5.5	4.7	3.9	3.9	17.6	25.5	25.3	25.5	24.3	25.3	Pays-Bas
New Zealand	-	0.4	0.1	0.1	0.1	0.1	0.1	-	20.3	11.6	11.7	9.5	7.1	8.4	Nouvelle-Zélande
Norway	0.5	1.4	2.0	1.8	1.7	2.3	2.3	29.4	43.1	40.0	35.0	36.1	38.3	38.3	Norvège
Sweden	2.6	4.4	4.7	3.7	3.5	3.1	2.8	33.9	36.2	37.5	32.1	34.3	32.6	31.0	Suède
Switzerland	0.3	0.5	0.6	1.1	1.1	1.1	1.3	19.5	19.5	25.7	32.7	32.1	32.1	30.4	Suisse
United Kingdom	7.3	4.0	5.8	6.2	5.7	4.6	3.9	15.0	19.5	22.4	25.4	22.3	26.1	24.1	Royaume-Uni
United States	31.3	20.6	8.4	10.4	10.2	11.8	12.9	9.6	22.0	13.4	15.8	15.0	15.6	16.1	Etats-Unis
Total bilateral concessional	77.2	66.2	63.8	63.1	62.0	63.7	60.0	11.2	19.7	19.8	20.0	18.7	20.4	19.0	**Total des apports bilatéraux concessionnels**
B. Multilateral donors															**B. Donneurs multilatéraux**
AfDF	0.1	0.1	1.1	1.5	1.5	1.5	2.2	-	100.0	96.0	84.1	84.1	67.8	72.0	FAfD
AsDB	0.1	1.0	1.3	1.4	1.2	1.1	1.5	46.7	35.0	51.5	53.0	45.2	33.2	36.4	BAsD
EEC/EDF	6.7	10.5	8.0	8.3	9.3	7.2	7.1	29.9	40.0	32.7	42.8	33.6	34.2	30.7	CEE/FED
IBRD	-	-	0.4	0.3	0.2	0.1	0.0	-	-	18.2	17.5	11.1	5.2	5.3	BIRD
IDA	6.2	9.9	10.3	9.2	11.0	12.9	14.1	30.9	24.9	37.5	32.1	30.0	29.5	32.6	AID
IDB	0.1	0.5	0.3	0.2	0.2	0.2	0.3	0.4	4.6	4.7	2.7	2.3	3.4	4.1	BID
IFAD	-	-	0.0	0.2	0.4	0.5	1.0	-	-	42.3	24.0	30.2	27.6	35.7	FIDA
IMF Trust Fund	-	-	4.3	4.6	0.1	-	-	-	-	29.2	15.1	9.5	-	-	Fonds fiduciaire du FMI
UN	9.7	11.8	10.5	11.2	14.2	12.8	13.9	16.0	22.3	29.2	25.2	27.1	26.1	27.9	ONU
Total multilateral concessional	22.8	33.8	36.2	36.9	38.0	36.3	40.0	17.5	25.3	28.7	26.9	28.4	28.0	29.8	**Total des apports multilatéraux concessionnels**
Total concessional flows	100.0	100.0	100.0	100.0	100.0	100.0	100.0	12.2	21.3	22.3	22.1	21.5	22.6	22.2	**Total des apports concessionnels**

Source: UNCTAD secretariat, based on information from the OECD/DAC secretariat.

Source: Secrétariat de la CNUCED, d'après des renseignements du secrétariat de l'OCDE/CAD.

Table 27 / Tableau 27

Concessional assistance from DAC member countries and multilateral agencies a/ to individual LDCs, 1970-1983

Aide concessionnelle reçue par chacun des PMA en provenance des pays du CAD et/ des institutions multilatérales, a/ 1970-1983

Net disbursements in $ million — Versements nets en millions de dollars

Country	1970	1971	1972	1973	1974	1975	1976	1977	1978	1979	1980	1981	1982	1983	Pays
Afghanistan	28.4	47.3	56.0	57.1	31.7	53.5	63.9	75.3	76.4	99.5	30.8	2.6	9.0	15.7	Afghanistan
Bangladesh	227.4	186.2	223.8	421.7	486.7	956.4	521.1	586.0	961.7	1132.0	1208.0	1014.9	1197.8	957.4	Bangladesh
Benin	14.9	29.3	20.1	26.6	33.2	52.0	50.9	45.0	57.7	81.1	86.3	77.6	76.0	80.4	Bénin
Bhutan	0.2	0.1	0.2	0.5	0.6	2.1	3.2	2.9	3.2	5.9	8.3	9.8	11.3	12.9	Bhoutan
Botswana	14.2	17.7	31.5	36.6	36.6	45.9	47.6	47.5	68.8	99.1	103.9	96.5	92.9	91.2	Botswana
Burkina Faso	22.0	28.9	34.3	56.9	90.7	86.1	83.1	107.4	157.9	193.4	205.4	208.2	201.0	187.5	Burkina Faso
Burundi	17.9	21.8	25.9	26.9	33.4	47.1	44.5	46.8	71.4	88.6	109.1	117.9	120.6	132.4	Burundi
Cape Verde	-	-	-	-	-	8.7	13.1	24.4	32.5	32.5	60.4	49.3	53.2	56.3	Cap-Vert
Central African Republic	14.4	15.5	25.6	25.7	35.6	55.4	38.1	40.4	51.3	82.3	101.6	88.7	88.7	93.0	République centrafricaine
Chad	22.3	30.6	30.9	42.2	65.3	57.1	60.9	81.9	117.8	79.7	35.3	59.8	60.9	86.2	Tchad
Comoros	7.9	8.8	10.2	17.6	27.3	21.7	11.6	8.6	7.6	13.5	25.4	32.1	26.1	29.5	Comores
Democratic Yemen	4.3	4.4	5.5	7.6	10.4	20.2	23.2	32.1	47.0	39.7	38.6	36.1	57.4	56.9	Yémen démocratique
Djibouti	11.8	10.7	13.3	19.5	29.0	34.4	28.1	34.5	32.0	23.1	30.6	50.1	54.8	51.3	Djibouti
Equatorial Guinea	-	-	1.0	1.0	0.6	0.7	0.4	0.4	0.6	2.7	9.3	9.8	13.0	12.0	Guinée équatoriale
Ethiopia	40.0	47.3	47.6	66.7	120.0	119.1	140.5	111.7	137.1	174.3	211.8	226.7	199.8	257.7	Ethiopie
Gambia	1.3	3.5	4.9	6.4	8.8	7.7	9.8	17.8	26.7	30.0	40.2	45.2	43.0	40.9	Gambie
Guinea	10.3	9.7	4.9	11.3	8.9	9.4	11.5	17.1	48.3	48.5	84.9	79.6	60.2	68.3	Guinée
Guinea-Bissau	0.1	0.2	-	-	1.1	15.5	18.7	35.9	47.7	49.8	55.6	63.7	59.7	52.7	Guinée-Bissau
Haiti	7.8	6.3	6.9	8.1	14.3	59.3	71.7	84.5	92.9	92.7	105.1	105.6	125.7	128.5	Haïti
Lao People's Dem. Republic	69.4	72.4	66.8	75.9	60.1	38.9	28.4	30.2	71.8	49.9	49.0	34.9	37.9	29.3	République dém. pop. lao
Lesotho	10.0	16.8	14.2	14.2	20.9	27.4	30.1	36.9	50.0	63.9	90.8	100.1	86.8	93.3	Lesotho
Malawi	36.9	31.6	36.3	29.7	41.6	63.9	63.3	79.4	98.5	141.7	142.0	137.3	121.2	117.0	Malawi
Maldives	0.2	0.8	0.7	0.6	0.6	5.0	1.5	2.8	1.8	2.5	5.5	5.0	3.0	6.9	Maldives
Mali	21.3	30.3	38.3	70.5	104.2	115.3	86.0	97.1	151.4	179.7	224.5	210.2	159.3	166.7	Mali
Nepal	23.6	23.9	30.2	35.4	32.2	45.4	50.0	71.4	75.1	133.3	156.3	169.2	195.3	199.3	Népal
Niger	31.7	38.0	43.1	70.5	136.0	124.1	125.4	91.0	134.9	167.6	161.6	164.3	167.6	150.3	Niger
Rwanda	21.8	25.2	30.1	38.8	45.6	81.6	78.9	90.5	121.1	145.4	148.1	145.2	148.9	147.9	Rwanda
Samoa	1.5	2.0	3.1	3.6	5.6	13.4	11.7	19.0	19.7	29.4	24.9	24.0	21.9	27.1	Samoa
Sao Tome and Principe	-	-	-	-	-	0.3	1.7	3.0	4.0	3.0	3.9	5.6	9.4	11.2	Sao Tomé-et-Principe
Sierra Leone	7.0	10.5	10.3	14.3	8.7	16.3	15.0	25.0	40.0	48.2	84.0	57.9	80.8	63.6	Sierra Leone
Somalia	27.9	30.7	23.7	35.7	31.9	72.7	67.4	68.2	88.0	101.9	290.2	307.2	279.0	292.6	Somalie
Sudan	6.6	10.6	37.2	42.6	54.4	110.3	115.6	109.4	224.2	261.7	441.1	482.8	554.4	602.9	Soudan
Togo	17.0	19.3	21.7	25.8	37.0	39.8	40.5	64.2	102.4	109.7	87.4	62.4	73.4	105.7	Togo
Uganda	33.1	31.8	29.5	14.8	11.3	13.3	20.1	14.1	17.1	41.3	112.1	135.5	127.4	123.9	Ouganda
United Republic of Tanzania	51.3	62.4	61.3	100.2	155.4	288.2	267.0	327.3	421.9	583.5	646.5	649.3	656.6	572.2	République-Unie de Tanzanie
Yemen	12.2	14.9	14.8	20.7	39.3	36.6	47.5	64.6	73.0	81.7	121.2	115.8	136.6	124.3	Yémen
All LDCs	816.7	889.5	1002.9	1425.7	1819.0	2742.8	2292.0	2593.5	3736.5	4512.8	5348.1	5193.8	5410.6	5245.0	Ensemble des PMA
All developing countries	6697.1	7530.1	7860.2	8690.9	10732	12891	12046	12626	16783	20622	24257	24122	23949	23583	Ensemble des pays en développement

Source : UNCTAD secretariat, based on information from the OECD/DAC secretariat.

Source : Secrétariat de la CNUCED, d'après des renseignements du secrétariat de l'OCDE/CAD.

a/ Multilateral institutions mainly financed by DAC countries.

a/ Institutions multilatérales essentiellement financées par les pays du CAD.

Table 27 (continued)

Concessional assistance from DAC member countries and multilateral agencies a/ to individual LDCS : Leading donors b/ in 1983

Tableau 27 (suite)

Aide concessionnelle reçue par chacun des PMA en provenance des pays du CAD et des institutions multilatérales a/: Principaux donneurs b/ en 1983

Country	Leading donors	Principaux donneurs	Pays
Afghanistan	UNDP, Norway, UNICEF, UNTA.	PNUD, Norvège, UNICEF, ATNU.	Afghanistan
Bangladesh	USA, IDA, Japan.	Etats-Unis, AID, Japon.	Bangladesh
Benin	IDA, France, Germany, Federal Republic of.	AID, France, Allemagne, République fédérale d'.	Bénin
Bhutan	UNDP, WFP.	PNUD, PAM.	Bhoutan
Botswana	Germany, Fed. Rep. of, UK, USA, Sweden, WFP.	Allemagne, R.F.d', Royaume-Uni, Etats-Unis, Suède, PAM.	Botswana
Burkina Faso	France, Netherlands, USA.	France, Pays-Bas, Etats-Unis.	Burkina Faso
Burundi	IDA, France, Germany, Fed.Rep. of, Belgium.	AID, France, Allemagne, Rép. féd. d', Belgique.	Burundi
Cape Verde	USA, Sweden, Germany, Fed. Rep. of, Netherlands.	Etats-Unis, Suède, Allemagne, Rép. féd. d', Pays-Bas.	Cap-Vert
Central African Rep.	France, EEC.	France, CEE.	République centrafricaine
Chad	France, EEC, WFP.	France, CEE, PAM.	Tchad
Comoros	France, WFP.	France, PAM.	Comores
Democratic Yemen	IDA, WFP.	AID, PAM.	Yémen démocratique
Djibouti	France.	France.	Djibouti
Equatorial Guinea	WFP, France, Italy, UNDP.	PAM, France, Italie, PNUD.	Guinée équatoriale
Ethiopia	EEC, IDA, WFP.	CEE, AID, PAM.	Ethiopie
Gambia	Germany, Fed. Rep. of, USA, IDA.	Allemagne, Rép. féd. d', Etats-Unis, AID.	Gambie
Guinea	IDA, EEC, France.	AID, CEE, France.	Guinée
Guinea-Bissau	IDA, Sweden, Netherlands.	AID, Suède, Pays-Bas.	Guinée-Bissau
Haiti	USA, IDA, IDB.	Etats-Unis, AID, BID.	Haïti
Lao People's Dem.Rep.	Sweden, IDA, AsDB, UNDP.	Suède, AID, BAsD, PNUD.	République dém. pop. lao
Lesotho	USA, Germany, Fed. Rep. of, WFP.	Etats-Unis, Allemagne, Rép. féd. d', PAM.	Lesotho
Malawi	IDA, UK, Germany, Fed. Rep. of.	AID, Royaume-Uni, Allemagne, Rép. féd. d'.	Malawi
Maldives	Japan, UNDP, UK, AsDB.	Japon, PNUD, Royaume-Uni, BAsD.	Maldives
Mali	France, IDA, Germany, Fed. Rep. of.	France, AID, Allemagne, Rép. féd. d'.	Mali
Nepal	IDA, Japan, AsDB, USA.	AID, Japon, BAsD, Etats-Unis.	Népal
Niger	France, Germany, Fed. Rep. of, USA.	France, Allemagne, Rép. féd. d', Etats-Unis.	Niger
Rwanda	Germany, Fed. Rep. of, Belgium, IDA.	Allemagne, Rép. féd. d', Belgique, AID.	Rwanda
Samoa	Australia, EEC, New Zealand, AsDB, Japan.	Australie, CEE, Nouvelle-zélande, BasD, Japon.	Samoa
Sao Tome and Principe	EEC, France, AfDF.	CEE, France, FafD.	Sao Tomé-et-Principe
Sierra Leone	EEC, Germany, Fed. Rep. of, USA, IDA.	CEE, Allemagne, Rép. féd. d', Etats-Unis, AID.	Sierra Leone
Somalia	Italy, USA, UNHCR.	Italie, Etats-Unis, UNHCR.	Somalie
Sudan	USA, Germany, Fed. Rep. of.	AID, Allemagne, Rép. féd. d'.	Soudan
Togo	IDA, France, EEC, Germany, Fed. Rep. of.	AID, France, CEE, Allemagne, Rép. féd. d'.	Togo
Uganda	IDA, EEC.	AID, CEE.	Ouganda
United Rep.of Tanzania	Sweden, IDA.	Suède, AID.	Rép. Unie de Tanzanie
Yemen	IDA, USA.	AID, Etats-Unis.	Yémen.

Source : UNCTAD secretariat, based on information from the OECD/DAC secretariat.

a/ Multilateral institutions mainly financed by DAC countries.

b/ Accounting for 10 per cent or more of total concessional assistance received by the given LDC.

Source : Secrétariat de la CNUCED, d'après des renseignements du secrétariat de l'OCDE/CAD.

a/ Institutions multilatérales essentiellement financées par les pays du CAD.

b/ Donnant 10 pour cent ou davantage de l'aide concessionnelle totale reçue par le PMA en question.

Table 28

Bilateral ODA from DAC member countries to individual LDCs, 1970-1983

Net disbursements in $ million

Tableau 28

APD bilatérale reçue par chacun des PMA en provenance des pays membres du CAD, 1970-1983

Versements nets en millions de dollars

Country	1970	1971	1972	1973	1974	1975	1976	1977	1978	1979	1980	1981	1982	1983	Pays
Afghanistan	21.4	37.9	41.0	43.2	16.9	32.5	34.8	27.6	32.0	47.0	11.4	-7.9	0.4	5.2	Afghanistan
Bangladesh	..	..	199.7	307.0	344.1	703.9	319.8	384.0	666.5	774.8	850.2	672.0	822.0	582.4	Bangladesh
Benin	8.2	20.8	12.1	13.5	18.5	29.1	27.5	26.6	30.3	48.6	35.7	45.0	40.9	41.6	Bénin
Bhutan	0.2	0.1	0.2	0.5	0.3	0.6	1.0	0.6	0.7	1.2	1.7	2.6	3.2	2.9	Bhoutan
Botswana	9.3	13.6	29.2	30.9	29.9	38.5	40.6	38.1	55.1	73.6	83.5	75.9	83.2	74.5	Botswana
Burkina Faso	13.7	15.9	22.5	34.7	50.2	53.1	60.1	71.7	96.6	132.0	151.1	158.0	147.0	134.2	Burkina Faso
Burundi	11.6	13.5	16.9	15.2	18.7	26.4	25.9	28.8	38.6	44.1	59.7	64.9	75.2	69.7	Burundi
Cape Verde	-	-	-	-	-	2.1	6.8	15.8	25.0	27.2	39.0	36.2	42.6	41.7	Cap-Vert
Central African Republic	9.2	8.5	14.1	15.1	18.6	33.3	25.8	30.2	29.7	51.2	75.1	72.8	68.8	65.1	République centrafricaine
Chad	14.7	22.0	24.9	26.4	37.9	28.2	43.2	49.6	70.9	49.4	20.2	31.3	35.3	42.3	Tchad
Comoros a/	6.8	8.1	10.0	17.0	27.1	17.5	8.4	1.8	1.8	6.3	13.4	17.8	14.2	15.7	Comores a/
Democratic Yemen	1.3	2.1	1.7	2.8	5.0	6.1	9.0	6.9	12.9	4.7	4.1	4.7	9.7	6.2	Yémen démocratique
Djibouti	10.9	10.2	13.1	19.4	28.3	34.1	28.1	32.7	29.3	19.0	32.0	36.3	44.4	40.4	Djibouti
Equatorial Guinea	-	0.1	-	0.0	-	-	-	-	-	0.1	1.2	4.3	5.1	5.3	Guinée équatoriale
Ethiopia	32.7	37.6	37.7	49.6	79.8	72.9	72.8	59.0	56.0	70.5	91.4	76.2	76.9	81.5	Ethiopie
Gambia	1.0	2.3	3.2	3.3	3.7	3.5	5.4	12.6	14.8	13.2	16.5	19.2	23.6	21.4	Gambie
Guinea	7.0	6.4	1.4	8.8	6.7	5.5	4.4	5.1	9.9	14.2	32.5	31.2	26.8	27.5	Guinée
Guinea-Bissau	-	0.1	-	0.0	0.1	8.1	11.8	26.1	36.8	33.9	34.4	41.4	33.7	27.1	Guinée-Bissau
Haiti	5.2	4.3	5.0	5.0	9.4	24.8	32.1	39.6	49.8	48.5	62.8	67.0	78.7	75.0	Haïti
Lao People's Dem. Republic	68.5	71.0	65.5	72.5	57.3	32.6	24.0	26.7	20.7	26.4	16.7	16.8	21.3	12.6	République dém. pop. lao
Lesotho	6.2	12.0	9.7	8.2	12.6	14.7	18.0	20.7	29.1	43.7	60.2	59.2	53.4	58.1	Lesotho
Malawi	25.9	22.9	26.7	22.0	30.5	47.1	46.2	54.1	56.4	92.0	75.6	82.1	65.0	56.3	Malawi
Maldives	-	0.7	0.5	0.5	0.2	2.0	0.3	1.2	3.7	0.9	1.9	2.8	0.9	3.2	Maldives
Mali	9.8	16.6	22.7	35.0	60.2	55.7	53.3	60.9	93.0	93.9	131.4	133.0	96.3	95.0	Mali
Nepal	20.4	19.3	24.7	25.1	20.5	28.6	29.2	37.5	39.6	82.4	84.0	88.0	111.4	108.6	Népal
Niger	21.2	24.7	26.3	42.1	82.6	80.2	80.1	59.4	77.7	116.7	105.0	122.5	123.6	99.5	Niger
Rwanda	16.7	19.8	23.3	26.2	31.6	53.7	56.6	61.4	78.3	88.4	96.6	102.6	99.0	94.2	Rwanda
Samoa	0.3	0.3	1.3	2.1	4.3	8.8	7.3	11.1	11.3	20.7	13.7	14.2	15.4	16.7	Samoa
Sao Tome and Principe	-	-	-	-	-	0.0	0.7	1.6	1.8	1.4	1.2	1.8	3.8	3.5	Sao Tomé-et-Principe
Sierra Leone	5.2	8.7	7.7	7.5	4.5	9.8	7.5	12.0	13.5	28.4	56.8	33.7	55.7	34.7	Sierra Leone
Somalia	17.9	21.7	11.6	19.3	7.3	23.3	20.1	25.2	46.0	49.8	139.8	139.8	141.6	160.7	Somalie
Sudan	-0.1	-1.7	10.2	16.8	33.2	60.2	54.4	55.8	113.0	149.3	271.6	294.7	357.3	442.1	Soudan
Togo	7.7	10.0	13.0	17.1	23.0	23.5	20.5	42.4	66.5	68.9	52.1	36.9	50.4	48.1	Togo
Uganda	24.4	20.3	21.4	9.1	6.8	4.7	9.6	3.8	7.5	16.1	42.3	48.6	52.8	43.2	Ouganda
United Republic of Tanzania	37.9	49.8	53.4	90.5	140.2	234.7	212.0	257.3	332.3	457.4	523.1	484.7	483.7	436.5	République-Unie de Tanzanie
Yemen	7.9	9.2	9.0	14.4	27.4	15.0	11.3	34.2	37.1	51.0	78.5	77.4	85.1	72.2	Yémen
All LDCs	(630.8)	(671.0)	759.7	1000.7	1237.4	1814.8	1408.8	1622.1	2307.5	2846.9 b/	3365.9 c/	3217.7	3448.4	3145.1	Ensemble des PMA
All developing countries	5632.0	6236.0	6489.9	6728.6	8037.7	9221.6	8628.7	8972.9	11917	14809	16896	17161	16941	16542	Ensemble des pays en développement

Source : UNCTAD secretariat, based on information from the OECD/DAC secretariat.

a/ Excluding grants from France to Mayotte.

b/ Excluding $13.8 million and $69.7 million from Canada and France respectively, not allocated by recipient country.

c/ Excluding $19.5 million from Canada not allocated by recipient country.

Source : Secrétariat de la CNUCED, d'après des renseignements du secrétariat de l'OCDE/CAD.

a/ Non compris l'aide versée au titre de dons par la France à Mayotte.

b/ Non compris 13,8 millions de dollars et 69,7 millions de dollars, en provenance du Canada et de la France respectivement, non alloués par pays bénéficiaires.

c/ Non compris 19,5 millions de dollars en provenance du Canada, non alloués par pays bénéficiaire.

Table 29

Bilateral grants from DAC member countries to individual LDCs, 1970-1983

Net disbursements in $ million

Tableau 29

Dons reçus par chacun des PMA en provenance des pays membres du CAD, 1970-1983

Versements nets en millions de dollars

Country	1970	1971	1972	1973	1974	1975	1976	1977	1978	1979	1980	1981	1982	1983	Pays
Afghanistan	20.2	24.8	35.2	25.6	14.6	19.6	18.8	27.9	31.8	42.7	17.5	1.9	7.0	11.6	Afghanistan
Bangladesh	..	..	186.2	220.6	226.8	255.0	147.5	222.3	531.2	538.6	1044.7	542.7	617.6	480.3	Bangladesh
Benin	8.9	12.7	20.2	11.2	13.8	22.4	16.1	16.9	36.4	33.3	42.0	41.3	36.4	33.7	Bénin
Bhutan	0.2	0.1	0.1	0.5	0.3	0.6	1.0	0.6	0.7	1.3	1.7	2.6	3.2	2.9	Bhoutan
Botswana	8.7	7.0	4.9	10.8	17.8	24.8	31.5	31.6	86.2	69.9	81.3	76.4	83.9	75.8	Botswana
Burkina Faso	12.9	15.6	27.6	31.9	42.8	47.0	48.1	62.0	91.8	165.9	133.2	161.4	125.9	112.0	Burkina Faso
Burundi	11.4	13.5	16.9	15.2	18.6	26.5	26.0	27.5	36.5	42.7	56.9	64.8	60.6	59.6	Burundi
Cape Verde	-	-	-	-	-	2.1	6.8	15.8	25.0	27.2	38.9	35.8	42.5	41.7	Cap-Vert
Central African Republic	9.5	8.2	21.3	15.3	18.3	33.4	24.0	30.8	29.0	52.9	71.9	58.5	60.7	51.1	République centrafricaine
Chad	14.0	21.5	35.1	25.6	37.0	27.4	40.3	45.7	64.7	51.3	20.4	46.5	35.3	40.9	Tchad
Comoros a/	6.8	7.9	9.9	16.4	25.8	16.9	8.0	1.1	0.6	7.5	14.0	22.7	11.9	14.3	Comores a/
Democratic Yemen	1.3	2.1	1.7	2.8	4.2	4.1	8.5	6.0	6.6	4.9	7.6	5.1	5.8	4.8	Yémen démocratique
Djibouti	9.6	10.5	11.2	18.5	26.6	25.6	26.3	29.7	30.3	20.5	34.1	37.8	44.3	36.8	Djibouti
Equatorial Guinea	-	-	-	0.0	-	-	-	-	-	0.1	1.2	4.3	5.1	5.3	Guinée équatoriale
Ethiopia	21.2	18.1	23.4	33.7	54.0	42.6	47.1	55.1	60.9	65.7	87.6	78.3	71.8	83.7	Ethiopie
Gambia	0.6	1.4	2.9	2.4	2.9	1.9	3.7	10.4	11.4	10.8	23.9	17.6	20.7	21.9	Gambie
Guinea	1.3	0.8	1.1	-0.9	1.5	0.2	0.3	2.6	9.2	12.7	14.7	21.8	17.4	15.3	Guinée
Guinea-Bissau	-	0.1	-	0.0	0.1	8.1	11.8	25.2	34.9	33.3	31.8	39.7	33.3	26.9	Guinée-Bissau
Haiti	4.2	4.3	5.0	5.0	9.4	21.8	24.7	26.5	32.5	35.7	48.2	53.8	64.1	63.0	Haïti
Lao People's Dem. Republic	66.9	70.0	65.0	69.9	55.9	27.3	13.8	14.0	28.7	23.9	16.8	17.0	22.0	13.3	République dém. pop. lao
Lesotho	6.1	11.6	11.0	8.3	12.7	14.7	17.8	20.6	29.0	40.5	60.4	59.0	53.3	58.4	Lesotho
Malawi	14.3	21.4	11.8	9.4	12.2	16.4	27.3	21.3	78.8	120.3	58.2	78.3	64.2	56.5	Malawi
Maldives	0.1	0.7	0.5	0.4	0.2	0.8	0.6	1.2	2.6	0.6	1.9	3.0	2.3	3.6	Maldives
Mali	9.4	15.1	35.6	29.9	57.4	52.0	42.4	49.1	74.7	146.3	120.2	133.0	90.7	89.3	Mali
Nepal	20.9	16.3	21.3	22.9	19.4	25.9	27.6	38.7	40.5	69.8	95.3	84.3	108.8	103.0	Népal
Niger	17.5	16.5	24.8	36.7	22.6	61.4	58.7	41.4	91.8	125.9	86.9	104.9	116.9	94.2	Niger
Rwanda	16.8	19.9	23.5	26.2	31.6	52.4	50.4	56.5	75.6	101.3	91.6	92.5	93.8	91.8	Rwanda
Samoa	0.3	0.3	1.3	2.0	4.3	7.6	7.2	11.0	11.3	21.7	13.6	14.2	15.4	16.7	Samoa
Sao Tome and Principe	-	-	-	-	0.0	0.7	0.9	1.6	1.8	1.4	1.2	1.8	2.2	3.8	Sao Tomé-et-Principe
Sierra Leone	4.8	5.6	4.6	4.9	5.3	6.5	6.9	8.8	12.8	22.1	27.5	22.9	22.6	21.3	Sierra Leone
Somalia	12.3	20.3	9.7	15.7	8.4	24.2	18.5	25.9	27.2	39.4	157.0	117.1	105.2	118.5	Somalie
Sudan	1.4	0.6	11.3	9.4	14.1	27.5	27.5	43.1	92.9	112.1	376.9	273.6	336.9	373.0	Soudan
Togo	6.7	9.4	16.6	15.6	17.0	19.9	19.9	24.8	25.1	32.0	31.0	33.2	31.8	35.4	Togo
Uganda	12.6	15.4	32.1	9.6	5.5	3.5	3.1	4.0	8.6	27.5	41.3	90.9	54.2	68.6	Ouganda
United Republic of Tanzania	23.6	26.2	39.5	58.1	89.9	152.0	169.4	191.9	420.3	438.6	607.4	442.1	427.8	384.6	République-Unie de Tanzanie
Yemen	5.6	3.4	2.9	4.1	11.3	11.1	8.1	22.4	30.3	44.0	150.8	54.6	59.8	77.7	Yémen
All LDCs	(398.8)	(448.1)	714.3	757.7	932.1	1083.1	990.4	1214.0	2171.7	2584.1	3709.3	2935.2	2956.7	2791.0	Ensemble des PMA
All developing countries	3333.0	3632.0	4330.7	4322.3	5210.1	5752.4	5893.8	6404.8	8582.7	10784	13178	12134	12330	12555	Ensemble des pays en développement

Source : UNCTAD secretariat, based on information from the OECD/DAC secretariat.

Source : Secrétariat de la CNUCED, d'après des renseignements du secrétariat de l'OECD/CAD.

a/ Excluding grants from France to Mayotte.

a/ Non compris l'aide versée au titre de dons par la France à Mayotte.

Table 30

Tableau 30

Total assistance from multilateral agencies mainly financed by DAC member countries to individual LDCs, 1970-1983

Aide totale des institutions multilatérales essentiellement financées par les pays membres du CAD en faveur des PMA, 1970-1983

Net disbursements in $ million

Versements nets en millions de dollars

Country	1970	1971	1972	1973	1974	1975	1976	1977	1978	1979	1980	1981	1982	1983	Pays
Afghanistan	7.0	9.4	15.0	14.2	14.8	21.0	29.1	47.7	44.4	52.5	19.4	10.5	8.6	10.5	Afghanistan
Bangladesh	..	..	24.1	119.9	143.0	308.4	201.5	202.0	294.7	356.7	359.1	342.6	376.2	374.3	Bangladesh
Benin	6.7	8.5	8.0	13.2	14.9	23.0	24.5	21.9	29.9	33.7	54.0	35.1	34.7	38.9	Bénin
Bhutan	-	-	-	-	0.3	1.5	2.2	2.3	2.5	4.7	6.6	7.2	8.1	10.0	Bhoutan
Botswana	4.9	4.1	14.8	19.1	12.4	10.1	9.1	12.3	16.2	31.0	23.7	30.3	26.3	35.2	Botswana
Burkina Faso	8.3	13.5	12.1	23.4	41.4	33.0	24.0	35.5	62.0	60.9	54.3	49.7	53.6	55.9	Burkina Faso
Burundi	6.0	8.0	8.7	11.4	14.4	21.6	20.1	19.1	33.0	44.3	49.7	53.3	46.3	72.6	Burundi
Cape Verde	-	-	-	-	-	6.6	6.1	8.6	7.5	5.3	21.4	13.1	17.6	18.7	Cap-Vert
Central African Republic	5.2	7.0	11.5	10.6	17.0	22.7	12.6	10.2	21.6	31.0	34.0	28.8	19.8	28.7	République centrafricaine
Chad	7.6	8.6	6.0	15.8	27.4	28.9	17.7	32.3	46.9	30.3	15.1	28.5	25.6	43.9	Tchad
Comoros	1.1	0.7	0.2	0.6	0.2	4.2	3.2	6.8	5.8	7.2	12.0	14.3	13.0	16.4	Comores
Democratic Yemen	3.0	2.3	3.8	4.8	5.4	14.1	14.2	25.2	34.1	35.0	34.5	31.4	47.7	50.7	Yémen démocratique
Djibouti	0.9	0.5	0.2	0.1	0.7	0.3	-	1.8	2.7	4.1	8.6	13.8	10.4	10.9	Djibouti
Equatorial Guinea	-	-	-	1.0	0.6	0.7	0.4	0.4	0.6	2.6	8.8	7.0	10.5	7.9	Guinée équatoriale
Ethiopia	10.2	18.9	16.1	21.2	38.4	48.3	65.9	49.0	77.2	99.8	118.2	149.2	121.0	174.9	Ethiopie
Gambia	0.3	1.2	1.7	3.1	5.1	4.2	4.4	5.2	12.0	17.6	29.4	28.1	20.7	20.7	Gambie
Guinea	18.5	27.5	25.6	8.4	0.5	5.2	5.0	11.7	36.6	32.9	49.9	46.0	34.0	42.9	Guinée
Guinea-Bissau	0.1	0.1	-	1.0	1.0	7.4	6.9	9.8	10.9	15.9	21.2	22.7	28.0	29.6	Guinée-Bissau
Haiti	2.4	1.7	1.8	3.1	4.9	34.5	39.6	44.9	43.1	44.2	42.3	38.6	47.0	54.2	Haïti
Lao People's Dem. Republic	0.9	1.4	1.3	3.4	2.8	6.3	4.4	3.5	29.2	23.5	23.4	18.1	16.6	16.7	République dém. pop. lao
Lesotho	3.8	4.8	4.5	6.0	8.3	12.7	12.1	16.2	21.2	20.2	30.6	41.1	35.5	37.4	Lesotho
Malawi	11.0	10.2	10.5	8.5	11.4	17.2	34.0	34.0	54.0	71.5	82.2	81.9	78.2	63.2	Malawi
Maldives	0.1	0.1	0.2	0.2	0.4	1.0	0.9	0.8	1.1	1.6	3.6	2.2	2.1	3.7	Maldives
Mali	11.5	14.2	15.6	35.5	43.9	59.5	32.6	36.7	61.0	87.4	94.2	77.6	64.6	72.5	Mali
Nepal	3.2	4.6	5.6	10.4	13.0	16.9	20.7	36.0	36.0	50.7	72.0	80.8	83.6	90.7	Népal
Niger	10.5	13.3	16.8	29.2	53.9	44.1	45.2	31.5	58.1	58.3	63.4	45.6	44.7	65.3	Niger
Rwanda	5.1	5.4	6.8	12.6	14.0	27.9	22.3	29.4	42.4	57.0	51.7	42.7	51.1	54.3	Rwanda
Samoa	1.2	1.7	1.8	1.5	1.3	4.6	4.4	7.9	8.4	8.7	11.2	9.8	6.5	10.4	Samoa
Sao Tome and Principe	-	-	-	-	-	0.3	1.0	1.4	2.2	1.6	2.7	3.8	5.6	7.7	Sao Tomé-et-Principe
Sierra Leone	4.8	2.6	3.2	6.6	7.7	10.4	8.8	13.8	26.4	21.9	30.5	25.5	25.4	28.0	Sierra Leone
Somalia	10.0	9.0	12.2	16.7	25.2	50.9	47.4	43.0	41.2	51.9	150.9	167.6	137.3	131.5	Somalie
Sudan	12.3	13.6	27.5	21.8	17.1	47.2	61.6	50.5	114.9	115.1	167.1	187.6	194.0	155.4	Soudan
Togo	9.3	9.9	9.9	9.0	14.0	16.2	20.8	12.3	65.7	69.8	67.1	22.9	20.5	56.5	Togo
Uganda	8.2	11.0	7.7	7.9	4.7	9.5	13.1	12.8	10.1	28.3	71.6	61.7	80.6	87.3	Ouganda
United Republic of Tanzania	14.6	19.8	23.5	19.0	23.3	93.1	66.7	94.0	105.6	146.3	144.4	182.4	179.8	153.0	République-Unie de Tanzanie
Yemen	4.3	5.7	5.8	6.3	11.9	21.6	36.2	30.4	35.9	33.1	42.7	38.4	51.5	51.2	Yémen
All LDCs	(239.6)	(272.4)	302.5	464.5	595.3	1034.5	905.0	1012.2	1495.1	1756.6	2071.5	2039.9	2026.7	2181.7	Ensemble des PMA
All developing countries	1724.2	2162.0	2309.9	3165.7	4360.6	6002.6	5741.3	6175.7	7596.8	9379.2	11734	12212	13152	13897	Ensemble des pays en développement

Source : UNCTAD secretariat, based on information from the OECD/DAC secretariat.

Source : Secrétariat de la CNUCED, d'après des renseignements du secrétariat de l'OCDE/CAD.

Table 31

Non-concessional assistance from multilateral agencies mainly financed by DAC member countries to individual LDCs, 1970-1983

Net disbursements in $ million

Tableau 31

Aide non-concessionnelle reçue par chacun des PMA en provenance des institutions multilatérales essentiellement financées par les pays membres du CAD, 1970-1983

Versements nets en millions de dollars

Country	1970	1971	1972	1973	1974	1975	1976	1977	1978	1979	1980	1981	1982	1983	Pays
Afghanistan	..	..	-	0.3	-	55.9	0.2	-	-0.5	-0.5	1.3	-0.3	-	-	Afghanistan
Bangladesh	-	..	-	5.2	0.4	0.1	1.1	3.5	-2.5	1.2	3.4	2.5	0.4	-0.7	Bangladesh
Benin	-	-	-	0.1	0.2	-	-	-	-	-	-	-	-0.4	0.1	Bénin
Bhutan	-	-	12.5	13.4	-	-	-	-	-	-	-	-	-	-	Bhoutan
Botswana	-	-	-	-	5.7	2.7	2.1	2.9	2.5	5.5	3.3	9.7	16.6	18.5	Botswana
Burkina Faso	-0.3	-0.3	0.3	1.2	0.9	-	1.0	-0.2	0.7	-0.5	-	-0.5	-0.4	2.6	Burkina Faso
Burundi	-	-	-0.3	-0.3	-0.3	0.3	1.5	1.1	0.2	-0.2	0.3	0.3	0.9	9.9	Burundi
Cape Verde	-	-	-	-	-	0.6	0.2	-	-	-	0.2	-	7.0	4.1	Cap-Vert
Central African Republic	-	-	-	-	-	-	-	-	-	-0.1	0.2	-0.0	-0.1	0.8	République centrafricaine
Chad	-	-	-	-	-	-	-	-	-	-	-	-	-	-	Tchad
Comoros	-	-	-	-	-	-	-	-	-	-	-	-	1.1	2.6	Comores
Democratic Yemen	-	-	-	-	-	-	-	-	-	-	-	-	-	-	Yémen démocratique
Djibouti	-	-	-	-	-	-	-	-	-	-	-	-	-	-	Djibouti
Equatorial Guinea	-	-	-	-	-	-	-	-	-	-	0.7	1.5	2.6	1.2	Guinée équatoriale
Ethiopia	2.9	9.2	6.2	4.1	-1.8	2.1	-1.8	-3.7	-3.9	-4.0	-2.2	-1.3	-1.9	-1.3	Ethiopie
Gambia	15.2	24.2	22.1	5.9	-	-	-	-	0.1	0.8	5.7	2.1	1.3	2.1	Gambie
Guinea	-	-	-	-	-1.7	1.3	-2.1	-0.3	-1.8	-1.4	-2.5	-2.4	0.6	2.1	Guinée
Guinea-Bissau	-0.2	-0.3	-0.1	-	-	-	-	-	-	-	-	0.4	2.0	4.0	Guinée-Bissau
Haiti	-	-	-	-	-	-	-	-	0.3	-	-	-	-	0.7	Haïti
Lao People's Dem. Republic	-	-	-	-	-	-	-	-	-	-	-	-	-	-	République dém. pop. lao
Lesotho	-	1.5	0.9	0.8	0.3	0.4	-	8.7	11.9	21.8	15.8	0.2	2.1	2.4	Lesotho
Malawi	-	-	-	-	-	-	3.0	-	-	-	-	26.7	22.0	2.5	Malawi
Maldives	-	-	-	-	-	-	-	-	-	-	-	-	-	-	Maldives
Mali	-	0.5	0.1	0.1	-0.1	-0.1	-0.1	0.5	2.6	1.6	1.1	0.4	1.6	0.8	Mali
Nepal	-	-	-	0.8	1.3	0.1	-0.1	2.1	0.5	-0.2	-0.3	-0.4	-0.3	-	Népal
Niger	-	-	-	-	0.5	0.2	-0.1	-0.1	0.9	7.4	6.8	3.8	0.7	14.5	Niger
Rwanda	-	-	-	-	-	-	-	0.3	0.2	-	0.2	0.1	1.2	0.6	Rwanda
Samoa	-	-	-	-	-	-	-	-	-	-	-	-	-	-	Samoa
Sao Tome and Principe	3.0	0.8	0.6	-0.2	3.5	3.9	1.3	0.8	-0.1	2.1	3.3	1.3	0.3	-0.9	Sao Tomé-et-Principe
Sierra Leone	-	-	0.1	0.3	0.6	1.5	0.1	-	-	-0.2	-	-0.1	-0.1	-	Sierra Leone
Somalia	5.6	1.3	0.5	-4.0	-4.1	-2.9	0.4	-3.1	3.7	2.7	-2.4	-0.5	-3.1	-0.4	Somalie
Sudan	-	-	-	-	-	-	-	1.8	29.8	29.0	31.8	-2.6	-2.5	-5.4	Soudan
Togo	-0.5	-0.5	1.2	0.3	0.2	-0.1	0.8	2.5	0.5	3.1	1.8	4.8	-	-1.1	Togo
Uganda	-	-	-0.4	2.2	-	0.9	2.6	-	-	-	-	-	6.0	6.6	Ouganda
United Republic of Tanzania	1.2	7.2	15.6	9.3	8.1	39.6	11.7	24.0	16.0	20.2	21.0	17.8	6.9	17.3	République-Unie de Tanzanie
Yemen	-	-	-	-	-	-	-	-	-	2.4	-	-	-	-0.9	Yémen
All LDCs	(53.7)	(53.9)	59.3	39.5	13.7	106.5	21.8	40.8	66.1	90.7	89.3	63.8	64.5	81.8	**Ensemble des PMA**
All developing countries	659.1	867.9	939.6	1213.4	1666.1	2333.0	2323.8	2522.9	2730.9	3565.9	4373.4	5252.1	6144.1	6855.5	**Ensemble des pays en développement**

Source : UNCTAD secretariat, based on information from the OECD/DAC secretariat.

Source : Secrétariat de la CNUCED, d'après des renseignements du secrétariat de l'OCDE/CAD.

Table 32

Concessional assistance from multilateral agencies mainly financed by DAC member countries to individual LDCs, 1970-1983

Net disbursements in $ million

Tableau 32

Aide concessionnelle reçue par chacun des PMA en provenance des institutions multilatérales essentiellement financées par les pays membres du CAD, 1970-1983

Versements nets en millions de dollars

Country	1970	1971	1972	1973	1974	1975	1976	1977	1978	1979	1980	1981	1982	1983	Pays
Afghanistan	7.0	9.4	15.0	13.9	14.8	21.0	29.1	47.7	44.4	52.5	19.4	10.5	8.6	10.5	Afghanistan
Bangladesh	..	..	24.1	114.7	142.6	252.5	201.3	202.0	295.2	357.2	357.8	342.9	375.8	375.0	Bangladesh
Benin	6.7	8.5	8.0	13.1	14.7	22.9	23.4	18.4	27.4	32.5	50.6	32.6	35.1	38.8	Bénin
Bhutan	-	-	-	0.0	0.3	1.5	2.2	2.3	2.5	4.7	6.6	7.2	8.1	10.0	Bhoutan
Botswana	4.9	4.1	2.3	5.7	6.7	7.4	7.0	9.4	13.7	25.5	20.4	20.6	9.7	16.7	Botswana
Burkina Faso	8.3	13.0	11.8	22.2	40.5	33.0	23.0	35.7	61.3	44.5	54.3	53.0	54.0	53.3	Burkina Faso
Burundi	6.3	8.3	9.0	11.7	14.7	20.7	18.6	18.0	32.8	44.5	49.4	53.0	45.4	62.7	Burundi
Cape Verde	-	-	-	-	-	6.6	6.3	8.6	7.5	5.3	21.4	13.1	10.6	14.6	Cap-Vert
Central African Republic	5.2	7.0	11.5	10.6	17.0	22.1	12.4	10.2	21.6	31.1	33.8	28.8	19.9	27.9	République centrafricaine
Chad	7.6	8.6	6.0	15.8	27.4	28.9	17.7	32.3	46.9	31.0	15.1	28.5	25.6	43.9	Tchad
Comoros	1.1	0.7	0.2	0.6	0.2	4.2	3.2	6.8	5.8	7.2	12.0	14.3	11.9	13.8	Comores
Democratic Yemen	3.0	2.3	3.8	4.8	5.4	14.1	14.2	25.2	34.1	35.0	34.5	31.4	47.7	50.7	Yémen démocratique
Djibouti	0.9	0.5	0.2	-	0.6	0.3	-	1.8	2.7	4.1	8.6	13.8	10.4	10.9	Djibouti
Equatorial Guinea	-	-	-	1.0	0.6	0.7	0.4	0.4	0.6	2.6	8.1	5.5	7.9	6.7	Guinée équatoriale
Ethiopia	7.3	9.7	9.9	17.1	40.2	46.2	67.7	52.7	81.1	103.8	120.0	150.5	122.9	176.2	Ethiopie
Gambia	0.3	1.2	1.7	3.1	5.1	4.2	4.4	5.2	11.9	16.8	23.7	26.0	19.4	19.5	Gambie
Guinea	3.3	3.3	3.5	2.5	2.2	3.9	7.1	12.0	38.4	34.3	52.4	48.4	33.4	40.8	Guinée
Guinea-Bissau	0.1	0.1	-	-	1.0	7.4	6.9	9.8	10.9	15.9	21.2	22.3	26.0	25.6	Guinée-Bissau
Haiti	2.6	2.0	1.9	3.1	4.9	34.5	39.6	44.9	43.1	44.2	42.3	38.6	47.0	53.5	Haïti
Lao People's Dem. Republic	0.9	1.4	1.3	3.4	2.8	6.3	4.4	3.5	29.2	23.5	23.4	18.1	16.6	16.7	République dém. pop. lao
Lesotho	3.8	4.8	4.5	6.0	8.3	12.7	12.1	16.2	20.9	20.2	30.6	40.9	33.4	35.0	Lesotho
Malawi	11.0	8.7	9.6	7.7	11.1	16.8	17.1	25.3	42.1	49.7	66.4	55.2	56.2	60.7	Malawi
Maldives	0.1	0.1	0.2	0.2	0.4	1.0	0.9	0.8	1.1	1.6	3.6	2.2	2.1	3.7	Maldives
Mali	11.5	13.7	15.6	35.5	44.0	59.6	32.7	36.2	58.4	85.8	93.1	77.2	63.0	71.7	Mali
Nepal	3.2	4.6	5.5	10.3	11.7	16.8	20.8	33.9	35.5	50.9	72.3	81.2	83.9	90.7	Népal
Niger	10.5	13.3	16.8	28.4	53.4	43.9	45.3	31.6	57.2	50.9	56.6	41.8	44.0	50.8	Niger
Rwanda	5.1	5.4	6.8	12.6	14.0	27.9	22.3	29.1	42.2	57.0	51.5	42.6	49.9	53.7	Rwanda
Samoa	1.2	1.2	1.8	1.5	1.3	0.3	4.4	7.9	8.4	8.7	9.8	9.8	6.5	10.4	Samoa
Sao Tome and Principe	-	-	-	-	-	-	1.0	1.4	2.2	1.6	2.7	3.8	5.6	7.7	Sao Tomé-et-Principe
Sierra Leone	1.8	1.8	2.6	6.8	4.2	6.5	7.5	13.0	26.5	19.8	27.2	24.2	25.1	28.9	Sierra Leone
Somalia	10.0	9.0	12.1	16.4	24.6	49.4	47.3	43.0	41.2	52.1	150.9	167.4	137.4	131.9	Somalie
Sudan	6.7	12.3	27.0	25.8	21.2	50.1	61.2	53.6	111.2	112.4	188.1	188.1	197.1	160.8	Soudan
Togo	9.3	9.3	8.7	8.7	14.0	16.3	20.0	21.8	35.9	40.8	35.3	25.5	23.0	57.6	Togo
Uganda	8.7	11.5	8.1	5.7	4.5	8.6	10.5	10.3	9.6	25.2	69.8	56.9	74.6	80.7	Ouganda
United Republic of Tanzania	13.4	12.6	7.9	9.7	15.2	53.5	55.0	70.0	89.6	126.1	123.4	164.6	172.9	135.7	République-Unie de Tanzanie
Yemen	4.3	5.7	5.8	6.3	11.9	21.6	36.2	30.4	35.9	30.7	42.7	38.4	51.5	52.1	Yémen
All LDCs	(185.9)	(218.5)	243.2	425.0	581.6	928.0	883.2	971.4	1429.0	1665.9	1982.2	1976.1	1962.2	2099.9	Ensemble des PMA
All developing countries	1065.1	1294.1	1370.3	1952.3	2694.5	3669.6	3417.5	3652.8	4865.9	5813.3	7360.3	6960.4	7007.6	7041.2	Ensemble des pays en développement

Source : UNCTAD secretariat, based on information from the OECD/DAC secretariat.

Source : Secrétariat de la CNUCED, d'après des renseignements du secrétariat de l'OCDE/CAD.

Table 33

Grants from multilateral agencies mainly financed by DAC member countries to individual LDCs, 1970-1983

Net disbursements in $ million

Tableau 33

Dons reçus par chacun des PMA en provenance des institutions multilatérales essentiellement financées par les pays membres du CAD, 1970-1983

Versements nets en millions de dollars

Country	1970	1971	1972	1973	1974	1975	1976	1977	1978	1979	1980	1981	1982	1983	Pays
Afghanistan	7.0	7.8	12.0	12.6	11.7	16.4	13.5	20.2	21.9	34.0	9.4	9.5	9.2	11.0	Afghanistan
Bangladesh	..	..	24.1	45.5	54.4	107.4	82.3	87.4	107.8	105.2	95.7	130.6	153.3	123.0	Bangladesh
Benin	6.6	6.3	5.4	6.4	10.3	17.3	16.9	10.4	17.5	23.4	24.9	19.3	17.1	15.6	Bénin
Bhutan	-	-	-	0.0	0.3	1.5	2.3	2.5	2.5	4.7	6.6	6.9	7.4	9.3	Bhoutan
Botswana	3.3	3.3	2.3	3.8	4.5	6.2	5.5	7.4	11.0	20.8	16.8	17.4	9.6	16.1	Botswana
Burkina Faso	8.3	13.0	10.3	18.7	34.9	26.6	15.7	17.4	37.3	32.2	27.3	32.6	40.4	32.2	Burkina Faso
Burundi	5.9	7.8	8.5	11.5	14.2	20.4	17.4	12.0	16.6	24.9	26.9	38.6	18.9	25.9	Burundi
Cape Verde	-	-	-	-	-	6.6	6.3	8.6	7.5	5.1	10.9	9.3	8.5	12.9	Cap-Vert
Central African Republic	5.0	4.9	8.1	9.3	16.0	21.4	12.1	9.1	11.2	18.0	18.0	20.7	14.0	18.3	République centrafricaine
Chad	7.4	7.1	5.4	14.3	24.9	23.6	12.5	13.6	21.6	19.4	13.0	26.7	25.0	42.8	Tchad
Comoros	1.1	0.7	0.2	0.6	0.2	4.2	3.2	6.8	5.2	4.8	7.0	11.2	9.6	12.9	Comores
Democratic Yemen	3.0	2.1	3.5	4.2	4.4	12.3	7.3	17.2	15.1	17.3	19.0	22.2	29.6	24.0	Yémen démocratique
Djibouti	0.9	0.5	0.2	0.1	0.7	0.3	-	1.8	2.7	3.7	8.0	13.0	9.4	9.6	Djibouti
Equatorial Guinea	-	-	-	1.0	0.6	0.7	0.4	0.4	0.6	2.6	2.2	5.5	7.8	6.0	Guinée équatoriale
Ethiopia	4.5	6.0	5.5	8.6	31.0	27.5	30.7	18.3	33.0	42.4	81.1	111.0	87.9	117.5	Ethiopie
Gambia	0.3	1.1	1.2	1.5	3.8	3.3	3.4	2.2	7.5	11.2	16.0	22.0	14.6	10.2	Gambie
Guinea	3.3	3.1	3.5	-	2.2	3.9	5.9	5.7	18.5	17.1	28.9	21.5	20.0	16.9	Guinée
Guinea-Bissau	0.1	0.1	-	-	1.0	7.4	6.9	9.8	10.6	14.4	16.9	13.0	13.2	11.2	Guinée-Bissau
Haiti	1.6	1.8	2.1	3.2	3.2	10.9	9.3	7.6	13.1	13.7	14.3	12.7	18.5	13.1	Haïti
Lao People's Dem. Republic	0.9	0.9	1.2	1.6	1.9	3.8	4.0	3.6	20.3	16.6	13.2	11.5	8.2	8.2	République dém. pop. lao
Lesotho	3.8	4.8	4.5	6.0	6.9	10.9	9.8	10.4	14.8	14.4	20.1	28.1	16.1	22.9	Lesotho
Malawi	1.4	1.4	1.8	3.0	3.7	5.3	4.8	9.0	13.8	17.4	26.7	25.6	21.9	17.5	Malawi
Maldives	0.1	0.1	0.2	0.2	0.4	1.0	0.9	0.8	1.1	1.6	2.0	1.7	2.0	2.6	Maldives
Mali	10.3	10.3	10.6	31.0	37.4	45.1	17.0	19.7	31.9	49.0	56.4	49.3	39.0	39.6	Mali
Nepal	3.0	3.4	4.2	5.9	7.2	10.7	10.5	14.7	13.6	20.1	34.0	32.1	29.8	36.0	Népal
Niger	8.2	11.5	13.7	25.1	51.6	41.6	41.6	24.1	41.2	38.0	24.9	26.5	30.6	29.5	Niger
Rwanda	5.0	5.3	5.9	10.3	9.5	22.3	13.7	17.6	28.1	32.3	30.6	32.3	32.6	25.9	Rwanda
Samoa	0.7	0.8	1.1	1.1	1.1	1.8	2.5	4.0	2.4	4.3	5.0	5.2	3.8	2.6	Samoa
Sao Tome and Principe	-	-	-	-	2.0	0.3	1.0	1.4	2.2	1.6	2.7	1.8	3.0	6.0	Sao Tomé-et-Principe
Sierra Leone	1.8	1.7	1.8	2.0	2.0	4.1	5.5	7.9	6.6	7.9	14.1	17.7	13.5	18.3	Sierra Leone
Somalia	6.8	7.4	10.9	13.6	18.0	39.7	39.2	32.6	30.5	43.8	125.6	146.0	112.4	105.0	Somalie
Sudan	6.7	12.1	27.0	24.3	19.0	35.0	28.3	28.3	34.5	56.5	104.5	105.3	102.2	96.1	Soudan
Togo	8.2	8.7	8.1	8.5	13.8	15.6	15.6	11.7	16.1	14.0	13.0	14.5	8.7	23.0	Togo
Uganda	3.3	3.5	1.8	3.0	3.3	5.9	7.9	9.3	8.1	24.2	39.9	43.3	30.8	41.1	Ouganda
United Republic of Tanzania	4.0	4.5	5.1	6.7	9.5	36.0	26.3	23.5	36.3	48.4	50.3	66.4	60.9	52.3	République-Unie de Tanzanie
Yemen	4.3	5.7	5.8	5.4	10.8	14.5	18.3	13.6	13.7	17.0	20.5	20.9	26.6	20.4	Yémen
All LDCs	(133.8)	(157.0)	196.0	291.5	414.4	610.1	492.4	490.4	676.4	822.0	1026.4	1171.9	1056.1	1075.1	**Ensemble des PMA**
All developing countries	666.8	772.6	818.4	1036.7	1482.9	2139.2	1634.8	1812.9	2336.5	2972.0	3339.8	3946.2	3603.0	3663.0	**Ensemble des pays en développement**

Source : UNCTAD secretariat, based on information from the OECD/DAC secretariat.

Source : Secrétariat de la CNUCED, d'après des renseignements du secrétariat de l'OCDE/CAD.

Table 34

Technical assistance disbursements to individual LDCs, a/ 1970-1983

$ million

Tableau 34

Versements au titre de l'assistance technique en faveur des PMA a/ 1970-1983

Millions de dollars

A. Total

Country	1970	1971	1972	1973	1974	1975	1976	1977	1978	1979	1980	1981	1982	1983	Pays
Afghanistan	20.9	24.3	24.3	24.1	21.8	25.1	20.3	28.2	31.1	37.8	21.8	14.8	13.9	15.2	Afghanistan
Bangladesh	..	..	10.6	11.7	29.7	58.3	60.0	27.3	99.7	148.2	158.9	147.1	133.1	176.3	Bangladesh
Benin	6.1	9.9	8.3	10.3	12.3	19.8	16.0	13.7	16.9	20.4	25.9	25.1	27.9	25.8	Bénin
Bhutan	0.1	0.1	0.1	0.2	0.5	1.8	2.7	2.1	2.2	4.8	6.0	7.4	6.2	7.2	Bhoutan
Botswana	2.7	4.9	4.5	7.9	9.4	13.7	15.5	18.0	23.0	36.3	47.5	48.0	42.8	40.5	Botswana
Burkina Faso	8.2	9.6	12.9	15.4	19.6	32.6	37.5	37.6	49.1	60.7	73.0	72.0	73.7	65.2	Burkina Faso
Burundi	10.5	11.5	13.7	15.7	17.2	23.1	23.0	25.6	30.4	35.7	45.0	44.2	46.8	45.4	Burundi
Cape Verde	.	-	-	-	-	1.0	2.2	2.8	5.6	6.2	11.9	11.4	20.6	17.8	Cap-Vert
Central African Republic	8.1	8.5	12.4	12.1	12.9	19.5	19.4	20.8	24.6	32.9	34.2	33.6	31.2	29.3	République centrafricaine
Chad	9.9	12.3	15.0	20.0	19.8	25.4	22.0	24.6	29.2	21.4	11.9	16.8	15.3	21.7	Tchad
Comoros	4.8	6.5	3.0	8.6	13.4	7.0	1.3	2.3	1.3	2.9	7.0	10.1	9.6	10.1	Comores
Democratic Yemen	2.3	3.5	4.8	4.9	7.0	9.2	11.3	10.6	10.8	7.9	11.6	12.6	14.8	13.9	Yémen démocratique
Djibouti	6.2	8.1	5.1	9.6	13.7	11.1	14.0	15.2	14.3	19.0	27.8	29.8	30.8	29.3	Djibouti
Equatorial Guinea	-	-	-	1.0	0.6	0.7	0.4	0.4	0.6	2.2	2.0	4.5	4.1	3.9	Guinée équatoriale
Ethiopia	19.6	28.0	26.2	30.6	36.5	36.1	31.5	30.3	26.5	29.2	44.2	63.9	53.1	61.9	Ethiopie
Gambia	0.7	1.0	1.6	2.0	2.1	2.7	4.3	3.3	6.8	11.1	12.7	13.8	17.4	15.8	Gambie
Guinea	4.1	4.4	1.1	1.3	1.4	3.4	5.5	6.0	10.3	11.1	18.7	21.4	20.5	14.7	Guinée
Guinea-Bissau	0.1	0.1	-	0.0	0.3	2.5	7.0	4.6	6.7	9.0	12.1	12.7	15.2	16.2	Guinée-Bissau
Haiti	3.6	3.5	4.8	7.0	6.5	11.8	13.5	13.6	20.5	24.0	32.3	32.8	34.1	32.2	Haïti
Lao People's Dem. Republic	39.6	41.7	36.0	42.3	29.7	15.0	4.5	5.1	11.8	12.0	14.0	13.3	11.3	10.7	République dém. populaire lao
Lesotho	2.6	2.8	3.3	5.0	6.6	8.7	12.0	12.7	16.3	19.9	29.1	31.2	32.3	32.0	Lesotho
Malawi	9.1	9.2	11.1	11.6	14.6	16.3	17.4	17.6	24.0	30.0	36.4	38.1	37.2	34.8	Malawi
Maldives	0.2	0.2	0.4	0.3	0.6	0.8	1.0	1.0	1.5	2.2	2.5	2.5	3.6	3.8	Maldives
Mali	8.1	9.3	12.1	13.0	19.0	24.6	23.2	25.6	35.4	49.5	76.9	63.0	55.0	53.5	Mali
Nepal	8.0	10.9	10.1	12.7	14.0	24.7	20.5	26.0	30.6	38.1	50.5	52.7	63.8	68.0	Népal
Niger	11.1	11.9	14.6	14.0	24.6	29.2	27.9	30.5	38.4	47.3	62.1	59.2	68.2	60.9	Niger
Rwanda	11.7	13.7	16.5	19.2	23.4	31.4	32.3	41.2	42.8	50.9	54.5	53.2	49.6	53.8	Rwanda
Samoa	0.9	0.9	1.6	1.8	3.7	4.7	4.8	5.8	6.8	6.0	9.8	10.8	7.6	7.4	Samoa
Sao Tome and Principe	-	-	-	-	-	0.3	0.5	0.9	1.5	1.3	1.3	1.4	2.8	1.7	Sao Tomé-et-Principe
Sierra Leone	5.3	5.0	4.3	5.6	4.4	7.9	10.4	10.4	13.2	14.9	21.4	21.7	21.3	19.3	Sierra Leone
Somalia	10.6	10.3	9.8	12.1	12.7	19.6	16.0	19.4	21.5	32.1	92.9	103.2	92.0	120.2	Somalie
Sudan	6.5	6.2	21.9	19.4	15.6	28.1	30.9	37.7	60.3	69.1	102.4	131.5	117.9	127.4	Soudan
Togo	7.7	9.1	11.2	13.3	16.9	16.9	17.0	18.9	21.9	25.1	28.9	30.4	30.3	27.8	Togo
Uganda	14.4	17.7	16.2	12.0	8.1	9.0	8.4	7.7	12.0	16.4	21.0	33.8	29.5	33.6	Ouganda
United Republic of Tanzania	21.4	24.0	34.8	41.2	48.6	60.2	76.7	80.2	106.0	138.2	172.6	176.4	180.7	172.2	République-Unie de Tanzanie
Yemen	2.6	3.2	4.8	6.4	10.0	17.0	15.6	25.2	32.8	39.5	50.3	60.6	64.7	60.1	Yémen
All LDCs	(280.7)	(324.0)	357.1	412.3	475.3	619.2	627.4	652.9	886.4	1111.8	1431.4	1505.0	1478.9	1529.6	Ensemble des PMA
All developing countries	1907.3	2097.7	2310.7	2869.5	3214.0	3967.1	3803.0	4070.0	4991.2	6240.8	7242.3	7370.5	7349.6	7710.6	Ensemble des pays en développement

Source : UNCTAD secretariat, based on information from the OECD/DAC secretariat.

Source : Secrétariat de la CNUCED, d'après des renseignements du secrétariat de l'OCDE/CAD.

a/ Bilateral contributions from DAC member countries plus contributions from multilateral agencies mainly financed by them.

a/ Somme des contributions bilatérales des pays membres du CAD et des contributions des institutions multilatérales essentiellement financées par ceux-ci.

Table 34 (continued)

Technical assistance disbursements to individual LDCs a/ 1970-1983

Tableau 34 (suite)

Versements au titre de l'assistance technique en faveur des PMA, a/ 1970-1983

Dollars

B. Per capita
B. Par habitant

Country	1970	1971	1972	1973	1974	1975	1976	1977	1978	1979	1980	1981	1982	1983	Pays
Afghanistan	1.7	1.9	1.9	1.8	1.6	1.8	1.4	1.9	2.1	2.4	1.4	0.9	0.8	0.9	Afghanistan
Bangladesh	..	..	0.1	0.2	0.4	0.7	0.7	0.3	1.2	1.7	1.8	1.6	1.4	1.9	Bangladesh
Benin	2.3	3.6	3.0	3.6	4.2	6.5	5.1	4.3	5.2	6.1	7.5	7.0	7.6	6.8	Bénin
Bhutan	-	-	-	0.2	0.4	1.6	2.3	1.7	1.8	3.8	4.7	5.7	4.7	5.3	Bhoutan
Botswana	4.3	7.6	6.7	11.3	12.9	18.2	19.6	22.1	27.3	41.4	52.3	51.1	44.0	40.2	Botswana
Burkina Faso	1.6	1.9	2.4	2.9	3.6	5.9	6.6	6.5	8.3	10.0	11.8	11.4	11.4	9.9	Burkina Faso
Burundi	3.1	3.4	4.0	4.4	4.7	6.2	6.1	6.6	7.7	8.9	10.9	10.5	10.8	10.2	Burundi
Cape Verde	-	-	-	-	-	3.6	7.7	9.7	19.2	20.9	39.7	37.5	66.7	56.9	Cap-Vert
Central African Republic	4.3	4.4	6.4	6.1	6.4	9.5	9.2	9.7	11.8	14.9	14.9	14.4	13.0	12.0	République centrafricaine
Chad	2.7	3.3	3.9	5.2	5.0	6.3	5.3	5.9	6.2	4.9	2.7	3.7	4.1	4.5	Tchad
Comoros	17.7	23.2	10.3	28.7	43.1	21.7	6.6	6.6	3.6	7.7	17.9	24.9	23.0	23.4	Comores
Democratic Yemen	1.6	2.4	3.2	3.1	4.3	5.4	6.5	6.9	5.8	4.1	5.9	6.2	7.1	6.4	Yémen démocratique
Djibouti	38.8	47.6	28.3	50.1	67.8	51.9	60.3	60.3	52.4	64.8	89.7	92.0	91.9	84.0	Djibouti
Equatorial Guinea	-	-	-	3.2	1.9	2.2	1.2	1.2	1.8	6.4	5.7	12.5	11.2	10.4	Guinée équatoriale
Ethiopia	0.8	1.1	1.0	1.2	1.4	1.3	1.1	1.0	0.9	1.0	1.4	2.0	1.6	1.8	Ethiopie
Gambia	1.5	2.1	3.3	4.0	4.1	5.0	7.7	5.7	11.3	15.3	19.5	20.7	25.5	22.7	Gambie
Guinea	1.0	1.1	0.3	0.3	0.3	0.8	1.2	1.3	2.2	2.3	3.9	4.3	4.1	2.8	Guinée
Guinea-Bissau	0.2	0.2	-	0.0	0.5	4.0	10.6	6.6	9.0	11.6	15.0	15.3	17.9	18.8	Guinée-Bissau
Haiti	0.9	0.8	1.1	1.6	1.4	2.6	1.3	2.9	4.2	4.9	6.4	6.4	6.6	6.1	Haïti
Lao People's Dem. Republic	13.1	13.5	11.3	13.0	8.9	4.4	1.9	1.4	3.2	3.2	3.6	3.3	2.8	2.5	République dém. populaire lao
Lesotho	2.4	2.6	3.0	4.4	5.7	7.3	9.9	10.2	12.8	15.2	21.7	22.7	22.8	22.2	Lesotho
Malawi	2.0	2.1	2.3	2.3	2.9	3.1	3.2	3.2	4.2	5.2	6.1	6.2	5.9	5.4	Malawi
Maldives	1.8	1.6	2.0	2.4	4.7	3.9	3.7	7.1	10.3	14.7	18.2	15.7	22.1	22.6	Maldives
Mali	1.4	1.6	2.0	2.2	1.9	1.9	1.5	4.0	5.3	7.3	11.0	8.8	7.5	7.1	Mali
Nepal	0.7	0.9	0.8	1.0	1.1	1.9	1.5	1.9	2.2	2.7	3.4	3.5	4.1	4.3	Népal
Niger	2.7	2.8	3.4	3.1	5.4	6.3	5.8	6.2	7.6	9.1	11.7	10.8	12.2	10.6	Niger
Rwanda	3.1	3.6	4.2	4.7	5.5	6.3	7.2	8.0	8.9	10.2	10.6	10.0	9.0	9.4	Rwanda
Samoa	6.3	6.3	4.0	12.2	25.0	31.3	31.8	37.9	44.2	38.5	62.4	68.4	47.5	46.0	Samoa
Sao Tome and Principe	-	-	-	-	1.5	3.8	6.2	11.0	18.1	15.5	15.3	16.1	31.5	18.5	Sao Tomé-et-Principe
Sierra Leone	1.9	1.7	1.5	1.9	1.5	2.6	3.4	3.3	4.1	4.6	6.5	6.5	6.2	5.6	Sierra Leone
Somalia	3.8	3.6	3.4	4.1	4.3	6.3	4.8	5.3	5.4	7.4	20.1	21.2	18.1	22.8	Somalie
Sudan	0.5	0.4	1.5	1.3	1.3	1.8	1.9	2.2	3.4	3.8	5.5	6.8	6.0	6.3	Soudan
Togo	3.8	4.4	5.3	6.1	6.7	7.4	7.3	7.9	8.9	10.0	11.2	11.4	11.0	9.8	Togo
Uganda	1.5	1.8	1.6	2.1	0.7	0.8	0.7	0.6	1.0	1.3	1.6	2.5	2.1	2.3	Ouganda
United Republic of Tanzania	1.6	1.7	2.4	2.8	3.2	3.8	4.7	4.7	6.0	7.6	9.1	9.0	8.9	8.2	République-Unie de Tanzanie
Yemen	0.5	0.6	0.9	1.1	1.7	2.8	2.5	3.9	4.9	5.8	7.1	8.4	8.7	7.8	Yémen
All LDCs	(1.3)	(1.4)	1.5	1.7	2.0	2.5	2.4	2.5	3.3	4.0	5.0	5.1	4.9	5.0	Ensemble des PMA
All developing countries	1.1	1.2	1.3	1.5	1.7	2.0	1.9	2.0	2.4	2.9	3.3	3.2	3.1	3.2	Ensemble des pays en développement

For source and note, see table 34 p. 48.

Pour la source et la note, se rapporter au tableau 34 p. 48.

Table 35

Net ODA as per cent of donor's GNP, from individual DAC member countries to LDCs as a group, 1975-1983

Tableau 35

Apports nets de l'APD accordée par chaque pays membre du CAD à l'ensemble des PMA, en pourcentage du PNB du pays donneur, 1975-1983

Percentages   En pourcentage

COUNTRY	1975	1976	1977	1978	1979	1980	1981	1982	1983	PAYS
	Bilateral ODA				APD bilatérale					
Australia	0.04	0.02	0.02	0.03	0.04	0.02	0.04	0.05	0.03	Australie
Austria	0.00	0.00	0.01	0.01	0.00	0.01	0.01	0.01	0.01	Autriche
Belgium	0.08	0.08	0.07	0.08	0.09	0.08	0.09	0.08	0.08	Belgique
Canada	0.10	0.06	0.06	0.08	0.08	0.07	0.06	0.08	0.07	Canada
Denmark	0.14	0.12	0.14	0.15	0.16	0.18	0.14	0.16	0.18	Danemark
Finland	0.05	0.05	0.04	0.03	0.04	0.05	0.05	0.05	0.07	Finlande
France	0.07	0.07	0.06	0.05	0.06	0.06	0.08	0.08	0.07	France
Germany,Fed.Rep.of	0.06	0.05	0.05	0.06	0.07	0.07	0.08	0.08	0.07	Allemagne,Rép.féd.d'
Italy	0.01	0.01	0.01	0.01	0.01	0.01	0.02	0.03	0.04	Italie
Japan	0.01	0.01	0.02	0.02	0.03	0.04	0.03	0.04	0.02	Japon
Netherlands	0.08	0.09	0.15	0.17	0.17	0.19	0.21	0.19	0.16	Pays-Bas
New Zealand	0.08	0.03	0.04	0.03	0.03	0.03	0.02	0.02	0.02	Nouvelle-Zélande
Norway	0.14	0.13	0.17	0.20	0.20	0.17	0.16	0.22	0.22	Norvège
Sweden	0.18	0.16	0.18	0.17	0.21	0.16	0.16	0.17	0.17	Suède
Switzerland	0.02	0.02	0.03	0.05	0.03	0.05	0.06	0.06	0.06	Suisse
United Kingdom	0.05	0.04	0.05	0.06	0.07	0.06	0.06	0.05	0.04	Royaume-Uni
United States	0.04	0.02	0.01	0.02	0.02	0.02	0.02	0.02	0.02	Etats-Unis
Total DAC countries	0.05	0.03	0.03	0.04	0.05	0.05	0.04	0.05	0.04	Total pays du CAD
	Total ODA (method A)[a]				APD totale (méthode A)[a]					
Australia	0.05	0.03	0.02	0.05	0.06	0.04	0.05	0.09	0.06	Australie
Austria	0.01	0.01	0.01	0.01	0.02	0.01	0.04	0.03	0.02	Autriche
Belgium	0.14	0.12	0.10	0.12	0.13	0.11	0.15	0.13	0.13	Belgique
Canada	0.14	0.09	0.09	0.11	0.12	0.10	0.10	0.11	0.11	Canada
Denmark	0.21	0.18	0.20	0.22	0.24	0.26	0.23	0.25	0.26	Danemark
Finland	0.07	0.07	0.05	0.05	0.06	0.06	0.08	0.07	0.10	Finlande
France	0.11	0.09	0.08	0.07	0.09	0.09	0.11	0.11	0.10	France
Germany,Fed.Rep.of	0.10	0.08	0.08	0.09	0.10	0.10	0.11	0.11	0.11	Allemagne,Rép.féd.d'
Italy	0.03	0.02	0.02	0.03	0.02	0.04	0.05	0.06	0.07	Italie
Japan	0.03	0.02	0.03	0.03	0.05	0.06	0.04	0.05	0.05	Japon
Netherlands	0.16	0.16	0.20	0.22	0.24	0.25	0.28	0.26	0.22	Pays-Bas
New Zealand	0.10	0.05	0.05	0.04	0.04	0.04	0.03	0.03	0.03	Nouvelle-Zélande
Norway	0.20	0.20	0.24	0.27	0.29	0.24	0.26	0.31	0.33	Norvège
Sweden	0.24	0.22	0.24	0.23	0.28	0.21	0.24	0.27	0.23	Suède
Switzerland	0.04	0.03	0.04	0.06	0.05	0.07	0.07	0.07	0.09	Suisse
United Kingdom	0.08	0.07	0.09	0.10	0.12	0.19	0.10	0.09	0.08	Royaume-Uni
United States	0.05	0.03	0.03	0.03	0.02	0.04	0.03	0.04	0.04	Etats-Unis
Total DAC countries	0.07	0.05	0.05	0.06	0.07	0.07	0.07	0.07	0.07	Total Pays du CAD
	Total ODA (method B)[a]				APD totale (méthode A)[a]					
Australia	0.06	0.03	0.03	0.08	0.09	0.06	0.05	0.10	0.07	Australie
Austria	0.01	0.01	0.01	0.03	0.04	0.01	0.04	0.04	0.03	Autriche
Belgium	0.15	0.13	0.12	0.15	0.14	0.13	0.16	0.15	0.14	Belgique
Canada	0.15	0.11	0.12	0.14	0.15	0.12	0.11	0.12	0.14	Canada
Denmark	0.21	0.19	0.21	0.25	0.26	0.28	0.25	0.29	0.28	Danemark
Finland	0.07	0.08	0.06	0.06	0.07	0.07	0.09	0.08	0.11	Finlande
France	0.11	0.09	0.09	0.08	0.09	0.10	0.12	0.12	0.11	France
Germany,Fed.Rep.of	0.10	0.09	0.09	0.10	0.12	0.12	0.12	0.12	0.12	Allemagne,Rép.féd.d'
Italy	0.04	0.03	0.03	0.05	0.03	0.06	0.06	0.07	0.07	Italie
Japan	0.03	0.03	0.04	0.05	0.06	0.08	0.05	0.05	0.06	Japon
Netherlands	0.16	0.16	0.21	0.22	0.26	0.27	0.29	0.29	0.24	Pays-Bas
New Zealand	0.10	0.05	0.05	0.04	0.05	0.04	0.03	0.03	0.02	Nouvelle-Zélande
Norway	0.21	0.22	0.26	0.31	0.30	0.27	0.28	0.35	0.35	Norvège
Sweden	0.25	0.23	0.27	0.27	0.31	0.22	0.26	0.31	0.23	Suède
Switzerland	0.04	0.04	0.06	0.07	0.06	0.08	0.08	0.08	0.10	Suisse
United Kingdom	0.08	0.08	0.11	0.13	0.14	0.10	0.12	0.11	0.09	Royaume-Uni
United States	0.05	0.03	0.04	0.05	0.02	0.05	0.03	0.05	0.04	Etats-Unis
Total DAC countries	0.07	0.06	0.07	0.08	0.08	0.09	0.08	0.08	0.07	Total Pays du CAD

Source: UNCTAD secretariat, based on information from the OECD/DAC secretariat.

a/ For the description of the two different methods used to calculate the amount of ODA provided through multilateral channels, see "Explanatory Notes".

Source: Secrétariat de la CNUCED, d'après des renseignements du secrétariat de l'OCDE/CAD.

a/ La description des deux méthodes différentes utilisées pour calculer le montant de l'APD fournie à travers les voies multilatérales figure dans les "Notes explicatives".

Table 36 — Tableau 36

ODA commitments from individual DAC member countries and individual multilateral agencies a/ to all LDCs, 1973-1983

Engagements de l'APD de chaque pays membre du CAD et de chaque institution multilatérale a/ essentiellement financée par ceux-ci en faveur de l'ensemble des PMA, 1973-1983

$ million — Millions de dollars

		1973	1974	1975	1976	1977	1978	1979	1980	1981	1982	1983
Bilateral donors	**Donneurs bilatéraux**											
Australia	Australie	19.2	33.6	28.2	10.2	43.9	42.3	32.5	48.9	66.9	54.7	48.7
Austria	Autriche	1.5	0.8	0.5	0.8	0.3	2.4	0.3	0.9	1.0	6.2	5.6
Belgium	Belgique	-	41.0	62.9	68.4	76.1	101.0	104.8	112.9	89.8	72.1	65.3
Canada	Canada	109.3	121.0	185.5	138.8	349.1	509.2	197.4	121.3	203.5	236.7	304.6
Denmark	Danemark	24.3	59.8	34.4	46.2	49.7	217.9	117.5	108.5	58.1	113.1	88.1
Finland	Finlande	7.1	5.3	20.7	10.6	9.7	8.2	41.4	38.7	38.4	34.9	21.1
France	France	168.0	242.2	288.6	272.2	221.3	216.2	325.0	558.0	569.8	500.6	543.0
Germany, Fed.Rep. of	Allemagne, Rép.féd. d'	166.1	307.8	308.0	362.3	343.9	506.8	1000.2	1835.3	711.0	477.2	488.7
Italy	Italie	18.7	10.0	14.7	11.9	16.5	15.7	19.4	43.9	225.5	207.4	167.9
Japan	Japon	48.2	69.9	154.9	108.5	162.6	348.2	329.2	386.6	365.0	450.4	319.9
Netherlands	Pays-Bas	22.3	58.4	107.9	146.2	256.5	417.8	319.9	358.5	316.4	204.6	251.8
New Zealand	Nouvelle-Zélande	3.4	7.3	6.1	1.8	3.5	7.6	4.6	9.0	7.8	2.4	2.3
Norway	Norvège	26.7	48.4	47.6	34.9	57.0	71.5	67.8	67.9	121.0	101.8	85.3
Sweden	Suède	60.8	103.8	151.1	130.0	265.3	224.8	285.7	164.3	192.5	167.6	145.2
Switzerland	Suisse	5.5	7.1	14.4	7.7	34.6	41.5	24.0	56.3	101.4	35.7	80.1
United Kingdom	Royaume-Uni	149.3	96.4	207.2	231.0	110.2	410.1	429.8	380.4	220.4	140.0	176.2
United States	Etats-Unis	373.7	352.2	524.1	384.5	383.8	439.8	511.6	630.9	632.1	705.3	775.5
Total	**Total**	1024.0	1564.9	2156.9	1965.9	2383.9	3580.9	3810.9	4922.3	3920.6	3510.7	3569.3
Multilateral donors	**Donneurs multilatéraux**											
AfDB/AfDF	BAfD/FAFD	-	25.1	95.2	77.5	121.9	132.2	159.2	190.3	217.9	207.3	243.6
AsDB	BAsD	40.2	75.7	70.9	125.6	128.2	130.9	178.5	204.3	241.2	255.7	377.1
EEC/EDF	CEE/FED	194.5	227.5	172.9	375.1	462.8	360.8	421.9	473.1	574.9	570.6	461.6
IBRD	BIRD	-	-	-	62.7	31.5	-	-	-	-	-	-
IDA	AID	398.5	395.9	599.3	536.1	607.2	769.8	678.3	1222.8	1001.8	1180.2	1285.4
IDB	BID	22.2	-	41.1	5.0	15.7	43.5	4.1	9.1	32.6	32.6	17.4
IFAD	FIDA	-	-	-	-	-	62.3	120.1	134.9	154.8	58.3	82.8
UN	ONU	132.9	168.3	323.1	305.1	289.8	403.9	481.2	600.5	737.0	692.6	728.3
Total	**Total**	788.4	892.5	1302.5	1487.1	1657.1	1903.3	2043.2	2835.1	2927.7	2997.2	3196.2
GRAND TOTAL	**TOTAL GENERAL**	1992.4	2457.4	3459.4	3453.1	4041.0	5484.2	5854.2	7757.4	6848.3	6507.9	6765.5

Source: UNCTAD secretariat based on information from the OECD/DAC secretariat.

Source: Secrétariat de la CNUCED, d'après des renseignements du secrétariat de l'OCDE.

a/ Multilateral agencies mainly financed by DAC member countries.

a/ Institutions multilatérales essentiellement financées par les pays membres du CAD.

Table 37

ODA commitments from DAC member countries and multilateral agencies mainly financed by them to individual LDCs, 1970-1983

$ million

Tableau 37

Engagements de l'APD à chacun des PMA, en provenance des pays membres du CAD et des institutions multilatérales essentiellement financés par ceux-ci, 1970-1983

millions de dollars

Country	1970	1971	1972	1973	1974	1975	1976	1977	1978	1979	1980	1981	1982	1983	Pays
Afghanistan	34.7	67.1	70.4	84.7	61.7	71.8	117.3	112.1	134.8	148.0	17.3	13.9	14.5	16.9	Afghanistan
Bangladesh	-	33.4	579.0	518.7	691.6	1215.5	877.6	892.4	1411.3	1216.1	2007.0	1455.1	1511.5	1354.5	Bangladesh
Benin	20.1	18.8	63.5	33.7	43.6	47.3	57.7	73.7	120.7	78.8	99.0	125.6	154.5	61.7	Bénin
Bhutan	0.1	0.4	0.1	0.6	0.6	1.8	3.6	3.0	3.1	5.3	15.4	11.8	12.4	24.8	Bhoutan
Botswana	40.7	13.7	46.8	39.6	48.1	54.0	52.7	58.1	153.8	123.5	126.5	113.1	101.0	101.7	Botswana
Burkina Faso	27.9	35.8	67.2	64.1	101.6	111.6	134.2	139.7	202.0	255.5	244.8	321.9	268.6	195.8	Burkina Faso
Burundi	17.0	32.1	12.8	22.4	35.1	61.2	68.4	75.9	78.4	127.5	170.9	222.0	97.7	168.7	Burundi
Cape Verde	-	-	-	-	-	16.7	20.1	36.9	47.6	59.3	56.5	71.2	59.5	71.3	Cap-Vert
Central African Republic	14.6	15.5	42.9	38.6	31.3	57.2	32.4	61.6	62.4	85.3	129.9	85.4	145.8	142.0	République centrafricaine
Chad	22.4	27.6	59.2	45.4	67.2	73.6	113.5	66.4	134.5	50.6	35.2	96.1	67.9	90.2	Tchad
Comoros	7.0	9.7	11.9	20.0	28.6	20.9	11.6	15.8	15.7	22.0	35.4	56.2	43.8	33.3	Comores
Democratic Yemen	4.4	5.1	5.8	15.5	17.2	37.2	17.4	25.4	45.3	31.4	56.4	56.5	114.0	61.5	Yémen démocratique
Djibouti	10.5	11.7	18.2	3.0	34.6	34.8	20.4	32.7	23.6	31.5	46.2	58.0	71.7	74.5	Djibouti
Equatorial Guinea	-	-	-	-	0.6	0.7	-1.6	0.4	0.6	19.7	19.2	18.5	13.6	18.1	Guinée équatoriale
Ethiopia	47.0	103.2	90.1	132.9	159.6	195.2	132.1	177.5	117.9	145.3	227.2	295.9	295.7	420.6	Ethiopie
Gambia	3.9	5.3	5.4	7.6	14.6	9.2	29.3	13.6	35.2	66.8	72.7	64.6	48.3	59.8	Gambie
Guinea	18.2	11.5	9.8	7.8	10.2	36.4	17.4	45.8	95.9	90.1	148.5	69.7	106.4	121.5	Guinée
Guinea-Bissau	0.4	0.1	-	0.0	1.1	23.8	41.8	47.2	65.6	64.3	63.5	59.8	57.8	83.7	Guinée-Bissau
Haiti	11.3	7.6	16.7	34.1	35.1	95.8	102.1	104.7	130.3	86.6	76.5	136.8	195.9	153.9	Haïti
Lao People's Dem. Republic	74.0	77.0	66.2	63.9	81.4	37.3	30.6	36.1	68.7	65.5	81.0	46.6	19.4	53.9	République dém. pop. lao
Lesotho	12.5	17.0	9.3	34.8	23.1	38.7	53.1	81.0	58.9	125.0	119.4	108.5	67.8	94.2	Lesotho
Malawi	15.2	46.5	52.9	55.3	73.1	85.4	69.5	145.8	266.7	185.2	143.4	210.8	84.1	270.3	Malawi
Maldives	0.1	6.4	1.0	0.3	0.5	2.4	1.8	8.3	2.9	6.5	5.9	4.8	7.2	15.6	Maldives
Mali	28.1	33.6	69.6	103.7	110.5	146.7	163.1	154.1	165.6	249.2	158.8	265.0	210.2	257.6	Mali
Nepal	25.7	17.5	40.3	59.6	45.4	53.7	161.9	128.7	184.5	207.0	270.1	249.6	210.0	276.8	Népal
Niger	37.5	61.3	42.7	76.2	131.8	109.6	180.4	117.4	171.0	250.0	184.7	239.4	209.2	206.1	Niger
Rwanda	29.5	27.1	33.2	27.1	51.3	97.9	116.2	147.1	141.1	161.4	207.1	207.5	196.7	188.3	Rwanda
Samoa	1.1	1.6	5.9	6.1	6.5	17.8	8.0	21.9	32.0	29.1	24.9	45.7	14.1	17.7	Samoa
Sao Tome and Principe	-	-	0.0	-	-	0.3	1.6	3.8	14.1	3.6	4.4	7.9	7.4	9.6	Sao Tomé-et-Principe
Sierra Leone	20.1	7.6	15.1	9.3	11.3	33.6	17.2	51.6	42.7	108.1	67.3	114.8	74.0	58.4	Sierra Leone
Somalia	15.1	27.3	32.8	40.9	60.0	78.5	100.4	79.9	109.1	184.0	366.5	457.7	307.4	289.2	Somalie
Sudan	12.5	16.0	72.3	144.3	99.9	167.0	129.3	155.7	413.5	428.3	967.3	534.2	514.6	664.9	Soudan
Togo	14.0	28.1	23.5	51.8	35.4	43.1	66.8	150.9	61.7	77.9	137.2	80.4	111.7	147.8	Togo
Uganda	23.3	31.1	42.5	11.0	14.1	9.1	17.8	17.1	17.2	75.5	209.9	195.5	199.4	290.4	Ouganda
United Republic of Tanzania	58.5	70.8	75.6	182.8	291.2	307.7	404.1	626.2	757.0	847.2	890.5	637.6	706.3	519.2	République-Unie de Tanzanie
Yemen	12.1	27.1	17.3	33.1	39.6	65.8	77.2	112.7	98.8	159.7	270.4	110.4	187.9	151.0	Yémen
All LDCs	659.5	894.2	1700.0	1992.4	2457.4	3459.4	3453.1	4041.0	5484.2	5854.2	7757.4	6848.3	6507.9	6765.3	Ensemble des PMA

Source : UNCTAD secretariat based on information from the OECD/DAC secretariat.

Source : Secrétariat de la CNUCED d'après des renseignements du secrétariat de l'OCDE/CAD.

Table 38

Grant element of ODA commitments from individual DAC member
countries to LDCs and to all developing countries, 1973-1983[a]/

Tableau 38

Elément de libéralité des engagements de l'APD
de chaque pays membre du CAD aux PMA et à
l'ensemble des pays en développement, 1973-1983[a]/

Country		1973	1974	1975	1976	1977	1978	1979	1980	1981	1982	1983		Pays
Australia	A	100.0	100.0	100.0	100.0	100.0	100.0	100.0	100.0	100.0	100.0	100.0	A	Australie
	B	99.4	99.4	100.0	100.0	100.0	100.0	100.0	100.0	100.0	100.0	100.0	B	
Austria	A	39.5	0.0	100.0	100.0	35.5	99.0	95.9	93.2	93.9	94.9	99.4	A	Autriche
	B	57.4	48.6	94.8	97.3	67.5	65.8	86.1	70.3	55.1	58.8	61.1	B	
Belgium	A	100.0	100.0	100.0	99.0	98.7	98.9	98.4	98.1	98.5	98.3	98.2	A	Belgique
	B	95.6	97.4	98.1	98.2	98.3	98.6	98.0	97.9	97.6	98.6	97.7	B	
Canada	A	92.2	93.5	94.7	98.3	100.0	100.0	100.0	100.0	100.0	100.0	100.0	A	Canada
	B	94.1	97.2	(96.4)	97.3	97.5	96.6	97.2	98.0	97.2	98.8	99.3	B	
Denmark	A	90.3	91.4	88.6	91.5	94.9	96.4	96.8	93.5	95.2	96.9	99.1	A	Danemark
	B	96.1	94.6	96.0	96.6	97.3	95.3	96.7	97.3	95.4	95.7	96.4	B	
Finland	A	100.0	84.6	87.8	84.8	100.0	100.0	100.0	100.0	95.0	99.0	100.0	A	Finlande
	B	85.6	89.4	91.5	90.8	97.5	99.0	97.7	97.5	95.6	95.9	99.7	B	
France	A	95.4	97.4	97.0	87.9	94.6	(95.0)	(95.0)	79.2	88.7	81.5	79.5	A	France
	B	91.2	89.2	(90.9)	90.9	93.4	92.3	(93.5)	90.0	89.5	90.0	89.3	B	
Germany, Fed.Rep.of	A	93.5	92.2	93.0	91.1	93.8	92.7	97.8	98.8	99.3	99.4	96.2	A	Allemagne, Rép.féd.
	B	83.1	84.2	88.3	(86.8)	86.0	86.6	85.1	89.3	84.9	88.9	88.8	B	
Italy [b]/	A	81.4	100.0	100.0	100.0	100.0	100.0	100.0	90.0	54.7	71.0	80.6	A	Italie [b]/
	B	69.3	97.8	98.4	(97.3)	99.2	98.7	99.6	98.8	91.4	91.4	(89.5)	B	
Japan	A	69.3	77.8	86.0	72.7	72.5	76.2	75.4	80.2	85.4	82.1	87.9	A	Japon
	B	68.6	61.8	(69.5)	75.8	70.2	75.0	77.7	74.3	75.3	74.2	79.5	B	
Netherlands	A	95.3	93.5	95.0	93.1	97.2	99.3	98.5	99.8	98.2	99.5	99.1	A	Pays-Bas
	B	88.4	87.4	93.8	86.5	90.8	93.3	92.5	91.6	95.1	93.9	95.1	B	
New Zealand	A	100.0	100.0	100.0	100.0	100.0	100.0	100.0	100.0	100.0	100.0	100.0	A	Nouvelle-Zélande
	B	98.5	98.2	99.1	97.4	99.8	100.0	100.0	100.0	100.0	100.0	100.0	B	
Norway	A	100.0	100.0	100.0	100.0	100.0	100.0	100.0	100.0	100.0	100.0	99.9	A	Norvège
	B	99.8	100.0	100.0	100.0	100.0	100.0	100.0	100.0	99.7	99.2	98.6	B	
Sweden	A	100.0	100.0	100.0	100.0	100.0	100.0	100.0	100.0	100.0	100.0	100.0	A	Suède
	B	98.6	99.3	99.2	99.9	99.8	99.9	100.0	99.0	99.7	99.8	99.8	B	
Switzerland	A	100.0	100.0	90.0	98.2	100.0	100.0	100.0	100.0	100.0	100.0	100.0	A	Suisse
	B	93.0	96.9	93.0	92.1	96.9	95.1	95.8	96.9	97.0	96.6	98.5	B	
United Kingdom	A	87.7	86.3	99.0	99.7	93.6	(99.2)	99.0	99.7	100.0	100.0	100.0	A	Royaume-Uni
	B	87.1	(86.0)	(96.9)	97.5	96.7	93.9	96.1	96.4	96.9	98.5	98.3	B	
United States	A	88.1	89.7	92.0	82.7	90.0	92.1	96.5	95.0	96.3	97.6	95.7	A	Etats-Unis
	B	89.9	90.5	85.7	86.4	89.9	89.4	91.5	90.5	93.4	93.8	94.6	B	
Total DAC countries	A	91.2	93.1	95.4	92.1	94.2	93.9	95.7	94.7	93.4	92.8	93.6	A	Total des pays du CAD
	B	87.5	86.6	89.4	89.3	89.4	89.9	90.8	89.9	89.6	90.5	91.3	B	

Source : OECD, Development Co-operation (various issues).

A = Commitments to LDCs excluding Djibouti, Equatorial Guinea,
Sao Tome & Principe, Sierra Leone and Togo (1972-1980);
Guinea-Bissau (1972-1978); Bangladesh, Central African
Republic, Gambia and Democratic Yemen (1972-1976); and
Cape Verde and Comoros (1972-1975). The DAC target norm
for LDCs is 90 per cent. The SNPA, para. 70(a), calls
upon donor countries and institutions to provide as a
general rule assistance to LDCs as grants.

B = Commitments to all developing countries and territories,
as well as to Gibraltar, Greece, Israel, Portugal,
Yugoslavia and Viet Nam. The DAC target norm for all
developing countries is 84 per cent.

a/ ODA commitments include debt reorganisation in
1972 and 1973 and exclude it in other years.

b/ Italy has not subscribed to the 1972 DAC Terms
Recommendations.

Source : OCDE, Coopération pour le développement (divers numéros)

A = Engagements aux PMA, non compris Djibouti, la Guinée
équatoriale, Sao Tomé-et-Principe, Sierra Leone et le
Togo (1972 à 1980); la Guinée-Bissau (1972 à 1978); le
Bangladesh, la République centrafricaine, la Gambie et le
Yémen démocratique (1972 à 1976); et le Cap-Vert et les
Comores (1972 à 1975). L'objectif du CAD pour les PMA a
pour norme 90 pour cent. Le NPSA, au paragraphe 70(a),
demande aux pays et aux institutions donateurs de fournir
en règle générale, sous forme de dons, l'aide aux PMA.

B = Engagements à l'ensemble des pays en développement, ainsi
qu'à Gibraltar, la Grèce, Israël, le Portugal, la
Yougoslavie et le Viet-Nam. L'objectif du CAD pour
l'ensemble des pays en développement a pour norme 84 pour
cent.

a/ Les engagements de l'APD comprennent en 1972 et en
1973 la réorganisation de la dette et l'excluent pour
les autres années.

b/ L'Italie n'a pas souscrit aux Recommandations des
Conditions de l'Aide du CAD de 1972.

Table 39A

ODA commitments from DAC member countries and multilateral agencies a/ to LDCs as a group, by purpose, average 1981-1983

Tableau 39A

Engagements de l'APD de chaque pays membre du CAD et de chaque institution multilatérale, a/ en faveur de l'ensemble des PMA, par objet, moyenne 1981-1983

Per cent of total / En pourcentage du total (except Total column, in $ m. / en m.$)

Donors / Donneurs	Agriculture	Industry, mining, construction / Industries manufacturières, extraction, construction	Energy / Energie	Transport and communication / Transports et communications	Health / Santé	Education / Enseignement	Social infrastructure / Infrastructure sociale	Trade, banking, tourism and other services / Commerce, banques, tourisme et autres services	General economic support b/ / Soutien économique général b/	Technical cooperation / Coopération technique	Total c/ in $ m. / en m.$
A. Bilateral donors / A. Donneurs bilatéraux											
Australia / Australie	7.0	-	0.0	8.3	0.6	0.0	-	0.0	72.6	10.8	170
Austria / Autriche	-	0.0	-	-	-	-	-	0.0	100.0	75.0	13
Belgium / Belgique	36.2	18.9	8.4	-	-	6.1	0.2	0.8	2.7	-	227
Canada / Canada	31.9	0.7	2.1	10.7	4.2	1.4	-	0.0	5.4	6.1	745
Denmark / Danemark	15.6	7.8	1.3	9.0	25.1	-	-	-	15.6	15.8	259
Finland / Finlande	16.6	4.8	9.1	..	1.3	0.8	1.9	1.5	10.3	58.4	94
France / France	5.5	0.8	8.8	15.6	3.5	-	0.2	0.3	16.5	35.3	1613
Germany, Fed.Rep.of / Allemagne, Rép.féd.d'	11.7	1.9	23.1	16.4	3.6	0.2	0.5	-	23.7	46.8	1677
Italy / Italie	17.0	0.2	3.3	9.2	4.5	-	1.8	0.4	41.1	25.9	601
Japan / Japon	18.5	1.4	0.0	11.4	10.5	0.6	0.5	-	26.7	8.8	1135
Netherlands / Pays-Bas	35.7	-	-	7.3	7.3	1.2	1.8	0.4	0.0	28.1	773
New Zealand / Nouvelle-Zélande	-	7.9	-	0.0	0.0	0.0	0.0	0.0	12.6	35.7	12
Norway / Norvège	13.5	8.2	1.9	11.2	13.5	4.6	10.7	0.5	25.1	23.2	308
Sweden / Suède	19.6	1.2	1.2	2.3	7.6	11.2	1.4	0.3	0.4	18.6	505
Switzerland / Suisse	33.5	0.0	8.0	12.4	11.6	10.7	2.1	2.5	35.1	21.9	217
United Kingdom / Royaume-Uni	0.5	0.0	-	9.6	-	1.3	-	-	-	43.1	537
United States / Etats-Unis	16.7	0.1	2.2	1.6	6.8	2.6	0.4	0.3	37.7	31.4	2113
Total bilateral / Total bilatéral	15.7	2.6	6.3	8.9	6.4	2.3	0.9	0.4	25.7	29.2	11001
B. Multilateral donors / B. Donneurs multilatéraux											
AfDF / FAFD	30.0	2.5	3.2	24.7	29.7	7.3	2.5	-	-	-	669
AsDB / BAsD	46.5	2.1	30.5	4.0	6.2	3.2	-	0.6	5.9	-	874
EEC / CEE	40.0	3.3	4.2	13.8	11.3	2.9	0.6	0.3	22.1	-	1607
IDA / AID	39.5	5.3	14.8	18.3	3.5	9.9	2.0	1.1	4.7	-	3467
IDB / BID	67.4	18.6	..	..	..	-	..	..	14.0	-	50
UN / ONU	..	..	..	..	..	..	..	..	..	..	296 d/
IFAD / FIDA	100.0	-	-	-	-	-	-	-	-	-	2158
Total multilateral / Total multilatéral	42.2	4.1	12.2	15.5	7.8	6.8	1.4	0.7	8.3	-	9121
GRAND TOTAL (A+B) / TOTAL GENERAL (A+B)	25.7	3.2	8.5	11.4	6.9	4.0	1.1	0.5	19.2	18.2	20122

Source : OECD "Creditor Reporting System". — Source : "Système de notification des pays créanciers" de l'OCDE.

Note : For technical reasons the amounts to sectors may be understated. — Note : Pour des raisons techniques les données pour les secteurs peuvent être sous-estimées.

a/ Multilateral agencies mainly financed by DAC member countries. / Institutions multilatérales essentiellement financées par les pays membres du CAD.

b/ Including current imports financing, emergency and disaster relief, budget support, balance of payments support and debt re-organisation. / Comprend les contributions destinées à financer des importations courantes, le secours d'urgence, le soutien budgétaire, le soutien à la balance des paiements et le réaménagement de la dette.

c/ Including unallocated and other commitments. / Y compris les engagements non-ventilés et autres.

d/ Mainly technical cooperation. / Principalement coopération technique.

Table 39B

ODA commitments from DAC member countries and multilateral agencies to individual LDCs, by purpose, average 1981-1983

Tableau 39B

Engagements de l'APD à chacun des PMA en provenance des pays membres du CAD et des institutions multilatérales, par objet, moyenne 1981-1983

Recipient country	Agriculture	Industry mining construction	Energy	Transport and communication	Health	Education	Social infrastructure	Trade, banking, tourism and other services	General economic support[b]	Technical cooperation	Total[c] (in $ m.)	Pays bénéficiaire
	Agriculture	Industries manufacturières, extraction, construction	Energie	Transports et communications	Santé	Enseignement	Infrastructure sociale	Commerce, banques, tourisme et autres services	Soutien économique général[b]	Coopération technique	(en m.$)	
	Per cent of total / En pourcentage du total											
Afghanistan	0.0	-	14.1	-	7.1	1.1	-	-	7.1	78.6	45	Afghanistan
Bangladesh	33.7	4.5	6.3	4.3	4.2	9.9	0.4	0.0	28.2	9.0	4321	Bangladesh
Benin	31.3	1.1	-	16.9	7.0	3.9	2.1	0.7	2.5	21.1	342	Bénin
Bhutan	53.9	-	-	0.0	11.5	12.3	-	-	-	11.5	49	Bhoutan
Botswana	15.1	2.8	8.0	11.1	3.1	1.5	0.9	0.9	6.2	37.8	316	Botswana
Burkina Faso	29.3	2.7	1.5	22.0	6.2	6.3	0.6	0.5	7.6	27.2	786	Burkina Faso
Burundi	28.1	4.1	12.0	14.8	5.2	3.8	2.2	1.4	5.2	20.2	488	Burundi
Cape Verde	13.5	0.6	5.8	5.8	12.8	5.3	1.3	0.0	29.5	24.4	202	Cap-Vert
Central African R.	27.3	-	2.8	24.5	4.3	5.3	0.7	1.1	2.5	30.1	373	Rép. centrafricaine
Chad	30.2	-	0.0	9.3	7.0	0.8	16.3	1.6	20.9	11.6	254	Tchad
Comoros	9.5	2.7	4.0	36.5	5.4	3.9	0.0	4.0	6.8	23.0	133	Comores
Democratic Yemen	31.6	0.0	24.3	15.1	7.9	-	-	-	7.2	9.9	232	Yémen démocratique
Djibouti	2.1	-	7.7	12.7	13.4	1.4	0.7	-	5.6	54.2	204	Djibouti
Equatorial Guinea	42.3	0.0	11.5	0.0	0.0	-	3.8	-	3.8	38.5	50	Guinée équatoriale
Ethiopia	20.1	1.3	6.8	14.5	17.1	8.9	2.6	3.9	12.4	11.2	1012	Ethiopie
Gambia	36.8	-	4.2	14.6	7.6	1.4	0.4	0.0	6.9	28.5	173	Gambie
Guinea	5.7	17.0	17.7	23.8	1.8	9.2	1.6	-	11.3	10.3	298	Guinée
Guinea-Bissau	27.0	3.7	10.6	11.1	10.1	2.6	6.7	1.1	16.9	14.3	201	Guinée-Bissau
Haiti	23.1	3.3	10.0	13.6	5.6	4.2	0.0	-	18.9	16.9	486	Haïti
Lao P.D.R.	33.3	4.9	27.2	12.9	7.4	0.0	0.0	1.1	6.2	18.9	120	Rép.dém.pop.Lao
Lesotho	12.9	0.4	0.8	28.5	15.7	9.7	1.2	0.4	10.5	35.1	270	Lesotho
Malawi	16.6	1.8	-	7.7	7.5	20.6	0.2	0.2	2.9	20.6	565	Malawi
Maldives	38.5	0.0	-	-	-	23.1	0.0	-	7.7	23.1	28	Maldives
Mali	29.8	0.5	7.3	16.9	8.8	3.9	0.5	0.3	7.3	24.4	733	Mali
Nepal	31.6	3.3	19.6	7.7	8.0	4.1	0.7	0.3	2.5	18.9	736	Népal
Niger	21.5	4.1	5.4	16.1	11.5	4.9	0.2	0.0	4.7	31.0	655	Niger
Rwanda	31.8	0.2	2.9	19.1	8.7	2.9	1.3	3.6	7.8	19.8	592	Rwanda
Samoa	29.4	-	11.8	10.3	5.9	2.9	0.0	5.9	2.9	27.9	78	Samoa
Sao Tome & Principe	42.8	-	-	9.5	0.4	14.3	-	-	14.3	19.0	25	Sao Tomé-et-Principe
Sierra Leone	42.6	-	2.1	7.6	5.3	11.0	0.0	-	17.3	19.0	247	Sierra Leone
Somalia	12.5	2.5	0.0	11.6	3.2	1.2	0.1	0.5	42.2	23.3	1054	Somalie
Sudan	28.3	0.8	5.2	8.0	10.8	0.4	1.6	0.1	35.8	16.0	1714	Soudan
Togo	22.6	4.7	1.8	15.5	7.4	1.2	0.0	0.0	18.2	23.5	340	Togo
Uganda	27.5	6.0	-	7.2	9.1	6.2	0.0	-	33.4	10.3	685	Ouganda
U.R. of Tanzania	18.1	5.4	9.1	11.6	10.4	2.7	0.4	0.3	19.2	19.8	1863	Rép.-U. de Tanzanie
Yemen	17.8	0.4	6.6	11.7	10.4	9.5	3.3	-	7.0	31.5	449	Yémen
All LDCs	25.8	3.2	8.3	11.4	6.9	4.0	1.1	0.6	19.0	18.3	20122	Ensemble des PMA

Source : OECD "Creditor Reporting System".

Note : For technical reasons the amounts to sectors may be understood.

a/ Multilateral agencies mainly financed by DAC member countries.

b/ Including current imports financing, emergency and disaster relief, budget support, balance of payments support and debt re-organisation.

c/ Including unallocated and other commitments.

Source : "Système de notification des pays créanciers" de l'OCDE.

Note : Pour des raisons techniques les données pour les secteurs peuvent être sous-estimées.

a/ Institutions multilatérales essentiellement financées par les pays membres du CAD.

b/ Comprend les contributions destinées à financer des importations courantes, le secours d'urgence, le soutien budgétaire, le soutien à la balance des paiements et le réaménagement de la dette.

c/ Y compris les engagements non-ventilés et autres.

Table 40

Tying status of bilateral ODA from individual DAC member countries to all LDCs, 1980,a/ 1981 and 1982

Commitments

Tableau 40

Etat de déliement de l'APD bilatérale à l'ensemble des PMA, en provenance de chaque pays membre du CAD, 1980,a/ 1981 et 1982

Engagements

Donor country	Year / Année	Total ($ million) (millions de dollars)	Per cent of total — En pourcentage du total		Tied — Aide liée			Pays donneur
			Untied b/ Aide non-liée b/	Partially tied Aide partiellement liée	Including all technical co-operation — Y compris l'ensemble de la coopération technique	Excluding all technical co-operation — Non compris l'ensemble de la coopération technique	Of which: in kind — Dont: aide en nature	
Australia	1980	51	..	6	94	84	84	
	1981	67	13	–	87	75	54	Australie
	1982	55	2	2	96	87	71	
Austria	1980	1	..	..	..	..	..	
	1981	1	..	..	..	..	..	Autriche
	1982	6	..	..	..	..	..	
Belgium	1980	113	26	–	74	34	–	
	1981	90	41	–	59	9	–	Belgique
	1982	72	40	–	60	10	–	
Canada	1980	121	13	1	86	76		
	1981	204	(13)	–	(87)	(76)	18	Canada
	1982	237	15	–	85	65	15	
Denmark	1980	120	56	–	44	22	7	
	1981	60	(53)	–	47	(35)	23	Danemark
	1982	127	19	–	81	72	44	
Finland	1980	39	41	–	59	–	–	
	1981	38	32	32	36	–	–	Finlande
	1982	35	32	32	36	–	–	
France	1980	484	–	36	64	41	..	
	1981	570	–	31	69	43	6	France
	1982	501	–	37	63	45	7	
Germany, Fed. Rep. of	1980	1754	82	–	18	3	2	Allemagne, Rép. féd. d'
	1981	711	45	–	55	9	4	
	1982	477	42	–	58	10	9	
Italy	1980	44	16	–	84	57	–	
	1981	188	(35)	–	(65)	(45)	12	Italie
	1982	245	25	–	75	45	10	
Japan	1980	375	43	4	53	45	10	
	1981	365	67	13	20	10	5	Japon
	1982	450	48	22	30	22	20	
Netherlands	1980	363	12	59	29	1	–	
	1981	321	12	57	31	3	1	Pays-Bas
	1982	205	15	48	37	1	..	
New Zealand	1980	9	..	56	44	–	–	
	1981	8	25	–	75	38	–	Nouvelle-Zélande
	1982	2	50	–	50	–	–	
Norway	1980	68	59	9	32	13	13	
	1981	121	73	–	27	8	4	Norvège
	1982	102	75	–	25	10	3	
Sweden	1980	186	44	44	12	–	–	
	1981	228	61	23	16	–	–	Suède
	1982	210	55	9	36	16	3	
Switzerland	1980	56	55	24	21	12	12	
	1981	110	62	–	38	18	5	Suisse
	1982	36	65	–	35	20	4	
United Kingdom	1980	382	21	52	27			
	1981	220	17	7	76	35	10	Royaume-Uni
	1982	140	9	1	90	36	4	
United States	1980	614	–	4	96	48	38	
	1981	632	2	–	98	58	43	Etats-Unis
	1982	705	5	–	95	55	48	
Total DAC countries	1980	4780	42	16	42	20	8	
	1981	3934	29	12	59	30	13	Total des pays du CAD
	1982	3605	24	12	64	35	19	

Source : OECD secretariat estimates.

a/ Figures for 1980 do not include commitments to Djibouti, Equatorial Guinea, Sao Tome and Principe, Sierra Leone and Togo.

b/ Excluding technical co-operation.

Source : Estimations du secrétariat de l'OCDE.

a/ Les données pour 1980 ne comprennent pas les engagements à Djibouti, à la Guinée équatoriale, à Sao Tomé-et-Principe, au Sierra Leone et au Togo.

b/ Non compris la coopération technique.

Table 41A

Bilateral ODA from individual OPEC member countries and total financial flows from individual multilateral agencies mainly financed by them, to LDCs as a group, 1970-1983

Tableau 41A

APD bilatérale de chaque pays membre de l'OPEP et apports financiers totaux de chaque institution multilatérale essentiellement financée par ceux-ci, en faveur de l'ensemble des PMA, 1970-1983

	1970	1971	1972	1973	1974	1975	1976	1977	1978	1979	1980	1981	1982	1983
A. Bilateral donors / Donneurs bilatéraux														
Algeria / Algérie	-	-	-	1.0	2.2	2.6	4.9	2.5	0.5	14.4	20.0	9.6	0.2	-
Iran	-	8.0	10.0	-	10.0	3.1	5.7	-	15.0	-	-	-	-	-
Iraq	4.0	-	-	0.5	56.1	32.4	50.2	25.0	42.5	22.5	48.7	-	-	-
Kuwait / Koweit	-	-0.1	2.5	3.3	49.6	47.4	70.1	122.4	110.8	127.6	169.0	167.7	110.6	153.9
Libyan Arab Jamahiriya / Jamahiriya arabe libyenne	1.9	7.0	12.5	6.5	60.8	40.8	12.5	0.8	10.4	0.1	8.1	23.1	-	-
Nigeria / Nigéria	-	-	-	-	5.8	2.2	3.5	1.3	-	3.8	0.1	-	-	-
Qatar	-	-	-	2.2	23.0	32.8	12.9	5.0	8.4	-	38.3	23.2	7.7	7.4
Saudi Arabia / Arabie saoudite	-	-	-	5.7	89.8	271.0	432.8	579.5	305.5	421.9	450.2	382.7	721.0	612.4
United Arab Emirates / Emirats arabes unis	-	-	-	4.1	47.8	143.4	84.8	115.1	153.3	104.7	160.8	59.4	79.5	29.6
Total bilateral concessional / Total des apports bilatéraux concessionnels	5.9	14.9	25.0	23.3	345.1	575.7	677.4	851.6	646.4	695.0	895.2	665.7	919.0	803.3
B. Multilateral donors / Donneurs multilatéraux														
1. Concessional / Apports concessionnels														
BADEA	-	-	-	-	1.2	15.8	18.5	4.5	19.3	15.7	16.9	14.4	14.7	19.3
AFESD / FADES	-	-	-	-	-	-	-	23.2	48.3	34.3	45.6	58.4	38.9	36.8
Islamic Development Bank / Banque islamique de développement	-	-	-	-	-	-	-	-	4.9	11.2	5.2	17.1	7.5	14.1
OPEC Fund / Fonds de l'OPEP	-	-	-	-	-	-	-	79.7	17.2	34.8	64.3	114.2	101.4	71.0
OAPEC Special Account / Compte spécial de l'OPAEP	-	-	-	-	66.3	64.9	33.5	-	-	-	-	-	-	-
SAAFA / FSAAA	-	-	-	-	26.9	-	31.0	-	-	-	-	-	-	-
Total	-	-	-	-	94.4	80.7	83.0	107.4	89.7	96.0	132.0	204.1	162.5	141.2
2. Non-concessional / Apports non concessionnels														
BADEA	-	-	-	-	-	-	-	-	8.1	4.2	8.7	1.2	2.3	-0.3
Islamic Development Bank / Banque islamique de développement	-	-	-	-	-	-	-	4.9	8.7	104.0	95.0	95.3	-55.5	18.6
Total	-	-	-	-	-	-	-	4.9	16.8	108.2	103.7	96.5	-53.2	18.3
Total multilateral (B1+B2) / Total des apports multilatéraux (B1+B2)	-	-	-	-	94.4	80.7	83.0	112.3	106.5	204.2	235.7	300.6	109.3	159.5
Total concessional (A+B1) / Total des apports concessionnels (A+B1)	5.9	14.9	25.0	23.3	439.5	656.4	760.4	959.0	736.1	791.0	1027.2	869.8	1081.5	944.5
GRAND TOTAL (A+B) / TOTAL GENERAL (A+B)	5.9	14.9	25.0	23.3	439.5	656.4	760.4	966.0	752.9	899.2	1130.9	966.3	1038.2	1301.4

Source : UNCTAD secretariat estimates. For 1970-1976 : OECD secretariat estimates.

Note : The figures include only those amounts allocated to a specific recipient country and therefore understate financial flows to the extent that certain donors have recorded disbursements in favour of groups of countries including some LDCs. For abbreviations see pages x and xi.

Source : Estimations du secrétariat de la CNUCED. Pour 1970-1976 : estimations du secrétariat de l'OCDE.

Note : Les données ne comprennent que les montants imputables à un pays bénéficiaire déterminé. Par conséquent, les apports financiers sont sous-estimés dans la mesure où certains donneurs ont alloué des versements à des groupes de pays comprenant des PMA. Se reporter, pour les abréviations aux pages xvii et xviii.

Table 41B

Bilateral ODA from individual OPEC member countries and total financial flows from individual multilateral agencies mainly financed by them, to LDCs as a group, 1970-1983

Tableau 41B

APD bilatérale de chaque pays membre de l'OPEP et apports financiers totaux de chaque institution multilatérale essentiellement financée par ceux-ci, en faveur de l'ensemble des PMA, 1970-1983

	1970	1971	1972	1973	1974	1975	1976	1977	1978	1979	1980	1981	1982	1983
A. Bilateral donors / Donneurs bilatéraux														
Algeria / Algérie	-	-	-	2.6	4.2	4.7	8.7	4.1	0.7	17.5	20.0	9.9	0.2	-
Iran	-	-	-	-	19.3	5.6	10.1	-	22.1	-	-	-	-	-
Iraq / Iraq	-	28.1	32.7	1.3	108.2	58.2	89.3	40.6	62.7	27.3	48.7	-	-	-
Kuwait / Koweït	15.0	-0.4	8.2	8.6	95.6	85.1	124.7	198.6	163.6	154.8	169.0	172.8	119.0	173.2
Libyan Arab Jamahiriya / Jamahiriya arabe libyenne	7.1	24.6	40.9	17.0	117.2	73.3	22.2	1.3	15.4	0.0	8.1	23.8	-	-
Nigeria / Nigéria	-	-	-	-	11.2	4.0	6.2	2.1	-	0.0	0.1	-	-	-
Qatar	-	-	-	5.8	44.3	58.9	22.9	8.1	12.4	4.6	38.3	23.9	8.3	8.3
Saudi Arabia / Arabie saoudite	-	-	-	14.9	173.1	486.7	769.7	940.1	451.1	511.8	450.2	394.3	775.5	689.0
United Arab Emirates / Emirats arabes unis	-	-	-	10.7	92.2	257.5	150.8	186.7	226.3	127.0	160.8	61.2	85.5	33.3
Total bilateral concessional / Total des apports bilatéraux concessionnels	22.1	52.4	81.8	61.0	665.3	1033.9	1204.7	1381.6	954.4	843.0	895.2	685.9	988.5	903.8
B. Multilateral donors / Donneurs multilatéraux														
1. Concessional / Apports concessionnels														
BADEA	-	-	-	-	-	-	-	7.3	28.5	19.0	16.9	14.8	15.8	21.7
AFESD / FADES	-	-	-	-	2.3	28.4	32.9	37.6	71.3	41.6	45.6	60.2	41.8	41.4
Islamic Development Bank / Banque islamique de développement	-	-	-	-	-	-	-	-	7.2	13.6	5.2	17.6	8.1	15.9
OPEC FUND / Fonds de l'OPEP	-	-	-	-	-	-	-	129.3	25.4	42.2	64.3	117.7	109.1	79.9
OAPEC Special Account / Compte spécial de l'OPAEP	-	-	-	-	127.8	116.6	59.6	-	-	-	-	-	-	-
SAAFA / FSAAA	-	-	-	-	51.9	-	55.1	-	-	-	-	-	-	-
Total	-	-	-	-	182.0	144.9	147.6	174.2	132.4	116.4	132.0	210.3	174.8	158.9
2. Non-concessional / Apports non concessionnels														
BADEA	-	-	-	-	-	-	-	7.9	12.0	5.1	8.7	1.2	2.5	-0.3
Islamic Development Bank / Banque islamique de développement	-	-	-	-	-	-	-	-	12.8	126.2	95.0	98.2	-59.7	20.9
Total	-	-	-	-	-	-	-	7.9	24.8	131.2	103.7	99.4	-57.2	20.6
Total multilateral (B1+B2) / Total des apports multilatéraux (B1+B2)	-	-	-	-	182.0	144.9	147.6	182.2	157.2	247.7	235.7	309.7	117.6	179.5
Total concessional (A+B1) / Total des apports concessionnels (A+B1)	22.1	52.4	81.8	61.0	847.3	1178.9	1352.3	1555.8	1086.8	959.5	1027.2	896.2	1163.3	1062.7
GRAND TOTAL (A+B) / TOTAL GENERAL (A+B)	22.1	52.4	81.8	61.0	847.3	1178.9	1352.3	1563.7	1111.6	1090.7	1130.9	995.6	1106.1	1083.3

Source : Table 41A. — Source : Tableau 41A.

a/ Actual disbursements from 1970 to 1983 were converted to 1980 prices using the index for LDCs in table 8.

a/ Les versements effectifs de 1970 à 1983 ont été convertis aux prix de 1980 en utilisant l'indice pour les PMA qui figure au tableau 8.

Table 42

Concessional assistance from OPEC member countries and multilateral agencies mainly financed by them a/ to individual LDCs, 1970-1983

Net disbursements in $ million

Tableau 42

Aide concessionnelle reçue par chacun des PMA, en provenance des pays membres de l'OPEP et des institutions multilatérales essentiellement financées par ceux-ci,a/ 1970-1983

Versements nets en millions de dollars

Country	1970	1971	1972	1973	1974	1975	1976	1977	1978	1979	1980	1981	1982	1983	Pays
Afghanistan	-	-	-	-	28.6	21.6	14.7	4.3	15.5	8.3	1.4	20.4	0.4	-2.1	Afghanistan
Bangladesh	-	-	-	-	34.8	61.1	10.9	39.7	45.7	23.6	55.1	77.5	149.4	123.8	Bangladesh
Benin	-	-	-	-	4.5	2.4	3.6	4.6	5.4	3.4	2.3	9.9	1.6	6.4	Bénin
Bhutan	-	-	-	-	-	-	-	-	-	-	-	-	-	-	Bhoutan
Botswana	-	-	-	-	-	5.4	1.0	-	0.1	0.5	2.7	0.4	8.5	12.2	Botswana
Burkina Faso	-	-	-	0.1	6.1	2.9	1.0	3.0	2.7	5.8	7.9	10.6	8.7	2.8	Burkina Faso
Burundi	-	-	-	-	4.0	1.0	0.1	1.2	2.8	6.1	7.3	3.8	5.9	3.8	Burundi
Cape Verde	-	-	-	-	-	0.1	11.8	2.2	0.6	1.0	2.0	1.3	0.2	0.2	Cap-Vert
Central African Republic	-	-	-	-	1.2	1.4	-	1.7	-	1.3	2.1	0.6	1.1	0.2	République centrafricaine
Chad	-	-	-	3.1	13.8	8.1	1.5	1.6	7.5	6.0	2.0	0.6	0.5	0.2	Tchad
Comoros	-	-	-	-	-	-	13.8	22.5	2.6	3.0	16.3	12.9	10.3	9.8	Comores
Democratic Yemen	4.1	4.7	10.8	3.1	34.5	31.3	146.9	93.1	43.2	32.4	65.5	62.6	84.2	36.3	Yémen démocratique
Djibouti	-	-	-	-	-	-	-	19.7	64.0	-	30.6	13.1	13.1	14.8	Djibouti
Equatorial Guinea	-	-	-	-	-	-	-	0.5	-	-	-	-	1.0	0.5	Guinée équatoriale
Ethiopia	-	-	-	-	15.3	1.5	-	3.3	2.6	0.9	0.1	10.2	0.1	-	Ethiopie
Gambia	-	-	-	-	1.3	15.4	2.1	2.6	8.9	6.4	14.2	16.2	3.6	1.4	Gambie
Guinea	-	-	-	-	21.0	5.9	0.4	15.6	14.0	12.2	4.4	2.4	2.5	0.9	Guinée
Guinea-Bissau	-	-	-	-	3.1	3.2	3.8	2.2	2.5	2.8	3.8	1.8	3.7	6.8	Guinée-Bissau
Haiti	-	-	-	-	-	-	-	3.1	-	-	-	0.6	2.0	1.5	Haïti
Lao People's Dem. Republic	-	-	-	-	-	-	-	2.1	-	4.2	0.6	0.0	0.4	0.4	République dém. pop. lao
Lesotho	-	-	-	-	-	2.8	-	1.9	0.0	0.3	0.0	0.9	2.8	7.6	Lesotho
Malawi	-	-	-	-	-	-	-	-	-	-	1.3	0.3	0.0	-	Malawi
Maldives	-	-	-	0.8	13.6	0.2	2.9	1.5	3.3	4.0	17.3	7.3	2.5	4.5	Maldives
Mali	-	-	-	-	-	-	-	16.8	11.9	24.7	29.3	21.1	31.0	43.2	Mali
Nepal	-	-	-	-	-	-	-	41.5	21.6	3.5	6.8	9.0	5.4	1.3	Népal
Niger	-	1.3	1.3	0.5	1.0	16.8	4.1	8.8	21.4	7.1	8.1	32.6	82.6	18.2	Niger
Rwanda	-	-	-	-	1.0	9.2	0.4	5.8	4.0	2.7	7.1	8.3	1.7	1.6	Rwanda
Samoa	-	-	-	-	-	-	-	-	-	-	0.7	-	1.0	-	Samoa
Sao Tome and Principe	-	-	-	-	-	0.6	10.0	1.6	0.5	0.5	-	0.5	0.5	0.5	Sao Tomé-et-Principe
Sierra Leone	-	-	-	5.5	1.9	1.8	0.2	1.0	-	5.0	5.0	1.4	0.9	1.6	Sierra Leone
Somalia	1.5	-1.5	3.5	-4.9	49.6	79.3	41.5	213.8	113.9	106.2	143.6	50.1	182.9	48.0	Somalie
Sudan	-	-	-0.3	-	83.2	178.2	267.5	129.8	115.9	303.9	250.2	197.1	157.2	353.4	Soudan
Togo	-	-	-	-	1.8	2.0	2.6	0.1	-	-	0.0	0.1	2.7	5.0	Togo
Uganda	-	-	4.0	-	18.8	25.7	5.2	9.5	7.2	7.4	0.1	0.2	6.2	11.5	Ouganda
United Republic of Tanzania	-	10.4	5.8	-	7.1	7.3	0.6	12.8	2.0	4.7	19.6	24.0	29.0	32.4	République-Unie de Tanzanie
Yemen	0.3	-	-	15.1	92.0	141.1	211.8	289.3	234.2	201.5	320.0	269.5	285.6	193.3	Yémen
All LDCs	5.9	14.9	25.0	23.3	439.5	656.4	760.4	959.5	736.5	791.4	1027.7	870.1	1081.8	944.7	**Ensemble des PMA**
All developing countries	390.6	441.2	660.3	2031.5	4265.1	5797.0	5578.6	4470.0	7549.1	7156.7	9202.0	8294.7	5892.8	5189.8	**Ensemble des pays en développement**

Source : UNCTAD secretariat estimates. For 1970-1976 : OECD secretariat estimates.

Note : The figures relating to LDCs include only those amounts allocated to a specific recipient country and therefore understate financial flows to the extent that certain donors have recorded disbursements in favour of groups of countries including some LDCs.

a/ The members of OPEC and the multilateral agencies financed by them included here and providing assistance to LDCs are listed in table 41A.

Source : Estimations du secrétariat de la CNUCED. Pour 1970-1976 : estimations du secrétariat de l'OCDE.

Note : Les données se rapportant aux PMA ne comprennent que les montants imputables à un pays bénéficiaire déterminé. Par conséquent, les apports financiers sont sous-estimés dans la mesure où certains donneurs ont alloué des versements à des groupes de pays comprenant des PMA.

a/ La liste des membres de l'OPEP et des institutions multilatérales financées par ceux-ci qui sont inclus ici et qui fournissent de l'aide aux PMA figure au tableau 41A.

Table 43

Concessional assistance from OPEC member countries to individual LDCs, 1970-1983 a/

Net disbursements in $ million

Tableau 43

Aide concessionnelle reçue par chacun des PMA, en provenance des pays membres de l'OPEP, 1970-1983 a/

Versements nets en millions de dollars

Country	1970	1971	1972	1973	1974	1975	1976	1977	1978	1979	1980	1981	1982	1983	Pays
Afghanistan	-	-	-	-	28.6	21.6	14.7	0.6	15.5	8.3	1.4	20.4	0.4	-2.1	Afghanistan
Bangladesh	-	-	-	-	34.8	61.1	10.9	25.8	44.6	13.2	51.1	47.2	126.8	110.0	Bangladesh
Benin	-	-	-	-	4.5	-	3.6	1.2	-	2.1	1.8	1.2	0.0	2.1	Bénin
Bhutan	-	-	-	-	-	-	-	-	-	-	-	-	-	-	Bhoutan
Botswana	-	-	-	0.1	-	-	-	-	-	-	-	-	6.1	8.1	Botswana
Burkina Faso	-	-	-	-	6.1	0.2	1.0	0.1	0.9	0.9	1.0	2.0	-	0.3	Burkina Faso
Burundi	-	-	-	-	3.0	-	0.1	0.4	2.0	1.7	2.8	2.0	5.9	3.3	Burundi
Cape Verde	-	-	-	-	-	-	1.3	0.7	-	-	-	-	-	0.2	Cap-Vert
Central African Republic	-	-	-	-	-	-	-	-	-	1.3	2.1	0.0	1.1	0.3	République centrafricaine
Chad	-	-	-	3.1	9.4	3.7	1.5	0.4	6.0	6.0	0.0	-	-	0.2	Tchad
Comoros	4.1	4.7	-	-	-	-	3.3	22.3	2.1	2.8	15.8	11.4	7.9	6.3	Comores
Democratic Yemen	-	-	10.8	3.1	22.6	31.1	140.2	88.6	28.9	23.8	53.2	44.2	71.7	19.5	Yémen démocratique
Djibouti	-	-	-	-	-	-	-	19.7	64.0	-	30.6	12.4	1.6	11.5	Djibouti
Equatorial Guinea	-	-	-	-	15.0	1.2	-	-	-	-	-	-	-	-	Guinée équatoriale
Ethiopia	-	-	-	-	1.3	1.2	2.1	0.9	0.2	0.9	0.1	10.1	2.3	0.9	Ethiopie
Gambia	-	-	-	-	1.1	-	-	-	-	-	-	14.0	-	-	Gambie
Guinea	-	-	-	-	21.0	5.9	0.4	13.2	9.1	9.2	7.0	-0.2	2.3	-0.5	Guinée
Guinea-Bissau	-	-	-	-	2.8	3.2	3.8	0.6	1.9	1.8	1.3	0.0	2.7	6.1	Guinée-Bissau
Haiti	-	-	-	-	-	-	-	-	-	-	-	-	-	-	Haïti
Lao People's Dem. Republic	-	-	-	-	-	-	-	-	-	-	-	-	-	-	République dém. pop. lao
Lesotho	-	-	-	-	-	-	-	-	0.0	0.3	0.0	0.2	-	2.5	Lesotho
Malawi	-	-	-	-	-	-	-	-	-	-	-	-	-	-	Malawi
Maldives	-	-	-	-	-	-	-	-	5.2	3.6	19.0	7.0	1.6	26.6	Maldives
Mali	-	-	-	0.8	9.7	25.5	3.0	1.3	3.1	21.3	16.6	5.7	18.6	3.9	Mali
Nepal	-	-	-	-	-	-	-	-	1.6	-	6.8	8.7	0.0	-0.9	Népal
Niger	-	1.3	1.3	0.5	1.0	14.1	4.1	5.9	16.1	0.7	1.6	23.7	82.1	18.1	Niger
Rwanda	-	-	-	-	-	8.7	0.4	5.0	1.1	0.5	1.2	0.5	0.0	1.6	Rwanda
Samoa	-	-	-	-	-	-	-	-	-	-	-	-	-	-	Samoa
Sao Tome and Principe	-	-	-	-	-	0.1	0.2	-	-	-	-	-	0.2	0.0	Sao Tomé-et-Principe
Sierra Leone	-	-	3.5	5.5	0.1	-	0.2	-	-	4.0	4.0	0.0	0.2	0.0	Sierra Leone
Somalia	1.5	-1.5	-0.3	-4.9	42.4	71.8	37.3	208.2	106.0	95.7	127.6	34.9	161.3	26.2	Somalie
Sudan	-	-	-	-	45.8	164.1	239.0	114.3	97.5	288.2	227.5	170.4	137.5	351.9	Soudan
Togo	-	-	4.0	-	1.8	2.0	2.6	0.1	-	-	0.0	0.1	2.7	2.3	Togo
Uganda	-	-	-	-	13.1	-	5.2	6.9	7.2	7.4	0.1	0.0	1.3	2.9	Ouganda
United Republic of Tanzania	0.3	10.4	5.8	15.1	81.1	-	0.6	-	1.0	3.5	15.5	15.3	14.3	18.2	République-Unie de Tanzanie
Yemen	-	-	-	-	-	139.5	199.2	278.8	223.9	189.4	306.2	233.3	271.4	182.6	Yémen
All LDCs	5.9	14.9	25.0	23.3	345.1	575.7	677.4	852.0	646.6	695.3	895.5	665.8	919.2	803.4	Ensemble des PMA
All developing countries	390.6	441.2	660.3	2031.5	4148.4	5638.3	5160.4	4249.2	7248.2	6906.5	8916.6	7922.2	5541.6	4865.3	Ensemble des pays en développement

Source : UNCTAD secretariat estimates. For 1970-1976 : OECD secretariat estimates.

Note : The figures relating to LDCs include only those amounts allocated to a specific recipient country and therefore understate financial flows to the extent that certain donors have recorded disbursements in favour of groups of countries including some LDCs.

a/ The members of OPEC included here are the following : Algeria, Iran (Islamic Republic of), Iraq, Kuwait, Libyan Arab Jamahiriya, Nigeria, Qatar, Saudi Arabia and United Arab Emirates.

Source : Estimations du secrétariat de la CNUCED. Pour 1970-1976 : estimations du secrétariat de l'OCDE.

Note : Les données se rapportant aux PMA ne comprennent que les montants imputables à un pays bénéficiaire déterminé. Par conséquent, les apports financiers sont sous-estimés dans la mesure où certains donneurs ont alloués des versements à des groupes de pays comprenant des PMA.

a/ Les membres de l'OPEP considérés ici sont les suivants : Algérie, Arabie saoudite, Emirats arabes unis, Iran (République Islamique), Iraq, Jamahiriya arabe libyenne, Koweït, Nigéria et Qatar.

Table 44

Grants from OPEC countries to individual LDCs, 1970-1983 a/

Net disbursements in $ million

Tableau 44

Dons reçus par chacun des PMA, en provenance des pays membres de l'OPEP, 1970-1983 a/

Versements nets en millions de dollars

Country	1970	1971	1972	1973	1974	1975	1976	1977	1978	1979	1980	1981	1982	1983	Pays
Afghanistan	-	-	-	-	28.6	13.8	2.7	0.1	5.0	-	-	1.0	-	-	Afghanistan
Bangladesh	-	-	-	-	14.8	10.7	2.5	10.8	6.7	-	20.4	5.8	90.6	80.0	Bangladesh
Benin	-	-	-	-	4.5	-	-	0.5	-	-	-	-	-	-	Bénin
Bhutan	-	-	-	-	-	-	-	-	-	-	-	-	-	-	Bhoutan
Botswana	-	-	-	-	-	-	-	-	-	-	0.0	-	-	-	Botswana
Burkina Faso	-	-	-	0.1	6.1	0.2	1.0	0.1	0.9	0.9	1.0	2.0	-	0.3	Burkina Faso
Burundi	-	-	-	-	3.0	-	0.0	0.0	-	-	-	-	-	0.0	Burundi
Cape Verde	-	-	-	-	-	0.1	1.3	0.7	-	-	-	-	-	0.2	Cap-Vert
Central African Republic	-	-	-	-	-	-	-	-	-	-	-	-	-	-	République centrafricaine
Chad	-	-	-	3.1	9.4	3.7	1.5	0.4	6.0	6.0	0.0	-	-	0.2	Tchad
Comoros	-	-	-	-	-	-	2.3	19.7	0.6	1.1	1.9	7.5	0.7	1.9	Comores
Democratic Yemen	-	0.4	0.7	3.0	18.2	27.6	128.8	76.5	8.8	17.6	34.2	20.4	46.3	9.6	Yémen démocratique
Djibouti	-	-	-	-	-	-	-	19.7	64.0	-	25.0	12.2	0.1	5.7	Djibouti
Equatorial Guinea	-	-	-	-	15.0	1.2	-	-	-	-	-	-	-	-	Guinée équatoriale
Ethiopia	-	-	-	-	1.3	1.2	-	0.9	0.2	0.9	-	3.1	-	0.4	Ethiopie
Gambia	-	-	-	-	1.1	-	2.1	0.2	0.2	0.0	0.0	-	0.9	0.7	Gambie
Guinea	-	-	-	-	11.0	1.9	0.4	0.6	2.1	0.3	0.1	-	-	0.7	Guinée
Guinea-Bissau	-	-	-	-	2.8	1.2	3.8	0.6	-	0.0	0.0	-	0.0	0.5	Guinée-Bissau
Haiti	-	-	-	-	-	-	-	-	-	-	-	-	-	-	Haïti
Lao People's Dem. Republic	-	-	-	-	-	-	-	-	-	-	-	-	-	-	République dém. pop. lao
Lesotho	-	-	-	-	-	-	-	-	-	-	-	-	-	-	Lesotho
Malawi	-	-	-	-	-	-	-	-	-	-	-	-	-	-	Malawi
Maldives	-	-	-	0.8	4.5	0.2	1.8	1.2	0.0	1.0	1.1	1.2	0.0	0.8	Maldives
Mali	-	-	-	-	-	24.5	3.0	5.1	1.0	11.5	5.1	0.0	0.0	0.5	Mali
Nepal	-	-	-	-	-	-	0.2	33.0	-	-	-	-	-	-	Népal
Niger	-	1.3	-	0.5	1.0	0.4	3.1	3.0	15.9	0.4	1.6	1.9	1.7	0.8	Niger
Rwanda	-	-	-	-	-	5.2	0.1	0.6	-	-	-	0.1	-	0.1	Rwanda
Samoa	-	-	-	-	-	-	-	-	-	-	-	-	-	-	Samoa
Sao Tome and Principe	-	-	-	-	-	0.1	0.2	0.0	-	-	-	-	-	-	Sao Tomé-et-Principe
Sierra Leone	-	-	-	-	-	0.0	0.2	0.0	4.0	-	4.0	0.0	0.2	0.0	Sierra Leone
Somalia	-	-	-	4.0	25.1	52.3	14.4	191.3	50.7	32.4	78.7	24.0	148.7	1.5	Somalie
Sudan	-	-	-	0.8	32.5	120.1	42.4	82.9	36.9	12.1	27.8	15.7	104.9	338.3	Soudan
Togo	-	-	-	-	1.8	2.0	2.6	0.1	-	-	0.0	0.0	0.0	0.2	Togo
Uganda	-	-	4.0	-	0.6	20.0	2.2	-	4.8	0.1	0.0	0.0	0.0	0.0	Ouganda
United Republic of Tanzania	-	-	-	-	-	-	-	-	0.0	-	-	-	-	0.0	République-Unie de Tanzanie
Yemen	0.2	0.6	1.2	11.8	78.0	135.4	179.7	255.5	175.9	148.1	226.8	149.6	175.4	166.1	Yémen
All LDCs	0.3	2.2	5.9	24.0	259.3	436.2	395.9	704.6	380.4	233.1	428.4	245.5	570.2	609.0	Ensemble des PMA
All developing countries	363.7	368.6	480.4	1585.7	2727.0	3164.7	2594.1	3015.3	2261.4	3750.3	4014.7	3471.1	2982.7	2393.5	Ensemble des pays en développement

Source : UNCTAD secretariat estimates. For 1970-1976: OECD secretariat estimates.

Note : The figures relating to LDCs include only those amounts allocated to a specific recipient country and therefore understate financial flows to the extent that certain donors have recorded disbursements in favour of groups of countries including some LDCs.

a/ The members of OPEC included here are the following: Algeria, Iran (Islamic Republic of), Iraq, Kuwait, Libyan Arab Jamahiriya, Nigeria, Qatar, Saudi Arabia and United Arab Emirates.

Source : Estimations du secrétariat de la CNUCED. Pour 1970-1976 : estimations du secrétariat de l'OCDE.

Note : Les données se rapportant aux PMA ne comprennent que les montants imputables à un pays bénéficiaire déterminé. Par conséquent, les apports financiers sont sous-estimés dans la mesure où certains donneurs ont alloué des versements à des groupes de pays comprenant des PMA.

a/ Les membres de l'OPEP considérés ici sont les suivants : Algérie, Arabie saoudite, Emirats arabes unis, Iran (République Islamique), Iraq, Jamahiriya arabe libyenne, Koweit, Nigéria et Qatar.

Table 45

Concessional assistance from multilateral agencies a/ mainly financed by OPEC countries, to individual LDCs, 1974-1983

Net disbursements in $ million

Tableau 45

Aide concessionnelle reçue par chacun des PMA, en provenance des institutions multi-latérales a/ essentiellement financés par les pays membres de l'OPEP, 1974-1983

Versements nets en millions de dollars

Country	1974	1975	1976	1977	1978	1979	1980	1981	1982	1983	Pays
Afghanistan	–	–	–	3.7	1.1	10.4	4.0	30.3	22.6	13.8	Afghanistan
Bangladesh	–	2.4	–	13.9	5.4	1.3	0.5	8.7	1.6	4.3	Bangladesh
Benin	–	–	–	3.4	–	–	–	0.4	–	–	Bénin
Bhutan	–	–	–	–	–	–	–	–	–	–	Bhoutan
Botswana	–	–	–	–	0.1	0.5	2.7	8.6	8.7	4.1	Botswana
Burkina Faso	–	5.4	–	2.9	1.8	4.9	6.9	1.8	2.4	2.5	Burkina Faso
Burundi	1.0	2.7	–	0.8	0.8	4.4	4.5	1.3	0.2	0.5	Burundi
Cape Verde	1.2	1.0	10.5	1.5	0.6	1.0	2.0	0.6	0.5	–	Cap-Vert
Central African Republic	4.4	1.2	–	1.7	1.5	–	0.0	0.6	–	–	République centrafricaine
Chad	–	–	–	1.2	0.5	0.2	0.5	1.5	1.9	–	Tchad
Comoros	–	0.2	10.5	0.2	0.5	0.2	0.5	0.7	2.4	3.5	Comores
Democratic Yemen	11.9	–	6.7	4.5	14.3	8.6	12.3	18.4	12.5	16.8	Yémen démocratique
Djibouti	0.3	0.3	–	0.5	–	–	–	0.7	1.9	3.3	Djibouti
Equatorial Guinea	–	14.2	–	2.4	2.4	–	0.0	0.1	0.1	0.5	Guinée équatoriale
Ethiopia	0.4	0.4	–	1.6	1.4	2.3	0.0	0.1	1.3	–	Ethiopie
Gambia	–	–	–	2.4	1.4	3.0	7.2	2.2	1.8	0.5	Gambie
Guinea	–	–	–	1.6	4.9	3.0	4.3	2.6	1.0	1.4	Guinée
Guinea-Bissau	0.3	–	–	1.6	0.6	1.0	2.5	1.8	1.8	0.7	Guinée-Bissau
Haiti	–	–	–	3.1	0.6	4.2	–	0.6	2.0	1.5	Haïti
Lao People's Dem. Republic	–	2.8	–	2.1	0.0	–	0.6	0.0	0.4	0.4	République dém. pop. lao
Lesotho	–	–	–	1.9	–	–	–	–	2.8	5.1	Lesotho
Malawi	–	–	–	–	0.2	0.4	1.3	0.3	0.9	0.6	Malawi
Maldives	–	–	–	0.2	0.2	–	0.7	1.6	–	–	Maldives
Mali	3.9	3.9	–	4.4	6.7	3.4	10.3	14.1	12.4	16.6	Mali
Nepal	–	2.7	–	4.1	5.3	6.4	6.5	8.9	5.4	2.2	Népal
Niger	1.0	1.0	–	2.9	2.9	2.2	5.9	7.8	1.7	0.1	Niger
Rwanda	–	–	–	0.8	0.5	0.5	0.7	1.0	1.0	0.0	Rwanda
Samoa	–	–	–	1.6	0.1	–	–	–	–	–	Samoa
Sao Tome and Principe	1.8	0.5	10.0	0.1	–	–	0.7	0.5	–	0.5	Sao Tomé-et-Principe
Sierra Leone	7.2	1.8	–	1.0	–	1.0	1.0	1.4	0.7	1.6	Sierra Leone
Somalia	37.4	7.5	4.2	5.6	7.9	10.5	16.0	15.2	21.6	21.8	Somalie
Sudan	–	14.1	28.5	15.5	18.4	15.7	22.7	26.7	19.7	1.5	Soudan
Togo	–	–	–	–	–	–	–	–	–	2.7	Togo
Uganda	5.7	5.7	0.0	4.5	0.0	0.0	0.0	0.2	4.9	8.6	Ouganda
United Republic of Tanzania	7.1	7.1	–	5.9	1.0	1.2	4.1	8.7	14.7	14.2	République-Unie de Tanzanie
Yemen	10.9	1.6	12.6	10.5	10.3	12.1	13.8	36.2	14.2	10.7	Yémen
All LDCs	94.4	80.7	83.0	107.5	89.9	96.1	132.2	204.3	162.6	141.3	**Ensemble des PMA**
All developing countries	116.7	158.7	418.2	220.8	300.9	250.2	285.4	372.5	351.2	324.5	**Ensemble des pays en développement**

Source : UNCTAD secretariat estimates. For 1974-1976 : OECD secretariat estimates.

a/ For the list of multilateral agencies included, providing concessional assistance to LDCs, see table 41A.

Source : Estimations du secrétariat de la CNUCED. Pour 1974-1976 : estimations du secrétariat de l'OCDE.

a/ Pour la liste des institutions multilatérales qui sont incluses ici et qui fournissent de l'aide concessionnelle aux PMA, se référer au tableau 41A.

Table 46

Tableau 46

Grants from multilateral agencies a/ mainly financed by OPEC countries, to individual LDCs, 1974-1983

Dons reçus par chacun des PMA, en provenance des institutions multilatérales a/ essentiellement financées par les pays membres de l'OPEP, 1974-1983

Net disbursements in $ million

Versements nets en millions de dollars

Country	1974	1975	1976	1977	1978	1979	1980	1981	1982	1983	Pays
Afghanistan	-	-	-	-	-	-	-	-	-	-	Afghanistan
Bangladesh	-	-	-	-	-	-	-	-	-	-	Bangladesh
Benin	-	-	-	-	-	-	-	-	-	-	Bénin
Bhutan	-	-	-	-	-	-	-	-	-	-	Bhoutan
Botswana	-	-	-	-	-	-	-	-	-	-	Botswana
Burkina Faso	-	-	-	-	-	-	-	-	-	-	Burkina Faso
Burundi	-	-	-	-	-	-	-	-	-	--	Burundi
Cape Verde	-	-	-	-	-	-	-	-	-	-	Cap-Vert
Central African Republic	-	-	-	-	-	-	-	-	-	-	République centrafricaine
Chad	-	-	-	-	-	-	-	-	-	0.0	Tchad
Comoros	-	-	-	-	-	-	-	-	-	-	Comores
Democratic Yemen	-	-	-	-	0.0	0.0	-	0.0	0.2	0.3	Yémen démocratique
Djibouti	-	-	-	-	-	-	-	-	0.2	-	Djibouti
Equatorial Guinea	-	-	-	-	-	-	-	-	-	-	Guinée équatoriale
Ethiopia	-	-	-	-	-	-	-	-	-	-	Ethiopie
Gambia	-	-	-	-	-	-	-	-	-	-	Gambie
Guinea	-	-	-	-	-	-	-	-	-	-	Guinée
Guinea-Bissau	-	-	-	-	-	0.0	-	-	0.0	-	Guinée-Bissau
Haiti	-	-	-	-	-	-	-	-	-	-	Haïti
Lao People's Dem. Republic	-	-	-	-	-	-	-	-	-	-	République dém.pop. lao
Lesotho	-	-	-	-	-	-	-	-	-	-	Lesotho
Malawi	-	-	-	-	-	-	-	-	-	-	Malawi
Maldives	-	-	-	-	-	-	-	-	-	-	Maldives
Mali	-	-	-	-	-	-	-	-	-	-	Mali
Nepal	-	-	-	-	-	-	-	-	-	-	Népal
Niger	-	-	-	-	-	-	-	-	-	-	Niger
Rwanda	-	-	-	-	-	-	-	-	-	-	Rwanda
Samoa	-	-	-	-	-	-	-	-	-	-	Samoa
Sao Tome and Principe	-	-	-	-	-	-	-	-	-	-	Sao Tomé-et-Principe
Sierra Leone	-	-	-	-	-	-	-	-	-	-	Sierra Leone
Somalia	0.4	-	-	0.0	0.1	0.1	0.1	0.6	0.2	0.1	Somalie
Sudan	-	-	-	-	-	-	-	-	0.2	0.7	Soudan
Togo	-	-	-	-	-	-	-	-	-	-	Togo
Uganda	-	-	-	0.0	0.0	0.0	-	0.0	0.0	0.0	Ouganda
United Republic of Tanzania	-	-	-	-	-	-	-	-	-	-	République-Unie de Tanzanie
Yemen	-	-	-	0.0	-	0.1	0.0	0.3	0.1	0.0	Yémen
All LDCs	0.4	-	-	0.1	0.1	0.3	0.2	1.0	1.2	1.3	**Ensemble des PMA**
All developing countries	0.4	1.1	7.5	1.6	0.6	0.5	0.7	1.7	3.0	7.3	**Ensemble des pays en développement**

Source: UNCTAD secretariat estimates. For 1974-1976: OECD secretariat estimates.

Source: Estimations du secrétariat de la CNUCED. Pour 1974-1976: estimations du secrétariat de l'OCDE.

a/ For the list of multilateral agencies included, providing concessional assistance to LDCs, see table 41A.

a/ Pour la liste des institutions multilatérales qui sont incluses ici et qui fournissent de l'aide concessionnelle aux PMA, se référer au tableau 41A.

Table 47
Non-concessional flows from multilateral agencies a/ mainly financed by OPEC countries, 1977-1983

Net disbursements in $ million

Tableau 47
Apports non-concessionnels reçus par chacun des PMA, en provenance des institutions multilatérales a/ essentiellement financées par les pays membres de l'OPEP, 1977-1983

Versements nets en millions de dollars

Country	1977	1978	1979	1980	1981	1982	1983	Pays
Afghanistan	-	-	37.1	-14.7	34.0	-11.3	38.9	Afghanistan
Bangladesh	-	0.1	1.7	1.7	0.6	2.1	0.0	Bangladesh
Benin	-	-	-	-	-	-	-	Bénin
Bhutan	-	-	-	-	-	-	-	Bhoutan
Botswana	-	-	-	-	-	-	-	Botswana
Burkina Faso	-	-	-	2.6	2.5	0.2	0.2	Burkina Faso
Burundi	-	-	-	-	-	-	-	Burundi
Cape Verde	-	-	-	-	-	-	-	Cap-Vert
Central African Republic	-	-	-	-	-	-	-	République centrafricaine
Chad	-	-	-	-	-	-	-	Tchad
Comoros	-	-	-	12.8	3.7	-0.4	-2.4	Comores
Democratic Yemen	-	-	-	-	1.2	4.9	-20.4	Yémen démocratique
Djibouti	-	-	-	-	-	-	-	Djibouti
Equatorial Guinea	-	-	-	-	-	-	-	Guinée équatoriale
Ethiopia	-	-	-	-	-	-	-	Ethiopie
Gambia	-	2.3	10.5	18.0	6.5	-2.3	1.0	Gambie
Guinea	-	-	-	8.4	3.5	-8.5	-2.3	Guinée
Guinea-Bissau	-	-	-	-	5.0	-	-	Guinée-Bissau
Haiti	-	-	-	-	-	-	-	Haïti
Lao People's Dem. Republic	-	-	-	-	-	-	-	République dém. populaire lao
Lesotho	-	-	-	-	-	-	-	Lesotho
Malawi	-	-	-	-	-	-	-	Malawi
Maldives	-	-	-	-	3.3	-	-	Maldives
Mali	-	-	2.7	-0.3	-2.0	-	-	Mali
Nepal	-	-	-	-	-	-	-	Népal
Niger	-	4.6	10.1	7.1	14.5	-14.6	-4.0	Niger
Rwanda	-	-	-	-	-	-	-	Rwanda
Samoa	-	-	-	-	-	-	-	Samoa
Sao Tome and Principe	-	-	-	-	-	-	-	Sao Tomé-et-Principe
Sierra Leone	-	-	3.9	15.0	12.5	-6.2	-4.5	Sierra Leone
Somalia	4.9	1.7	39.0	32.5	7.2	-2.9	-7.1	Somalie
Sudan	-	2.2	1.0	0.0	-	0.0	0.0	Soudan
Togo	-	-	-	-	-	0.3	2.4	Togo
Uganda	-	5.8	1.4	0.5	0.0	0.4	0.0	Ouganda
United Republic of Tanzania	-	-	-	-	-	-	-	République-Unie de Tanzanie
Yemen	-	-	0.4	19.8	3.3	-14.9	16.7	Yémen
All LDCs	4.9	16.9	108.3	103.8	96.5	-53.2	18.3	Ensemble des PMA
All developing countries	38.7	158.5	258.6	104.5	327.9	-2.6	129.6	Ensemble des pays en développement

Source : UNCTAD secretariat estimates.

a/ For the list of multilateral agencies included, providing non-concessional flows to LDCs, see table 41A.

Source : Estimations du secrétariat de la CNUCED.

a/ Pour la liste des institutions multilatérales qui sont incluses ici et qui fournissent des apports non concessionnels aux PMA, se référer au tableau 41A.

Table 48

Net ODA as per cent of donor's GNP from individual OPEC
member countries to LDCs as a group, 1975-1983

Percentages

Tableau 48

Apports nets de l'APD accordée par chaque pays membre de l'OPEP à
l'ensemble des PMA, en pourcentage du PNB du pays donneur,1975-1983

En pourcentage

Country	1975	1976	1977	1978	1979	1980	1981	1982	1983	Pays
	Bilateral ODA				APD bilatérale					
Algeria	0.02	0.03	0.01	0.00	0.05	0.05	0.02	0.00	–	Algérie
Iran (Islamic Rep. of)	0.01	0.01	–	0.02	–	–	–	–	–	Iran (Rép. islamique)
Iraq	0.21	0.32	0.14	0.18	0.06	0.14	–	–	–	Iraq
Kuwait	0.36	0.48	0.77	0.61	0.46	0.52	0.52	0.42	0.59	Koweit
Libyan Arab Jamahiriya	0.36	0.08	0.00	0.06	0.00	0.02	0.09	–	–	Jamahiriya arabe libyenne
Nigeria	0.01	0.01	0.00	–	0.00	0.00	–	–	–	Nigéria
Qatar	1.30	0.39	0.16	0.24	0.07	0.58	0.32	0.12	0.12	Qatar
Saudi Arabia	0.76	0.92	0.98	0.47	0.55	0.39	0.24	0.47	0.55	Arabie saoudite
United Arab Emirates	1.60	0.74	0.79	1.10	0.55	0.58	0.20	0.29	0.12	Emirats arabes unis
Venezuela	–	–	–	–	–	–	–	–	–	Venezuela
Total OPEC countries	0.27	0.26	0.28	0.20	0.16	0.17	0.12	0.17	0.16	Total des pays de l'OPEP
	Total ODA (method A)a/				APD totale (méthode A)a/					
Algeria	0.02	0.03	0.05	0.04	0.08	0.07	0.06	0.03	0.01	Algérie
Iran (Islamic Rep. of)	0.01	0.01	0.03	0.04	0.01	0.01	0.00	0.00	0.00	Iran (Rép. islamique)
Iraq	0.22	0.52	0.16	0.23	0.09	0.17	0.04	0.02	0.04	Iraq
Kuwait	0.43	0.68	0.94	0.80	0.58	0.61	0.65	0.65	0.75	Koweit
Libyan Arab Jamahiriya	0.56	0.11	0.06	0.20	0.08	0.07	0.19	0.04	0.06	Jamahiriya arabe libyenne
Nigeria	0.01	0.02	0.03	0.01	0.01	0.01	0.05	0.02	0.01	Nigéria
Qatar	1.61	0.41	0.26	0.35	0.12	0.68	0.40	0.25	0.17	Qatar
Saudi Arabia	0.88	0.99	1.04	0.54	0.70	0.44	0.30	0.54	0.64	Arabe saoudite
United Arab Emirates	1.78	0.76	0.83	1.17	0.62	0.63	0.27	0.35	0.16	Emirats arabes unis
Venezuela	0.02	0.02	0.04	0.02	0.03	0.02	0.04	0.03	0.04	Venezuela
Total OPEC countries	0.32	0.30	0.32	0.25	0.22	0.20	0.17	0.22	0.21	Total des pays de l'OPEP
	Total ODA (method B)a/				APD totale (méthode B)a/					
Algeria	0.01	0.05	0.09	0.06	0.09	0.10	0.08	0.07	0.04	Algérie
Iran (Islamic Rép. of)	0.01	0.01	0.04	0.05	0.01	0.02	0.00	0.00	0.00	Iran (Rép. islamique)
Iraq	0.22	0.44	0.22	0.22	0.09	0.19	0.07	0.06	0.04	Iraq
Kuwait	0.43	0.71	1.21	0.99	0.72	0.72	0.71	0.83	0.97	Koweit
Libyan Arab Jamahiriya	0.55	0.16	0.16	0.31	0.16	0.12	0.22	0.10	0.18	Jamahiriya arabe libyenne
Nigeria	0.03	0.10	0.10	0.03	0.02	0.01	0.12	0.03	0.02	Nigéria
Qatar	1.57	0.42	0.29	0.49	0.20	0.76	0.41	0.29	0.22	Qatar
Saudi Arabia	0.90	1.00	1.06	0.60	0.83	0.48	0.31	0.59	0.71	Arabie saoudite
United Arab Emirates	1.76	0.77	0.86	1.25	0.74	0.67	0.28	0.41	0.20	Emirats arabes unis
Venezuela	0.02	0.02	0.06	0.04	0.03	0.03	0.04	0.04	0.05	Venezuela
Total OPEC countries	0.32	0.32	0.37	0.29	0.26	0.23	0.19	0.25	0.25	Total des pays de l'OPEP

Source: UNCTAD secretariat estimates. For 1975-1976,
the estimates are based on information from
the OECD secretariat.

a/ For the description of the two different
methods used to calculate the amount of
ODA provided through multilateral channels,
see "Explanatory Notes".

Source: Estimations du secrétariat de la CNUCED. Pour 1975-1976,
les estimations sont établies d'après des renseignements
du secrétariat de l'OCDE.

a/ La description des deux méthodes différentes utilisées
pour calculer le montant de l'APD fournie à travers les
voies multilatérales figure dans les
"Notes explicatives".

Table 49

ODA commitments from individual OPEC member countries and individual multilateral agencies mainly financed by them, to LDCs as a group, 1973-1983

$ million

Tableau 49

Engagements de l'APD de chaque pays membre de l'OPEP et de chaque institution multilatérale essentiellement financée par ceux-ci, en faveur de l'ensemble des PMA, 1973-1983

millions de dollars

	1973	1974	1975	1976	1977	1978	1979	1980	1981	1982	1983	
Bilateral donors												**Donneurs bilatéraux**
Algeria	1.0	3.0	3.6	4.9	2.5	0.5	34.4	-	20.0	0.2	-	Algérie
Iran (Islamic Rep.)	-	11.0	16.6	20.9	-	-	-	-	-	-	-	Iran (Rép. Islamique)
Iraq	12.5	109.2	51.1	64.0	1.3	53.5	324.5	289.4	48.8	37.3	-	Iraq
Kuwait	38.4	61.0	189.4	138.6	161.6	116.7	107.0	216.9	257.4	265.0	165.5	Koweit
Libyan Arab Jamahiriya	12.4	59.4	36.1	6.5	0.8	25.4	0.0	8.7	23.1	-	-	Jamahiriya arabe libyenne
Nigeria	-	5.8	3.0	0.2	0.1	0.9	1.6	2.5	-	-	-	Nigéria
Qatar	2.1	37.0	19.9	17.5	4.6	10.7	3.0	37.3	22.6	7.6	7.4	Qatar
Saudi Arabia	24.0	90.0	397.5	509.4	847.4	783.8	347.0	360.5	425.7	842.9	1073.3	Arabie saoudite
United Arab Emirates	11.2	60.8	157.9	140.6	253.2	135.9	58.1	306.2	36.0	83.0	7.1	Emirats arabes unis
Total	101.6	437.2	875.1	902.6	1271.5	1127.4	875.6	1221.5	833.6	1236.0	1253.3	**Total**
Multilateral donors												**Donneurs multilatéraux**
BADEA	-	-	-	42.6	29.8	22.6	8.2	44.8	10.0	32.0	20.0	BADEA
AFESD	-	52.3	65.9	103.6	95.0	0.5	14.4	43.6	68.6	65.7	145.4	FADES
Islamic Dev. Bank	-	-	-	-	30.6	12.8	18.3	11.4	18.4	39.9	8.3	Banque islamique de dév.
OPEC Fund	-	-	-	13.2	108.6	57.1	93.5	110.7	174.9	165.6	62.2	Fonds de l'OPEP
OAPEC	-	66.3	-	33.5	-	-	-	-	-	-	-	Compte spécial de l'OPAEP
SAAFA	-	59.3	33.0	30.5	-	-	-	-	-	-	-	FSAAA
Total	-	177.9	98.9	223.4	264.0	93.0	134.4	210.5	271.9	303.2	235.9	**Total**
GRAND TOTAL	101.6	615.1	974.0	1126.0	1535.5	1220.4	1010.0	1432.0	1105.5	1539.2	1489.2	**TOTAL GENERAL**

Source : UNCTAD secretariat estimates.
For 1973-1976 : OECD secretariat estimates.
For abbreviations see pages x and xi.

Source : Estimations du secrétariat de la CNUCED.
Pour 1973-1976 : estimations du secrétariat de l'OCDE.
Se reporter, pour les abréviations, aux pages xvii et xviii.

Table 50

ODA commitments from OPEC member countries and multilateral agencies mainly financed by them to individual LDCs, 1970-1983
$ million

Tableau 50

Engagements de l'APD à chacun des PMA, en provenance des pays membres de l'OPEP et des institutions multilatérales essentiellement financés par ceux-ci, 1970-1983
Millions de dollars

Country / Pays	1970	1971	1972	1973	1974	1975	1976	1977	1978	1979	1980	1981	1982	1983
Afghanistan / Afghanistan	–	–	–	–	40.1	68.6	23.6	42.3	20.0	3.6	–	1.0	–	–
Bangladesh / Bangladesh	–	–	–	–	66.3	102.0	13.6	85.4	75.0	50.0	78.7	227.5	311.2	334.2
Benin / Bénin	–	–	–	–	6.9	–	9.1	2.5	9.7	4.5	4.5	6.0	–	8.9
Bhutan / Bhoutan	–	–	–	–	–	–	–	–	–	–	–	–	–	10.3
Botswana / Botswana	–	–	–	0.1	6.1	5.4	–	1.0	–	4.2	26.6	3.9	24.1	–
Burkina Faso / Burkina Faso	–	–	–	1.0	4.0	2.9	5.5	23.3	8.1	14.4	7.0	12.0	20.2	16.2
Burundi / Burundi	–	–	–	–	–	–	2.2	11.8	6.0	4.5	9.5	33.3	9.0	14.6
Cape Verde / Cap-Vert	–	–	–	–	0.5	0.9	10.5	1.5	1.9	1.0	17.7	1.0	2.5	14.5
Central African Republic / République centrafricaine	–	–	–	–	2.4	0.2	1.8	–	–	3.6	2.1	2.5	10.1	5.8
Chad / Tchad	–	–	–	20.1	13.2	11.0	10.0	2.8	22.4	1.6	2.1	–	–	0.0*
Comoros / Comores	29.1	–	–	–	–	–	20.5	20.1	1.9	34.5	4.4	11.9	34.4	5.9
Democratic Yemen / Yémen démocratique	–	1.3	0.3	1.3	50.3	72.8	184.9	114.8	21.9	63.6	100.8	66.4	77.6	40.8
Djibouti / Djibouti	–	–	–	–	16.7	–	–	19.7	64.0	0.5	62.6	29.8	52.5	52.2
Equatorial Guinea / Guinée équatoriale	–	–	–	–	1.3	–	–	0.5	–	1.0	–	1.0	–	4.7
Ethiopia / Ethiopie	–	–	–	–	1.3	15.4	–	5.7	0.7	0.9	0.1	11.2	–	–
Gambia / Gambie	–	–	–	–	1.8	–	6.4	26.2	2.6	–	31.4	6.5	2.4	1.0
Guinea / Guinée	–	1.0	–	–	21.7	5.9	21.8	12.0	7.5	14.8	180.0	–	24.0	11.2
Guinea-Bissau / Guinée-Bissau	–	–	–	–	3.1	6.2	1.6	2.1	14.0	1.0	5.2	2.5	1.5	24.6
Haiti / Haïti	–	–	–	–	–	–	–	3.2	–	4.0	3.5	4.0	–	2.9
Lao People's Dem. Republic / République dém. pop. lao	–	–	–	–	–	–	–	–	5.0	–	1.5	2.2	–	–
Lesotho / Lesotho	–	–	–	–	3.8	–	–	1.9	5.1	3.0	17.0	3.5	–	3.0
Malawi / Malawi	–	–	–	–	–	–	–	1.8	–	–	–	1.0	0.0	–
Maldives / Maldives	–	–	–	–	–	1.3	6.8	1.5	12.2	2.3	35.4	8.1	3.4	1.4
Mali / Mali	–	–	–	2.3	16.0	25.5	49.1	28.6	20.0	26.3	46.7	25.5	141.1	7.8
Nepal / Népal	–	–	–	2.5	–	17.8	17.1	37.1	3.0	12.2	1.3	11.0	–	30.6
Niger / Niger	–	25.3	–	–	1.1	–	15.8	11.5	17.7	5.2	46.7	100.6	46.9	5.0
Rwanda / Rwanda	–	–	–	–	2.1	11.6	5.0	15.6	–	4.8	3.0	9.3	10.0	18.8
Samoa / Samoa	–	–	–	–	–	0.6	1.6	0.4	1.0	–	0.8	1.0	2.0	0.5
Sao Tome and Principe / Sao Tomé-et-Principe	–	–	–	–	3.7	0.2	10.0	7.1	0.0	5.6	13.9	7.0	–	1.2
Sierra Leone / Sierra Leone	–	5.0	3.0	5.5	73.6	96.8	67.1	430.7	68.3	80.8	13.9	90.0	7.6	1.1
Somalia / Somalie	–	0.1	5.9	30.3	117.1	258.2	286.3	215.9	401.9	169.6	268.5	130.2	205.8	22.4
Sudan / Soudan	–	–	–	–	–	2.0	2.5	0.1	–	–	–	–	118.9	585.1
Togo / Togo	–	–	–	–	24.4	79.8	2.1	14.7	27.2	8.4	10.5	7.4	16.2	21.1
Uganda / Ouganda	–	–	4.0	–	14.2	15.7	5.0	11.6	5.1	–	36.6	85.0	22.0	5.0
United Republic of Tanzania / République-Unie de Tanzanie	–	–	–	–	–	–	–	–	–	–	–	–	–	5.0
Yemen / Yémen	2.2	8.8	6.5	38.6	122.8	172.6	346.4	379.3	397.5	482.2	284.6	192.8	394.8	237.2
All LDCs / Ensemble des PMA	31.3	41.6	19.8	101.6	615.0	974.0	1126.2	1536.0	1220.8	1010.1	1432.3	1105.8	1539.5	1489.4

Source : UNCTAD secretariat estimates.
For 1970-1976 : OECD secretariat estimates.

Source : Estimations du secrétariat de la CNUCED.
Pour 1970-1976 : estimations du Secrétariat de l'OCDE.

Table 51

Tableau 51

ODA commitments from individual OPEC member countries and multilateral agencies mainly financed by them, to LDCs as a group, by purpose, average 1981-1983

Engagements de l'APD de chaque pays membre de l'OPEP et de chaque institution multilatérale essentiellement financée par ceux-ci, en faveur de l'ensemble des PMA, par objet, moyenne 1981-1983

	Agriculture / Agriculture	Mining / Industries extractives	Manufacturing / Industries manufacturières	Electricity gas and water / Électricité gas et eau	Transport and storage / Transports et entrepôts	Other services / Autres services	Multi-purpose / Objet multiple	Balance of payments support / Soutien à la balance des paiements	Distress relief / Secours d'urgence	Other and un-allocated / Autres et non-ventilésa/	Total in $ m. / en m.$	
	Per cent of total / En pourcentage du total											
Bilateral donors												**Donneurs bilatéraux**
Algeria	-	-	-	-	41.2	1.2	-	98.8	-	-	20	Algérie
Iraq	5.8	-	16.0	-	41.2	2.2	-	-	-	34.8	86	Iraq
Kuwait	13.2	-	7.0	25.4	22.7	-	5.4	-	0.4	25.9	688	Koweit
Libyan Arab Jamahiriya	-	-	-	-	-	-	-	-	-	100.0	23	Jamahiriya arabe libyenne
Qatar	-	-	-	-	-	-	-	-	-	100.0	38	Qatar
Saudi Arabia	0.7	1.9	4.0	2.6	6.7	0.9	2.4	21.7	3.6	55.4	2342	Arabie saoudite
United Arab Emirates	-	-	22.7	17.8	9.8	-	-	-	2.9	46.8	126	Emirats arabes unis
Total	3.4	1.4	5.5	7.7	10.9	0.7	2.8	15.9	2.8	48.9	3323	Total
Multilateral donors												**Donneurs multilatéraux**
BADEA	-	-	16.1	8.1	75.3	-	-	-	-	0.5	62	BADEA
AFESD	8.0	-	16.6	41.0	32.7	-	-	-	-	1.8	280	FADES
Islamic Dev. Bank	-	-	-	30.6	28.9	-	11.1	-	-	29.4	67	Banque islamique de développement
OPEC Fund	2.3	6.7	4.5	24.0	11.1	1.2	-	35.5	-	14.6	403	Fonds de l'OPEP
Total	3.9	3.3	9.2	29.2	25.0	0.6	0.9	17.6	-	10.3	811	Total
GRAND TOTAL	3.5	1.7	6.2	12.0	13.6	0.7	2.5	16.2	2.2	41.3	4134	TOTAL GENERAL

Source : UNCTAD secretariat estimates.

Source : Estimations du secrétariat de la CNUCED.

a/ Mainly budget support in the case of bilateral flows.
Mainly technical assistance in the case of multilateral flows.

a/ Principalement soutien budgétaire dans le cas des apports bilatéraux.
Principalement assistance technique dans le cas des apports multilatéraux.

Table 52

Grant element of ODA commitments from individual OPEC member countries and multilateral agencies mainly financed by them, to LDCs as a group, 1977-1983

Tableau 52

Elément de libéralité des engagements de l'APD de chaque pays membre de l'OPEP et de chaque institution multilatérale essen- tiellement financée par ceux-ci, à l'ensemble des PMA, 1977-1983

	1977	1978	1979	1980	1981	1982	1983	Donneurs bilatéraux
Bilateral donors								**Donneurs bilatéraux**
Algeria	100.0	100.0	94.2	-	54.8	100.0	-	Algérie
Iran (Islamic Rep.)	-	-	-	-	-	-	-	Iran (Rép. islamique)
Iraq	50.0	66.6	52.5	56.1	42.4	42.1	-	Iraq
Kuwait	68.2	74.7	71.9	69.6	70.3	66.7	68.5	Koweit
Libyan Arab Jamahiriya	100.0	70.5	100.0	58.7	78.1	-	-	Jamahiriya arabe libyenne
Nigeria	50.0	100.0	100.0	98.0	-	-	-	Nigéria
Qatar	100.0	74.2	100.0	100.0	100.0	100.0	100.0	Qatar
Saudi Arabia	83.9	63.4	71.6	76.8	64.7	82.7	93.1	Arabie saoudite
United Arab Emirates	71.8	83.6	99.1	60.7	51.1	61.4	100.0	Emirats arabes unis
Total	79.6	67.5	67.4	67.2	65.6	76.7	89.9	**Total**
Multilateral donors								**Donneurs multilatéraux**
BADEA	47.4	60.1	39.5	35.7	31.3	32.3	31.7	BADEA
AFESD	42.2	100.0	41.1	37.4	40.1	38.6	38.5	FADES
Islamic Dev. Bank	56.3	49.0	53.0	52.5	51.7	60.6	59.5	Banque islamique de dév.
OPEC Fund	67.8	57.1	60.4	56.0	56.6	61.1	54.4	Fonds de l'OPEP
Total	55.0	57.0	56.0	47.6	51.2	53.1	42.8	**Total**
GRAND TOTAL	75.3	66.7	65.9	64.3	62.1	72.1	82.5	**TOTAL GENERAL**

Source : UNCTAD secretariat estimates.

For abbreviations see pages x and xi.

Source : Estimations du secrétariat de la CNUCED.

Se reporter, pour les abréviations, aux pages xvii et xviii.

Table 53

IMF oil facility, a/ 1974-1983

Net drawings in $ million

Tableau 53

Mécanisme pétrolier du FMI a/ 1974-1983

Tirages nets en millions de dollars

Country	1974	1975	1976	1977	1978	1979	1980	1981	1982	1983	Pays
Afghanistan	-	-	-	-	-	-	-	-	-	-	Afghanistan
Bangladesh	48.6	44.8	17.0	-0.9	-15.3	-27.4	-29.8	-26.2	-12.0	-1.9	Bangladesh
Benin	-	-	-	-	-	-	-	-	-	-	Bénin
Bhutan	-	-	-	-	-	-	-	-	-	-	Bhoutan
Botswana	-	-	-	-	-	-	-	-	-	-	Botswana
Burkina Faso	-	-	-	-	-	-	-	-	-	-	Burkina Faso
Burundi	-	1.5	-	-	-1.5	-	-	-	0.0	-	Burundi
Cape Verde	-	-	-	-	-	-	-	-	-	-	Cap-Vert
Central African Republic	3.2	2.8	1.2	-	-1.0	-1.7	-2.0	-2.0	-0.7	-0.1	République centrafricaine
Chad	2.6	-	-	-	-0.6	-0.8	-0.7	-0.7	-	-	Tchad
Comoros	-	-	-	-	-	-	-	-	-	-	Comores
Democratic Yemen	11.2	8.6	8.5	-	-3.9	-6.5	-7.7	-7.1	-3.2	-1.0	Yémen démocratique
Djibouti	-	-	-	-	-	-	-	-	-	-	Djibouti
Equatorial Guinea	-	-	-	-	-	-	-	-	-	-	Guinée équatoriale
Ethiopia	-	-	-	-	-	-	-	-	-	-	Ethiopie
Gambia	4.2	-	-	-	-	-	-	-	-	-	Gambie
Guinea	-	-	-	-	-0.8	-1.2	-1.4	-0.8	-0.2	-	Guinée
Guinea-Bissau	-	-	-	-	-	-	-	-	-	-	Guinée-Bissau
Haiti	4.6	3.2	3.0	-0.1	-1.6	-2.5	-2.9	-2.6	-1.1	-0.3	Haïti
Lao People's Dem. Republic	-	-	-	-	-	-	-	-	-	-	République dém. pop. lao
Lesotho	-	-	-	-	-	-	-	-	-	-	Lesotho
Malawi	-	2.5	1.5	-	-	-0.9	-1.3	-1.1	-1.0	-0.2	Malawi
Maldives	-	-	-	-	-	-	-	-	-	-	Maldives
Mali	4.8	1.2	4.6	-	-1.5	-2.2	-3.0	-2.6	-1.2	-0.5	Mali
Nepal	-	-	-	-	-	-	-	-	-	-	Népal
Niger	-	-	-	-	-	-	-	-	-	-	Niger
Rwanda	-	-	-	-	-	-	-	-	-	-	Rwanda
Samoa	-	0.4	0.1	-	-	-0.1	-0.1	-0.1	-0.1	-	Samoa
Sao Tome and Principe	-	-	-	-	-	-	-	-	-	-	Sao Tomé-et-Principe
Sierra Leone	5.2	0.7	5.8	-	-1.5	-2.7	-3.1	-2.9	-1.4	-0.4	Sierra Leone
Somalia	-	-	-	-	-	-	-	-	-	-	Somalie
Sudan	34.5	22.2	-	-0.7	-8.3	-14.5	-16.8	-11.9	-5.0	-1.2	Soudan
Togo	-	-	-	-	-	-	-	-	-	-	Togo
Uganda	6.0	17.2	-	-	-12.5	-10.3	-	-0.4	-1.0	-	Ouganda
United Republic of Tanzania	34.2	28.8	-	-1.9	-9.8	-16.8	-16.9	-14.9	-4.5	-	République-Unie de Tanzanie
Yemen	-	-	-	-	-	-	-	-	-	-	Yémen
All LDCs	159.1	134.3	41.7	-3.6	-58.3	-87.6	-85.7	-73.3	-31.4	-5.6	Ensemble des PMA
All developing countries	919.4	1579.0	452.0	-207.6	-783.3	-537.2	-559.1	-535.5	-325.8	-62.6	Ensemble des pays en développement

Source : IMF, International Financial Statistics (various issues).

Source : FMI, International Financial Statistics (divers numéros).

a/ The net contribution by members of OPEC to the IMF oil facility (as measured by their share in IMF borrowings) was 86.1 per cent in 1974, 77.3 per cent in 1975 and 48.6 per cent in 1976.

a/ La contribution nette des membres de l'OPEP au financement du mécanisme pétrolier du FMI (mesurée d'après leur part de montants nets de prêts au FMI) s'est élevée à 86,1 pour cent en 1974, 77,3 pour cent en 1975 et 48,6 pour cent en 1976.

Table 54 / Tableau 54

Balance of payments summary for all LDCs, 1973-1983

Situation récapitulative de la balance des paiements de l'ensemble des PMA, 1973-1983

$ million / Millions de dollars

		1973	1974	1975	1976	1977	1978	1979	1980	1981	1982	1983
1. Exports of goods and services / Exportations de biens et services		3899	4452	4748	5740	6662	6913	8731	10514	10639	9617	9553
1a. Goods f.o.b. / Marchandises f.o.b.		3058	3530	3583	4516	5403	5382	6731	7928	7669	6694	6788
1b. Non-factor services / Services non facteurs		841	922	1165	1224	1259	1531	2000	2586	2970	2923	2765
2. Imports of goods and services / Importations de biens et services		5666	7386	8719	8518	10524	13247	16233	20483	20674	19052	17767
2a. Goods f.o.b. / Marchandises f.o.b.		4255	5589	6665	6468	8028	10067	12405	15938	16313	15201	13909
2b. Non-factor services / Services non facteurs		1411	1797	2054	2050	2496	3180	3828	4544	4361	3852	3858
3. Merchandise balance (1a-2a) / Balance "marchandises" (1a-2a)		-1197	-2060	-3082	-1953	-2625	-4685	-5674	-8010	-8644	-8507	-7121
4. Balance of goods and services (1-2) / Balance des biens et services (1-2)		-1767	-2934	-3971	-2778	-3862	-6334	-7502	-9969	-10035	-9435	-8214
5. Investment income receipts / Revenu des investissements, recettes		92	137	126	154	198	275	392	550	480	437	309
6. Investment income payments / Revenu des investissements, paiements		236	251	281	378	419	559	603	805	872	1004	1041
7. Private transfers (net) / Transferts privés (nets)		333	388	516	1090	1524	1716	1823	2246	2285	2110	2740
8. Current account balance (4+5-6+7) / Balance "compte courant" (4+5-6+7)		-1579	-2661	-3611	-1912	-2561	-4904	-5889	-7970	-8165	-7895	-6208
9. Government transfers (net) / Transferts publics (nets)		1065	1239	1563	1281	1718	2168	3123	3044	3047	3321	2955
10. Long term loans (net) / Prêts à long terme (nets)		879	1360	1508	1092	1094	1828	2231	2728	2187	1677	1745
10a. Government / Publics		730	1218	1364	1056	939	1672	1965	2457	2240	2057	2018
10b. Others / Autres		149	142	144	36	155	156	266	271	-53	-380	-273
11. Direct investment and other long-term capital (net) / Investissements directs et autres capitaux à long terme (nets)		10	18	86	110	88	259	353	356	259	447	309
12. Short-term capital (net) / Capitaux à court terme (nets)		-21	106	511	134	431	688	418	805	1289	318	93
13. Errors and ommissions (net) / Erreurs et omissions (nets)		-147	-99	-62	-45	168	362	128	631	45	269	223
14. Overall balance a/ (8+9+10+11+12+13) / Balance générale a/ (8+9+10+11+12+13)		206	-37	-4	660	938	401	364	-406	-1338	-1863	-883

Source: UNCTAD secretariat estimates based on information from IMF and UNCTAD, Handbook of International Trade and Development Statistics, Supplement 1984 and ibid 1985.

Source: Estimations du secrétariat de la CNUCED d'après des renseignements du FMI et CNUCED, Manuel de statistiques du commerce international et du développement, supplément 1984 et ibid. 1985.

a/ The "overall balance" equals change in reserves (including SDR allocations and gold monetization). A balance with a positive sign corresponds to an increase in reserve holdings and a negative sign indicates a decrease in such holdings. For a description of the balance of payments categories used in this table, see the general notes to table 5.1A of the UNCTAD Handbook of International Trade and Development Statistics, Supplement 1985.

a/ La "balance générale" est égale à la variation des réserves (y compris les allocations de DTS et la monétisation de l'or). Une balance comportant un signe positif correspond à une augmentation des disponibilités en réserves et un signe négatif indique une diminution de ces disponibilités. Pour la description des catégories utilisées dans ce tableau, se référer aux notes générales du tableau 5.1A du Manuel de statistiques du commerce international et du développement, supplément 1985 de la CNUCED.

Table 55

Tableau 55

External debt outstanding a/ 1975, and 1979-1983

Encours de la dette extérieure a/ 1975, et 1979-1983

A. $ million

A. millions de dollars

Country	1975	1979	1980	1981	1982	1982 b/	1983 b/	Pays
Afghanistan	819	1285	1195	1142	1324	1607	1728	Afghanistan
Bangladesh	1601	3348	3614	3938	4359	4314	4623	Bangladesh
Benin	90	237	484	574	566	641	603	Bénin
Bhutan	-	-	-	-	-	2	2	Bhoutan
Botswana	278	295	283	286	389	284	315	Botswana
Burkina Faso	62	260	295	312	367	385	453	Burkina Faso
Burundi	17	112	151	175	223	242	324	Burundi
Cape Verde	1	18	20	40	60	65	80	Cap-Vert
Central African Rep.	82	132	164	171	211	212	220	République centrafricaine
Chad	67	172	156	126	129	169	152	Tchad
Comoros	5	39	50	53	67	73	93	Comores
Democratic Yemen	120	427	549	798	941	1043	1314	Yémen démocratique
Djibouti	27	51	28	22	43	46	68	Djibouti
Equatorial Guinea	27	36	57	67	81	92	103	Guinée équatoriale
Ethiopia	386	616	704	963	1057	1084	1326	Ethiopie
Gambia	14	81	118	145	154	164	179	Gambie
Guinea	848	1064	1111	1291	1283	1346	1335	Guinée
Guinea-Bissau	7	66	104	111	127	131	146	Guinée-Bissau
Haiti	57	227	269	356	394	462	496	Haïti
Lao People's Dem.Rep.	25	77	75	65	60	308	375	République dém. pop. lao
Lesotho	13	54	76	91	131	131	167	Lesotho
Malawi	279	567	746	767	786	747	755	Malawi
Maldives	1	10	28	39	44	50	59	Maldives
Mali	337	533	692	739	811	822	905	Mali
Nepal	38	155	185	243	305	311	348	Népal
Niger	117	406	608	703	690	811	824	Niger
Rwanda	25	127	161	180	195	201	233	Rwanda
Samoa	16	49	57	56	60	64	68	Samoa
Sao Tome and Principe	-	-	-	-	-	18	26	Sao Tomé-et-Principe
Sierra Leone	169	360	389	392	394	445	433	Sierra Leone
Somalia	236	679	749	906	978	1126	1269	Somalie
Sudan	1481	3396	3953	4681	5450	5218	5688	Soudan
Togo	138	858	916	871	816	988	1000	Togo
Uganda	213	492	609	593	654	614	657	Ouganda
United Rep.of Tanzania	836	1592	1734	1951	1988	2059	2350	Rép.-Unie de Tanzanie
Yemen	248	627	984	1223	1406	1454	1805	Yémen
All LDCsc/	8679	18448	21313	24070	26544	27730	30525	Ensemble des PMAC/

For sources and notes see table 55 page 73.

Pour les sources et les notes, se référer au tableau 55, page 73.

Table 55 (continued)

External debt outstanding, 1975, and 1979-1983

Tableau 55 (suite)

Encours de la dette extérieure, 1975, et 1979-83

B. As ratio to exports d/

B. Rapport dette/exportations d/

Country	1975	1979	1980	1981	1982	1982b/	1983b/	Pays
Afghanistan	3.7	2.6	1.7	1.6	1.9	2.3	2.5	Afghanistan
Bangladesh	5.3	5.2	4.9	5.9	6.5	6.5	6.7	Bangladesh
Benin	2.8	7.4	9.0	15.3	16.9	19.1	13.4	Bénin
Bhutan	-	-	-	-	-	..	..	Bhoutan
Botswana	2.0	0.7	0.6	0.8	0.9	0.6	0.5	Botswana
Burkina Faso	1.4	3.4	3.3	4.2	6.6	6.9	7.9	Burkina Faso
Burundi	0.5	1.1	2.3	2.5	2.5	2.8	4.3	Burundi
Cape Verde	0.2	7.2	4.8	12.9	15.4	16.7	20.0	Cap-Vert
Central African Rep.	1.7	1.7	1.4	2.2	1.9	1.9	2.2	République centrafricaine
Chad	1.0	1.2	1.1	0.9	1.0	1.3	1.0	Tchad
Comoros	0.5	2.2	4.4	3.2	3.3	3.7	5.0	Comores
Democratic Yemen	0.7	0.9	0.7	1.3	1.2	1.3	1.9	Yémen démocratique
Djibouti	1.7	4.6	1.5	1.0	2.2	2.3	2.7	Djibouti
Equatorial Guinea	1.0	1.2	4.1	4.2	4.8	5.4	5.2	Guinée équatoriale
Ethiopia	1.6	1.5	1.7	2.6	2.6	2.7	3.3	Ethiopie
Gambia	0.3	1.4	3.7	5.3	3.5	3.7	3.7	Gambie
Guinea	4.4	3.2	2.8	3.1	3.5	3.5	3.1	Guinée
Guinea-Bissau	1.0	4.7	9.5	7.9	10.6	10.9	12.2	Guinée-Bissau
Haiti	0.7	1.5	1.2	2.3	2.4	2.9	3.0	Haïti
Lao People's Dem.Rep.	2.3	2.2	2.4	2.0	1.5	7.7	7.1	République dém. pop. lao
Lesotho	1.0	1.2	1.3	1.9	3.6	3.6	7.2	Lesotho
Malawi	2.0	2.4	2.6	2.8	3.2	3.0	3.3	Malawi
Maldives	0.4	2.1	3.6	4.6	3.3	3.7	5.9	Maldives
Mali	6.2	3.6	3.4	4.8	5.6	5.6	5.4	Mali
Nepal	0.4	1.4	2.3	1.7	3.5	3.6	3.7	Népal
Niger	1.3	0.9	1.1	1.5	2.1	2.4	2.4	Niger
Rwanda	0.6	1.1	2.1	2.0	2.2	2.2	2.9	Rwanda
Samoa	2.2	2.7	3.3	5.1	4.6	4.9	3.6	Samoa
Sao Tome and Principe	-	-	1.9	-	-	1.8	2.6	Sao Tomé-et-Principe
Sierra Leone	1.4	1.7	1.9	2.6	3.5	4.0	3.6	Sierra Leone
Somalia	2.7	6.1	5.6	4.4	4.9	5.7	6.0	Somalie
Sudan	3.4	6.3	7.3	7.1	10.9	10.5	9.1	Soudan
Togo	1.1	3.9	2.7	4.1	4.6	5.6	6.2	Togo
Uganda	0.8	1.1	1.8	2.4	2.0	1.8	1.8	Ouganda
United Rep.of Tanzania	2.2	3.1	3.4	3.4	4.5	4.6	6.5	Rép.-Unie de Tanzanie
Yemen	22.5	44.8	42.8	26.0	36.0	37.3	40.1	Yémen
All LDCsc/	2.4	2.7	2.7	3.4	3.8	4.0	4.2	Ensemble des PMAc/

Source : UNCTAD secretariat based on information from the OECD secretariat.

a/ Disbursed at year end.
b/ Data not comparable with those for previous years.

c/ Total of LDCs for which data are shown
d/ Goods only.

Source : Secrétariat de la CNUCED d'après des renseignements du secrétariat de l'OCDE.

a/ Dette à la fin de l'année (montants versés).
b/ Les données ne sont pas comparables à celles des années précédentes.

c/ Total des PMA pour lesquels les données sont montrées.
d/ Marchandises seulement.

Table 56 / Tableau 56

Debt service payments, 1975 and 1979-1983

Paiements effectués au titre du service de la dette, 1975 et 1979-1983

A. $ million
A. Millions de dollars

Country	1975	1979	1980	1981	1982	1982[a/]	1983[a/]	Pays
Afghanistan	27	13	180	140	112	113	124	Afghanistan
Bangladesh	61	99	109	151	138	138	199	Bangladesh
Benin	9	16	24	55	52	44	56	Bénin
Bhutan	-	-	-	-	-	-	0	Bhoutan
Botswana	22	46	40	36	31	52	23	Botswana
Burkina Faso	8	10	17	15	19	23	17	Burkina Faso
Burundi	2	4	7	6	6	17	18	Burundi
Cape Verde	0	0	0	4	1	1	2	Cap-Vert
Central African Rep.	7	3	2	5	4	3	9	République centrafricaine
Chad	6	15	12	8	1	1	1	Tchad
Comoros	1	2	2	1	1	1	2	Comores
Democratic Yemen	4	13	23	68	46	51	57	Yémen démocratique
Djibouti	4	11	6	5	3	3	3	Djibouti
Equatorial Guinea	2	1	2	4	3	3	5	Guinée équatoriale
Ethiopia	31	28	35	55	61	58	80	Ethiopie
Gambia	0	1	2	7	6	13	6	Gambie
Guinea	54	117	128	118	78	90	80	Guinée
Guinea-Bissau	-	4	4	4	4	4	2	Guinée-Bissau
Haiti	8	12	22	16	16	16	15	Haïti
Lao People's Dem.Rep.	2	3	2	2	2	2	4	République dém. pop. lao
Lesotho	0	2	6	7	14	9	14	Lesotho
Malawi	20	46	70	91	76	65	56	Malawi
Maldives	-	0	0	1	3	3	7	Maldives
Mali	6	21	17	13	12	7	12	Mali
Nepal	5	5	13	8	10	10	13	Népal
Niger	9	46	87	116	151	144	95	Niger
Rwanda	1	2	3	4	6	8	6	Rwanda
Samoa	1	4	5	4	2	3	2	Samoa
Sao Tome and Principe	-	-	-	-	-	3	0	Sao Tomé-et-Principe
Sierra Leone	22	54	43	55	38	20	37	Sierra Leone
Somalia	5	9	20	31	33	23	27	Somalie
Sudan	166	96	100	135	180	132	104	Soudan
Togo	22	52	78	58	38	39	36	Togo
Uganda	20	17	15	61	70	66	98	Ouganda
United Rep.of Tanzania	40	108	115	93	88	87	126	Rép.-Unie de Tanzanie
Yemen	5	23	47	110	89	76	55	Yémen
All LDCs [b/]	570	886	1238	1482	1392	1325	1392	Ensemble des PMA [b/]

For sources and notes, see table 56, page 75.

Pour les sources et les notes, se référer au tableau 56, page 75.

Table 56 (continued)

Debt service payments, 1975, and 1979-1983

Tableau 56 (suite)

Paiements effectués au titre du service de la dette, 1975, et 1979-1983

B. Per cent of exports c/

B. En pourcentage des exportations c/

Country	1975	1979	1980	1981	1982	1982 a/	1983 a/	Pays
Afghanistan	12.2	2.7	25.6	20.2	15.8	16.0	18.2	Afghanistan
Bangladesh	20.1	15.5	14.8	22.8	20.6	20.6	28.8	Bangladesh
Benin	28.6	50.5	44.9	145.6	154.2	131.0	124.4	Bénin
Bhutan	-	-	-	-	-	..	..	Bhoutan
Botswana	15.8	10.6	7.9	9.5	6.8	11.5	3.6	Botswana
Burkina Faso	17.4	13.4	18.9	20.0	33.9	41.1	29.8	Burkina Faso
Burundi	4.9	4.1	11.1	9.2	6.2	19.3	23.7	Burundi
Cape Verde	10.0	6.6	4.2	9.7	39.2	39.2	50.0	Cap-Vert
Central African Rep.	15.8	4.1	2.1	5.2	3.7	2.8	9.0	République centrafricaine
Chad	9.1	11.0	8.3	6.0	0.9	0.9	0.6	Tchad
Comoros	5.0	13.0	15.2	4.2	5.4	5.4	10.9	Comores
Democratic Yemen	2.2	2.7	3.0	11.3	5.8	6.4	8.1	Yémen démocratique
Djibouti	26.9	103.6	32.6	23.5	16.5	16.5	12.0	Djibouti
Equatorial Guinea	6.9	3.4	14.3	25.0	17.6	17.6	25.0	Guinée équatoriale
Ethiopia	13.1	6.7	8.3	14.6	15.2	14.4	19.9	Ethiopie
Gambia	0.9	1.3	4.9	25.1	13.6	29.5	12.2	Gambie
Guinea	27.7	35.8	32.5	28.0	20.2	23.3	18.6	Guinée
Guinea-Bissau	-	25.5	39.9	29.6	29.4	29.4	16.7	Guinée-Bissau
Haiti	9.3	8.2	9.7	10.4	9.9	9.9	9.0	Haïti
Lao People's Dem.Rep.	19.1	9.4	7.4	5.5	3.8	3.8	7.5	République dém. pop. lao
Lesotho	3.3	4.0	10.1	14.3	38.9	25.0	60.3	Lesotho
Malawi	14.5	19.6	24.5	33.9	30.9	26.4	24.5	Malawi
Maldives	-	3.8	4.9	11.2	21.2	21.2	70.0	Maldives
Mali	11.3	14.2	8.1	8.4	8.2	4.8	7.2	Mali
Nepal	4.5	4.9	16.4	5.8	11.1	11.1	13.9	Népal
Niger	10.4	10.3	15.4	25.4	45.3	43.2	27.9	Niger
Rwanda	2.4	2.2	4.2	4.6	6.3	8.9	7.6	Rwanda
Samoa	17.1	20.1	26.9	32.1	15.9	23.1	10.5	Samoa
Sao Tome and Principe	-	-	-	-	-	30.0	..	Sao Tomé-et-Principe
Sierra Leone	18.0	26.3	21.1	35.9	34.2	18.0	31.1	Sierra Leone
Somalia	5.7	8.4	15.1	14.9	16.4	11.6	12.9	Somalie
Sudan	37.9	17.8	18.4	20.5	36.1	26.5	16.7	Soudan
Togo	17.4	23.9	23.2	27.4	21.5	22.0	22.2	Togo
Uganda	7.8	3.9	4.4	24.9	20.9	19.7	26.7	Ouganda
United Rep.of Tanzania	10.7	21.1	22.7	16.0	19.8	19.6	34.7	Rép.-Unie de Tanzanie
Yemen	48.7	161.8	202.4	234.0	228.2	194.9	122.2	Yémen
All LDCs b/	16.0	13.2	15.9	20.8	20.1	19.1	19.4	Ensemble des PMA b/

Source : UNCTAD secretariat, based on information from the OECD secretariat.

a/ Data not comparable with those for previous years.

b/ Total of LDCs for which data are shown.

c/ Goods only.

Source : Secrétariat de la CNUCED, d'après des renseignements du secrétariat de l'OCDE.

a/ Les données ne sont pas comparables à celles des années précédentes.

b/ Total des PMA pour lesquels des données sont montrées.

c/ Marchandises seulement.

Table 57 A

Area and population distribution

Tableau 57A

Superficie du pays et distribution de la population

Country	Area / Superficie		Population			Labour force participation rate[b] / Taux d'activité[b] /			Pays
	Total Totale (000 km2/)	% of arable land and land under permanent crops % de terres arables et sous cultures permanentes	Density Densité Pop./km2	Total Totale (mill.)	Urban Urbaine %	M	F	T	
	1982	1982	1983	1983	1983	1980-1982			
Afghanistan	647.5	12.4	27	17.2	17	53	13	34	Afghanistan
Bangladesh	144.0	63.4	657	94.7	17	57	13	36	Bangladesh
Benin	112.6	16.0	34	3.8	16	51	39	45	Bénin
Bhutan	47.0	2.0	29	1.4	4	..	..	56	Bhoutan
Botswana	600.4	2.3	2	1.0	22[a]/	43	40	42	Botswana
Burkina Faso	274.2	9.6	24	6.6	11	55	47	51	Burkina Faso
Burundi	27.8	46.9	160	4.5	2	53	41	47	Burundi
Cape Verde	4.0	9.9	78	0.3	27[a]/	56	6	29	Cap-Vert
Central African Rep.	623.0	3.1	4	2.5	44	58	50	54	Rép. Centrafricaine
Chad	1284.0	2.5	4	4.8	20	57	17	37	Tchad
Comoros	2.2	42.4	199	0.4	22[a]/	48	26	37	Comores
Democratic Yemen	333.0	0.6	6	2.2	37	47	3	24	Yémen démocratique
Djibouti	22.0	0.0	16	0.3	66[a]/	..	..	..	Djibouti
Equatorial Guinea	28.1	8.2	13	0.4	56[a]/	54	3	28	Guinée équatoriale
Ethiopia	1221.9	11.5	28	33.9	15	54	28	41	Ethiopie
Gambia	11.3	14.2	62	0.7	19[a]/	50	41	46	Gambie
Guinea	245.9	6.4	21	5.2	26	54	34	44	Guinée
Guinea Bissau	36.1	7.9	24	0.9	25[a]/	58	2	29	Guinée-Bissau
Haiti	27.8	32.3	191	5.3	27	53	42	47	Haïti
Lao P.D.R.	236.8	3.8	18	4.2	15	50	40	45	Rép. dém. pop. lao
Lesotho	30.4	9.8	48	1.4	13	58	44	51	Lesotho
Malawi	118.5	19.7	54	6.4	11	53	30	42	Malawi
Maldives	0.3	10.0	564	0.2	21[a]/	55[c]/	36[c]/	46[c]/	Maldives
Mali	1240.0	1.7	6	7.5	19	55	48	52	Mali
Nepal	140.8	16.6	112	15.7	7	58	37	48	Népal
Niger	1267.0	2.9	5	5.8	14	56	6	31	Niger
Rwanda	26.3	39.3	216	5.7	5	55	49	52	Rwanda
Samoa	2.8	42.7	57	0.2	24[a]/	..	..	..	Samoa
Sao Tome & Principe	1.0	37.5	95	0.1	32[a]/	..	..	30	Sao Tomé-et-Principe
Siera Leone	71.7	24.7	48	3.5	23	48	25	36	Sierra Leone
Somalia	637.7	1.8	8	5.3	33	55	21	38	Somalie
Sudan	2505.8	5.0	8	20.4	20	55	7	31	Soudan
Togo	56.8	25.1	50	2.8	22	49	32	40	Togo
Uganda	236.0	24.7	62	14.6	7	54	27	40	Ouganda
U. R. of Tanzania	945.1	5.5	22	21.0	14	53	29	41	R.-U. de Tanzanie
Yemen	195.0	14.3	39	7.7	18	50	3	25	Yémen
ALL LDCs	13404.7	6.7	23	308.4	16	55	22	39	Ensemble des PMA
All developing countries	67967.7	10.4	35	2401.2	34	51	22	37	Ensemble des pays en développement

Source: United Nations, Demographic Yearbook, 1981 and 1983;
FAO, Production Yearbook, 1983; World Bank, World
Development Report (various issues); World Bank, Social
Indicators Data Sheets (various issues).

Source: Nations Unies, Annuaire démographique 1981 et 1983;
FAO, Annuaire de la production 1983; Banque
mondiale, Rapport sur le développement dans le
monde (divers numéros); Banque mondiale, Social
Indicators Data Sheets (divers numéros).

a/ Year other than 1982.
b/ Economically active population as a percentage of total
population of sex(es) specified of all ages.
c/ 1977.

a/ Année autre que 1982.
b/ Population active en pourcentage de la population
totale de tous âges du sexe ou des sexes précisés.
c/ 1977.

Table 57B

Birth and death rates, life expectancy

Tableau 57B

Taux de natalité et de mortalité, espérance de vie

Country	Infant mortality rate (per 1000 live births) Taux de mortalité infantile (pour 1000 naissance vivantes)		Average life expectancy at birth (Years) Espérance de vie moyenne à la naissance (années)						Crude bith rate (per 1000) Taux brut de natalité (pour 1000)		Crude death rate (per 1000) Taux brut de mortalité (pour 1000)		Pays
	1975-80	1980-85	1975-80			1980-85			1975-80	1980-85	1975-80	1980-85	
			M	F	T	M	F	T					
Afghanistan	205	205	37	37	37	37	37	37	48.9	49.6	27.0	27.3	Afghanistan
Bangladesh	140	133	47	46	47	48	47	48	47.2	44.8	18.9	17.5	Bangladesh
Benin	160	149	39	42	41	41	44	43	51.1	51.0	24.6	22.5	Bénin
Bhutan	156	144	45	43	44	47	45	46	40.0	38.4	19.8	18.1	Bhoutan
Botswana	87	79	51	54	53	53	56	55	50.5	50.0	14.0	12.7	Botswana
Burkina Faso	160	149	39	42	40	40	44	42	48.1	47.8	24.0	22.2	Burkina Faso
Burundi	149	137	40	44	42	42	46	44	48.3	47.6	23.0	20.9	Burundi
Cape Verde	87	77	53	56	55	55	59	57	25.9	23.9	11.3	10.3	Cap-Vert
Central African Rep.	154	143	39	43	41	41	45	43	44.9	44.7	23.5	21.8	Rép. centrafricaine
Chad	154	143	39	43	41	41	45	43	44.1	44.2	23.1	21.4	Tchad
Comoros	97	88	46	50	48	48	52	50	46.5	46.3	17.1	15.9	Comores
Democratic Yemen	153	138	43	45	44	46	48	47	47.6	47.6	20.9	18.8	Yémen démocratique
Djibouti	30a/	..	..	..	..	..	..	50e/	..	49.2e/	..	18.3e/	Djibouti
Equatorial Guinea	149	137	40	44	42	42	46	44	42.5	42.5	22.7	21.0	Guinée équatoriale
Ethiopia	155	143	39	43	41	41	45	43	49.3	49.2	23.4	21.5	Ethiopie
Gambia	204	193	32	35	34	34	37	35	48.3	48.4	30.4	29.0	Gambie
Guinea	171	159	37	40	38	39	42	40	46.9	46.8	25.3	23.5	Guinée
Guinea-Bissau	154	143	39	43	41	41	45	43	40.9	40.7	21.9	21.7	Guinée-Bissau
Haiti	121	108	49	52	51	51	54	53	41.8	41.3	15.7	14.2	Haïti
Lao P.D.R.	135	122	46	49	48	48	51	50	43.1	40.6	17.3	15.5	Rép. dém. pop. lao
Lesotho	120	110	46	49	47	48	51	49	41.9	41.7	17.8	16.4	Lesotho
Malawi	179	165	41	45	43	43	47	45	52.6	52.1	21.6	19.9	Malawi
Maldives	120b/	79c/	..	..	..	..	..	..	45.6b/	44.5	14.3b/	13.3c/	Maldives
Mali	160	149	39	42	40	40	44	42	50.4	50.2	24.4	22.4	Mali
Nepal	156	144	45	43	44	47	45	46	44.6	41.7	20.5	18.4	Népal
Niger	151	140	39	42	41	41	44	43	50.9	51.0	25.0	22.9	Niger
Rwanda	119	110	46	49	48	48	51	50	51.1	51.1	18.1	16.6	Rwanda
Samoa	13d/	..	..	..	..	..	..	65e/	17.3d/	..	3.1d/	..	Samoa
Sao Tome & Principe	72b/	70c/	..	..	..	..	..	62e/	38.5b/	38.7c/	10.2b/	10.2c/	Sao Tomé-et-Principe
Sierra Leone	215	200	31	34	32	33	36	34	47.8	47.4	31.9	29.7	Sierra Leone
Somalia	155	143	39	43	41	41	45	43	46.3	46.5	21.1	21.3	Somalie
Sudan	131	118	44	46	45	47	49	48	47.1	45.9	19.4	17.4	Soudan
Togo	124	113	45	48	47	47	51	49	45.5	45.4	18.6	16.9	Togo
Uganda	100	94	48	52	50	50	54	52	50.1	49.9	16.2	14.7	Ouganda
U. R. of Tanzania	107	98	47	51	49	49	53	51	50.9	50.4	16.8	15.3	Rép.-Unie de Tanzanie
Yemen	170	154	40	42	41	43	45	44	48.6	48.5	24.1	21.6	Yémen
ALL LDCs	145	136	44	45	44	45	47	46	47.9	46.8	20.7	19.1	Ensemble des PMA
All developing countries	124	115	50	51	50	51	52	52	38.6	36.7	14.2	12.9	Ensemble des pays en développement

Source: United Nations, Demographic Indicators By Countries assessed in 1980 and 1982); United Nations Demographic Yearbook 1981 and 1983; World Bank, Social Indicators Data Sheets, (various issues); World Bank, World Development Report,(various issues).

Source: Nations Unies, Indicateurs démographiques par pays (estimés en 1980 et 1982); Nations Unies, Annuaire démographique 1981 et 1983; Banque mondiale, Social Indicators Data Sheets, (divers numeros); Banque mondiale, Rapport sur le développement dans le monde, (divèrs numeros).

a/ 1978.
b/ 1979.
c/ 1982.
d/ 1980.
e/ Most recent estimates available between 1980 and 1982.

a/ 1978.
b/ 1979.
c/ 1982.
d/ 1980.
e/ Année la plus récente disponible entre 1980 et 1982.

Table 57C

Health at birth

Tableau 57C

Santé à la naissance

Country	Low-birth-weight infants (percentage) Enfants de poids insuffisant à la naissance (pour cent) 1979	1982	Year[b]/ année[b]/	% of women attended during childbirth by trained personnel % de femmes ayant reçu des soins prodigués par du personnel qualifié pendant l'accouchement Trained personnel[c]/ Personnel qualifié[c]/	Institutional delivery[d]/ Accouchement dans une institution[d]/	Pays
Afghanistan	..	20.0	(1978)	5		Afghanistan
Bangladesh	50.0	50.0	1984		1	Bangladesh
Benin	..	9.6	(1982)		19	Bénin
Bhutan	..	..	(1982)		1	Bhoutan
Botswana	..	12.0	(1984)	52		Botswana
Burkina Faso	21.0	..	1979	5		Burkina Faso
Burundi	13.5	..	1978		15	Burundi
Cape Verde	..	..	1979	53[e]/	51[e]/	Cap-Vert
Central African Rep.	23.0	..	..	..	..	République centrafricaine
Chad	10.5	10.5	1978	45		Tchad
Comoros	..	..	(1982)		35	Comores
Democratic Yemen	..	..	..	..	..	Yémen démocratique
Djibouti	..	..	..	..	..	Djibouti
Equatorial Guinea	..	..	..	..	..	Guinée équatoriale
Ethiopia	13.1	13.1	(1980)	10-15		Ethiopie
Gambia	14.0	14.0	1978		25	Gambie
Guinea	18.0	..	(1980)		90	Guinée
Guinea Bissau	9.0	13.0	..	..	..	Guinée-Bissau
Haiti	..	..	(1984)		15	Haiti
Lao People's Dem. Rep.	18.0	..	..	..	..	Rép. dém. pop. lao
Lesotho	14.5	7.6	..	..	..	Lesotho
Malawi	..	12.0	1979	40		Malawi
Maldives	..	..	..	..	..	Maldives
Mali	12.7	..	(1981)	14		Mali
Nepal	..	..	(1982)		4	Népal
Niger	..	15.0	1980	25		Niger
Rwanda	17.0	19.9	1979	25		Rwanda
Samoa	..	..	..	..	..	Samoa
Sao Tome and Principe	..	..	(1983)	88		Sao Tomé-et-Principe
Sierra Leone	..	17.0	1976	30		Sierra Leone
Somalia	..	..	(1983)	2		Somalie
Sudan	16.7	16.7	(1976)	33[f]/	25[g]/	Soudan
Togo	..	16.9	1978		50	Togo
Uganda	10.0	..	..	..	..	Ouganda
United Rep. of Tanzania	13.0	14.4	(1983)	50		R.-U de Tanzanie
Yemen	..	..	1982	11[h]/	6[h]/	Yémen
All LDCs[a]/	29.3	27.1		16	9	Ensemble des PMA[a]/
All developing countries	21.4	20.6		35	..	Ensemble des pays en développpement

Source: WHO, World Health Statistics Quarterly 33(3) (1980) and 38(3), 1985; Weekly Epidemiological Record No. 27, 6 July 1984.

a/ Average of LDCs which data are shown. b/ The year to which the information refers, or if this is not known, the year of publication of the information, in brackets. c/ Trained personnel includes physicians, nurses, midwives, trained primary health care and other workers and trained traditional birth attendants. d/ "Institution" includes public and private hospitals, clinics, health centres. e/ Survey or sample, Sao Vicente only. f/ Rural areas only (1976). g/ Khartoum only (1983). h/ Survey or sample.

Source: OMS, Rapport Trimestriel de statistiques sanitaires mondiales 33(3) 1980 et 38(3) 1985; OMS, Relevé épidémiologique hebdomadaire No. 27, 6 juillet 1984.

a/ Moyenne des PMA pour lesquelles les données sont disponibles. b/ Année à laquelle se rapporte les données, ou si cette année n'est pas connue, année de publication des données, entre parenthèses. c/ Sont englobés dans l'appelation "Personnel qualifié" les médicins, sages-femmes, agents de santé communautaires et autres personnels qualifiés ainsi que les accoucheurs traditionnels ayant reçu une formation. d/ Institution: comprend les hopitaux publics et privés, les cliniques et les centres de soins. e/ Sondage ou échantillon, Sao Vicente uniquement. f/ Zones rurales uniquement (1976). g/ Khartoum uniquement. h/ Sondage ou échantillon.

Table 57D   Tableau 57D

Food and Water   **Alimentation et eau**

Country / Pays	Average daily calorie intake per capita — Disponibilités alimentaires (calories par personne par jour)		Percentage of population with access to safe water or adequate sanitation — Pourcentage de la population disposant d'eau saine ou de mesures suffisantes d'hygiène du milieu							
			Urban/urbain				Rural			
			Water — Eau		Sanitation — Hygiène du milieu		Water — Eau		Sanitation — Hygiène du milieu	
	Average — Moyenne 1982	As % of requirements — En % des besoins 1982	1980	1983	1980	1983	1980	1983	1980	1983
Afghanistan	2285	94	28	..	..	..	8	..	..	..
Bangladesh	1922	83	26	29	21	21	40	43	1	2
Bénin	2154	101	26	..	48	..	15	14	4	..
Bhutan	..	..	50	40b/	..	90	5	47	..	23
Botswana	2222a/	85a/	..	98	..	..	..	..	..	..
Burkina Faso	1879	79	27	..	38	50	31	22	5	..
Burundi	2206	95	90	90	40	50	20	22	35	52
Cape Verde	2716a/	130a/	100	99	34	49	21	27	10	8
Central African Rep.	2194	97	..	..	..	..	..	..	..	..
Chad	1620	68	..	..	..	..	..	..	..	..
Comoros	2291a/	104a/	..	..	..	..	..	..	..	..
Democratic Yemen	2329	97	85	73	70	69	25	39	15	33
Djibouti	..	..	50	80	43	75	20	40	20	18
Equatorial Guinea	..	..	..	47	..	99	..	..	..	..
Ethiopia	2162	93	85	..	..	..	..	36	..	..
Gambia	2260a/	88a/	69	100	54	..	..	..	..	..
Guinea	1987	86	18	..	21	22	2	37	1	18
Guinea-Bissau	2282a/	70a/	48	21	..	..	8	25	13	12
Haiti	1903	84	21	58	..	41	12	20	..	13
Lao People's Dem.Rep.	1992	90	37	28	..	13	..	..	14	4
Lesotho	2285	100	77	66	13	..	11	11	..	1
Malawi	2242	97	11	54	100	75	37	49	81	1
Maldives	1983a/	97a/	37	46	60	71	3	7	1	1
Mali	1731	74	83	71	79	91	0	8	0	3
Nepal	2018	86	41	41	16	16	7	11	1	1
Niger	2456	105	48	55	36	36	32	33	3	3
Rwanda	2202	95	48	95	60	60	55	60	50	60
Samoa	2527a/	88a/	97	..	86	82	94	94	83	86
Sao Tome & Principe	2351a/	92a/	..	61	31	52	..	6	..	..
Sierra Leone	2049	85	50	65	..	48	2	21	6	10
Somalia	2102	91	60	100	..	73	20	31	..	5
Sudan	2250	96	100	100	24	24	31	31	..	..
Togo	2167	94	70	68	..	34c/	31	26	10	8
Uganda	1807	78	45	45	..	83	8	12	..	10
U. R. of Tanzania	2331	101	100	88	60	75	18	39	..	47
Yemen	2346	97	100	100	..	..	..	21	..	..
ALL LDCs d/	2067	89	49	58	36	47	28	34	8	12
All developing countries	2451	107	74	74	50	53	33	40	11	11

Pays (in order): Afghanistan, Bangladesh, Bénin, Bhoutan, Botswana, Burkina Faso, Burundi, Cap-Vert, République centrafricaine, Tchad, Comores, Yémen démocratique, Djibouti, Guinée équatoriale, Ethiopie, Gambie, Guinée, Guinée-Bissau, Haïti, République dém. pop. lao, Lesotho, Malawi, Maldives, Mali, Népal, Niger, Rwanda, samoa, Sao Tomé-et-Principe, Sierra Leone, Somalie, Soudan, Togo, Ouganda, République-Unie de Tanzanie, Yémen, Ensemble des PMA d/, Ensemble des pays en développement.

Source: World Bank, World Development Report 1985, WHO, The International Drinking Water Supply and Sanitation Decade: Review of National Baseline Data (as at 31 December 1980) and other data supplied by WHO.

Source: Banque mondiale, Rapport sur le développement dans le monde 1985; OMS, The International Drinking Water Supply and Sanitation Decade: Review of National Baseline Data (au 31 déc. 1980) et autres données fournies par l'OMS.

a/ Year other than 1982. b/ House connection. c/ Sewer connection. d/ Average of countries for which data are available.

a/ Année autre que 1982. b/ Raccordement à domicile. c/ Raccordement à l'égout. d/ Moyenne des pays sur lesquels les données sont disponibles.

Table 57E

Tableau 57E

Education and literacy

Enseignement et alphabétisme

Country / Pays	Adult literacy rate (%) – Taux d'alphabétisme (adultes) around/vers 1985 M	F	T	Number of illiterates (000) – nombre d'illettrés around 1985/vers 1985 M	F	T	School enrolment ratio (% of relevant age group) – Taux d'inscription scolaire – Primary/Primaire 1980 M	F	T	Primary 1982 M	F	T	Secondary/Secondaire 1980 M	F	T	Secondary 1982 M	F	T
Afghanistan	39	8	24	3114	4491	7605	54	12	34	56	13g	35g	16	4	10	18g	5g	12g
Bangladesh	43	22	33	16313	20961	37274	78	48	63	68d	51d	60d	23	7	15	24g	6g	15g
Benin	37	16	26	679	951	1630	84	39	62	87	42	65	24	9	16	30	12	21
Bhutan	..	..	..	56	83	139	15f	7f	11f	30d	16d	23d	2e	..	1f	5d	1d	3d
Botswana	73	69	71	..	..	..	92	111	102	94g	110g	102g	21	23	22	21g	25g	23g
Burkina Faso	21	6	13	1697	2079	3776	24	14	19	28	16	22	4	2	3	4	2	3
Burundi	43a/b	26a/b	34a/b	..	..	..	34	22	28	41f	25g	33g	4	2	3	4g	2g	3g
Cape Verde	61	39	47	..	..	..	..	..	..	..	..	..	..	..	..	..	..	..
Central African Rep.	53	29	40	327	560	887	89	49	68	92f	50g	70g	20	6	13	21g	7g	14g
Chad	..	..	..	..	..	..	..	..	..	..	..	..	..	..	..	..	..	..
Comoros	..	..	..	..	..	..	120	85	103	..	..	..	33	17	25	..	..	..
Democratic Yemen	59	25	41	233	451	684	93	37	65	94f	34g	64g	26	11	18	24g	11g	18g
Djibouti	..	..	37c	..	..	..	..	..	..	..	..	..	..	..	..	..	..	..
Equatorial Guinea	..	..	55b/d	..	..	105c	..	..	..	60g	33g	46g	..	..	..	..	..	..
Ethiopia	..	..	..	..	..	..	56	30	43	71	41	56	14	8	11	16g	8g	12g
Gambia	36	15	25	120	165	285	62	33	48	..	..	..	18	8	13	22	10	16
Guinea	..	..	..	..	..	..	44	22	33	..	..	..	23	9	16	..	..	..
Guinea-Bissau	46	17	31	101	160	261	128	59	93	119	57	88	14	3	9	23	6	15
Haiti	40	35	38	1080	1238	2318	75	64	69	74f	64g	69g	14	12	13	13g	12g	13g
Lao People's Dem. Rep.	92e	76e	84e	..	..	..	105	89	97	..	..	..	22	14	18	..	..	20
Lesotho	..	..	..	..	..	..	84f	123f	104f	95	129	112	13f	20f	17f	..	..	..
Malawi	..	..	..	..	..	..	70	49	59	..	..	..	5	2	4	..	..	..
Maldives	..	..	..	..	..	..	..	..	..	..	..	..	..	..	..	..	..	..
Mali	23	11	17	1625	1979	3604	35h	20h	27h	34g	19g	26g	13h	5h	9h	..	..	..
Nepal	39	12	26	2892	4001	6893	126	53	91	102	42	73	33	9	21	32	9	21
Niger	..	..	..	562	1025	1587	29h	17h	23h	..	..	..	5h	2h	4h	..	..	5g
Rwanda	61	33	47	..	..	..	74	67	70	72	67	70	3	1	2	..	..	2
Samoa	..	..	..	..	..	..	..	..	..	..	..	..	..	..	..	..	..	..
Sao Tome & Principe	..	..	..	..	..	..	..	..	..	..	..	..	..	..	..	..	..	..
Sierra Leone	18	6	12	1088	1683	2771	45i	30i	37i	..	..	..	16i	7i	12i	..	..	..
Somalia	..	..	..	..	..	..	38	21	30	..	..	..	16	6	11	..	..	..
Sudan	..	..	..	376	606	982	60	43	51	61g	43g	52g	20	12	16	20g	15g	18g
Togo	54	28	41	..	..	..	144	89	116	129	84	106	49	16	33	41	14	27
Uganda	..	..	..	..	..	..	58	44	51	69	51	60	7	3	5	11	5	8
U. R. of Tanzania	..	..	..	1166	1924	3090	107	95	101	101	95	98	5	2	4	4g	2g	3g
Yemen	27	3	14	..	..	..	82	12	47	99	17	59	9	2	5	12	2	7
All LDCs / Ensemble des PMA	42	20	35	..	..	..	72	44	58	71j	47j	59j	17	7	12	19j	7j	13j
All developing countries / Ensemble des pays en développement	65	46	56	..	..	..	95	77	86	98j	84j	91j	37	25	31	40j	31j	36j

Source: UNESCO

a/ 1982. b/ Age group 10+. c/ 1980. d/ 1983. e/ Age group 15-45. f/ 1979. g/ 1981. h/ 1978. i/ 1977. j/ Average of countries for which data are shown.

a/ 1982. b/ Groupe d'âge 10+. c/ 1980. d/ 1983. e/ Groupe d'âge 15-45. f/ 1979. g/ 1981. h/ 1978. i/ 1977. j/ Moyenne des pays pour lesquels les données sont disponibles.

Table 57F
Communications and media

Tableau 57F
Communications et médias

Country / Pays	Newsprint consumption — Consommation de papier journal (Kg per 1000 inhabitants / Kg pour 1000 habitants)		Mail traffic — Courrier postal (number of items per 100 inhabitants / nombre d'envois pour 100 habitants)			Number of calls per telephone — Nombre d'appels par téléphone	Telephones per 1000 inhabitants — Téléphones pour 1000 habitants	Radio receivers per 1000 inhabitants — Postes récepteurs de radio pour 1000 habitants	
			Domestic / Intérieur	Foreign / Étranger					
	1980	1982	1983	Received / Reçu 1983	sent / Envoyé 1983	1983	1983	1980	1982
Afghanistan	6	6	56b/	10b/	8b/	4.0c/	1.6k/	75	80
Bangladesh	127	340	287c/	80c/	37c/	3342.3h/i/	1.8k/	8l/	8l/
Benin	29	27	61d/	207d/	104d/	45.2b/	4.0k/	72	73
Bhutan	..	..	1380c/e/	29c/e/	21c/e/	..	1.5k/	5l/	8l/
Botswana	..	..	..	..	..	303.5i/	17.8	75	103
Burkina Faso	..	..	19d/	13d/	5d/	4.9b/	2.1	18	19
Burundi	..	..	143	75	63	379.3	1.3	36	38
Cape Verde	..	..	..	..	..	..	5.6i/	137	139
Central African Rep.	..	..	..	..	..	43.0i/	1.7k/	52	56
Chad	..	..	..	..	..	140.7k/	0.5k/	26	26
Comoros	254	430	181	458	174	..	4.8k/	107	120
Democratic Yemen	..	..	70	227	174	530.0b/	20.9	51	55
Djibouti	..	..	..	..	..	5.5i/		55	51
Equatorial Guinea	64	61	5f/	6f/	3f/	562.1i/	3.0k/	284	300
Ethiopia	..	..	48c/g/	9c/g/	4c/g/	..	3.3	97	91
Gambia	..	..	..	..	..	32.1i/	6.2k/	107	111
Guinea	124	118	346d/	168d/	167d/	954.1h/	3.2k/	28	30
Guinea-Bissau	120	115	380d/	16930d/	4726d/	1032.2d/	3.8k/	31	32
Haiti	51	49	9c/	40c/	12c/	..	4.0k/	20	21
Lao People's Dem. Rep.	..	..	727b/e/	1094b/	423b/e/	..	2.2k/	90	95
Lesotho	101	16	..	530	188	98.6d/	4.3k/	22l/	28l/
Malawi	..	..	526	312c/	428c/	..	5.7	46	46
Maldives	29	27	16c/	31	21	46.8	13.0k/	45	74
Mali	..	..	20	..	..	3863.9h/	1.2k/	15	16
Nepal	19	18	42	42	15	..	1.2	20	23
Niger	..	..	159b/	75b/	98b/	28.2i/j/	1.7i/	47	48
Rwanda	..	..	368b/	6623b/	2482b/	38.8h/	0.9k/	29	29
Samoa	..	3125	10	52	39	..	25.6k/	204	400
Sao Tome and Principe	61	59	..	..	..	834.5	23.8	271	281
Sierra Leone	43	39	..	..	..	..	4.7k/	137	191
Somalia	86	81	232c/e/	69c/e/	59c/e/	..	1.6k/	19	25
Sudan	..	..	67c/	587c/	235c/	43.7d/	3.4k/	74	73
Togo	15	14	..	..	..	..	4.2	213	209
Uganda	..	173	368c/	188c/f/	122c/	5568.9k/	3.7	22	22
United Rep. of Tanzania	186	..	29	138	41	94.7	5.0k/	27	26
Yemen	..	..	..	..	..	..	5.0k/	16	16
All LDCs — Ensemble des PMA	94a/	175a/	215a/	438a/	147a/	..	2.8	40	41
All developing countries — Ensemble des pays en développement	1280	1370	1050	179	112	..	25.8	110	130

Source: UNESCO, Statistical Yearbook 1984, Universal Postal Union Statistics des services postaux 1980 and 1983; United Nations, Statistical Yearbook 1979,1980 and 1981; ITU, Yearbook of Common Carrier Telecommunication Statistics (12th edition) and ITU, "Telecommunication for all" Nov. 1983.

a/ Total of LDCs for which data are shown. b/ 1978. c/ 1980. d/ 1977. e/ Excluding "small packets". f/ Letters only. g/ Excluding "Printed Matter". h/ 1979. i/ Total national traffic only. j/ 1982. k/ 1981. l/ The number of licences issued or sets declared.

Source: UNESCO, Annuaire statistique 1984; Union Postale Universelle, Statistique des services postaux 1980 et 1983; Nations Unies, Annuaire statistique 1979,1980 et 1981; UIT, Annuaire statistique des télécommunications du secteur public (12e édition); UIT, "Télécommunications for all" nov. 1983.

a/ Total des PMA pour lesquels les données sont indiquées. b/ 1978. c/ 1980. d/ 1977. e/ "Petits paquets" non compris. f/ Lettres seulement. g/ Non compris "Imprimés". h/ 1979. i/ Trafic national total seulement. j/ 1982. k/ 1981. l/ Nombre de licences délivrées ou de postes déclarés.

Table 57G   Tableau 57G

Energy   Energie

Country	Coal, oil, gas and electricity Charbon, pétrole, gaz et électricité Consumption per capita in Kg of coal equivalent Consommation par habitant en Kg équivalent en charbon			Fuelwood, charcoal & bagasse Bois de chauffage, charbon de bois et bagasse	Installed electricity capacity (Kw./1000 pop.) Puissance électrique installée (Kw./1000 hab.)			Pays
	1980	1981	1982	1981	1980	1981	1982	
Afghanistan	48	48	50	141	25	24	23	Afghanistan
Bangladesh	44	46	50	38	11	11	11	Bangladesh
Benin	50	41	40	342	4	4	4	Bénin
Bhutan	3	3	3	751	9	8	8	Bhoutan
Botswana	424a/	377b/	..	..	..	..	..	Botswana
Burkina Faso	33	31	32	336	6	6	6	Burkina Faso
Burundi	14	20	17	58	2	2	2	Burundi
Cape Verde	150	148	184	..	20	20	26	Cap-Vert
Central African Rep.	42	40	42	362	13	13	13	Rép. centrafricaine
Chad	23	22	21	541	8	8	8	Tchad
Comoros	46	44	43	..	10	10	10	Comores
Democratic Yemen	499	567	759	..	51	64	62	Yémen démocratique
Djibouti	358	327	301	..	81	77	75	Djibouti
Equatorial Guinea	71	89	84	384	20	19	19	Guinée équatoriale
Ethiopia	31	31	31	248	10	10	10	Ethiopie
Gambia	115	111	113	441	17	16	16	Gambie
Guinea	87	84	84	212	36	35	35	Guinea
Guinea-Bissau	54	52	51	169	9	8	8	Guinée-Bissau
Haiti	65	66	62	327	24	25	24	Haïti
Lao People's Dem. Rep.	55	67	62	283	64	62	61	Rép. dém. pop. lao
Lesotho	..	..	..	..	..	..	..	Lesotho
Malawi	59	54	52	574	18	18	18	Malawi
Maldives	39	44	55	..	13	13	12	Maldives
Mali	29	27	29	1396	6	6	6	Mali
Nepal	11	12	11	297	5	5	5	Nepal
Niger	49	49	50	172	4	4	4	Niger
Rwanda	19	23	21	316	8	7	7	Rwanda
Samoa	306	323	344	164	83	82	81	Samoa
Sao Tome & Principe	200	195	191	..	47	46	45	Sao Tomé-et-Principe
Sierra Leone	90	110	91	773	29	28	28	Sierra Leone
Somali	95	108	103	56	7	6	6	Somalie
Sudan	82	86	86	595	16	16	16	Soudan
Togo	112	162	197	68	14	13	13	Togo
Uganda	27	23	24	111	12	12	12	Ouganda
U. R. of Tanzania	46	45	45	602	14	13	13	R.-U. de Tanzanie
Yemen	78	84	99	12	9	14	14	Yémen
All LDCs	49	53	55	260	13	13	13	Ensemble des PMA
All developing countries	468	463	473	206	106	111	114	Ensemble des pays en développement

Source: United Nations, Yearbook of World Energy Statistics 1982 and World Bank, Social Indicators Data Sheets (various issues).

Note: The various types of energy are defined in the explanatory notes.

a/ 1978-1980.
b/ 1979-1981.

Source: Nations Unies, Annuaire des statistiques mondiales de l'énergie 1982 et Banque mondiale, Social Indicators Data Sheets (divers numéros).

Note: Les différentes formes d'énergie sont définies dans les notes explicatives.

a/ 1978-1980.
b/ 1979-1981.